AF769491

The Fundamentals of Contract Law and Clauses

For Seth, Mina and Amelia, as always.

The Fundamentals of Contract Law and Clauses

A PRACTICAL APPROACH

Nancy S. Kim

Proflowers Distinguished Professor of Internet Studies and Professor of Law, California Western School of Law and Visiting Professor, Rady School of Management, University of California, San Diego, USA

Edward Elgar
PUBLISHING

Cheltenham, UK • Northampton, MA, USA

© Nancy S. Kim 2016

All rights reserved. No part of this publication may be reproduced, stored in a retrieval system or transmitted in any form or by any means, electronic, mechanical or photocopying, recording, or otherwise without the prior permission of the publisher.

Published by
Edward Elgar Publishing Limited
The Lypiatts
15 Lansdown Road
Cheltenham
Glos GL50 2JA
UK

Edward Elgar Publishing, Inc.
William Pratt House
9 Dewey Court
Northampton
Massachusetts 01060
USA

A catalogue record for this book
is available from the British Library

Library of Congress Control Number: 2016938588

MIX
Paper from responsible sources
FSC® C013604

ISBN 978 1 78347 941 2 (cased)
ISBN 978 1 78347 942 9 (paperback)
ISBN 978 1 78347 943 6 (eBook)

Typeset by Servis Filmsetting Ltd, Stockport, Cheshire
Printed and bound by CPI Group (UK) Ltd, Croydon, CR0 4YY

Contents in brief

Full contents

Table of cases

Table of legislation

Federal Law

State Law

California

Georgia

New Jersey

New Mexico

New York

North Dakota

Pennsylvania

Utah

International Law

Part I

Introduction

This book introduces a novel way to learn contract law. It is intended to help those who work with contracts understand what common clauses mean, how they might affect a transaction, and how to use them effectively. The audience for this book is broad and includes business and law students, business lawyers, contracts managers, and business people.

This book contains select case summaries, problems, and many citations and references; however, it depends primarily upon contract clauses to illustrate doctrinal concepts and how they may affect a transaction.

Most of the contract law topics discussed in this book are covered in first year contracts courses. Unfortunately, they are often taught without reference to an actual contract. This book is intended to make abstract concepts more concrete. Students may find it much easier to understand legal concepts when they can view how those concepts are applied in a written agreement. The focus throughout the book is on preventive lawyering and students are encouraged to ask: What does this contract clause mean? How can it affect what I want from a deal? What problems can it cause? What can I do to minimize the likelihood of problems?

Most first year courses use casebooks and a litigation-oriented approach to introduce students to contracts doctrine. While cases are indispensable to understanding how disputes are resolved, they provide only some guidance as to how to avoid disputes or prevent misunderstandings. This text adopts a transactions-centered approach to teaching contracts by showing students how doctrinal concepts are captured in contract clauses. Students learn the material in a more active manner and learn how to preempt problems, reduce risk, and add value to transactions.

Much has been made of the disruptive impact of technology on the legal profession. In response, many law schools are revamping their curriculum to incorporate more skills-based training. Such training must include much more than technical expertise, which can be easily outdated and replaced by technology. The ability to anticipate and prevent problems is an essential skill for today's lawyer. For a transactional lawyer, this includes understanding the doctrinal foundations of common contract clauses.

This book is a guide to understanding what common contract clauses mean and how they might affect a business transaction. It is intended for those who negotiate and sign contracts as part of their job. Because every contract you sign will be interpreted and construed within the context of contract doctrine, you must understand that context. This book provides a brief summary of basic contract law concepts within the framework of standard contract provisions. In other words, this book does what most first year contract law books do not – it provides a working knowledge of contracts. Other contract law books help you learn how to read cases; this book helps you learn to read *contracts*.

I've told you what this book is – and now, I'll tell you what this book is *not*. It is not a casebook. It is intended to be accessible to lawyers and non-lawyers. Because the intended readership includes non-lawyers and international lawyers, the Case Highlights are summaries of cases. This book is not a drafting book. Contract drafters should strive for clear, concise writing and the avoidance of legalese and readers of this book are encouraged to familiarize themselves with one of the many excellent contract drafting textbooks available. This book is not one of them. Instead, this book explains the meaning of common clauses in the context of contract law but generally avoids discussion of whether these clauses could be drafted in a way that is stylistically better. Because a primary purpose of this text is to familiarize readers with common contract clauses, many of the Example Clauses contain what many legal drafting books consider unnecessary legalese or stylistic blunders. The reality is that many common contract clauses *are* poorly drafted but those working with contracts must still understand their meaning. In addition, it may not always be practical or wise for an attorney to make extensive stylistic revisions to a contract. While it is not a drafting text, this book does indicate where drafting ambiguities may create problems. It also explains how a lawyer may harm his or her client through "greedy drafting" where, in an attempt to gain advantage, a lawyer may actually leave the client more vulnerable. These greedy drafting references illustrate the importance of ethical drafting.

This book is primarily concerned with written contracts. Specifically, it is concerned with written contracts in a business setting. That business setting may involve two companies, but it may also involve two individuals or an individual and a business. This book's focus is U.S. contract law; however, given the increasingly global nature of business transactions, every U.S. business lawyer should be aware that there are differences between U.S. contract law and contract law in other countries. Conversely, non-U.S. business lawyers will benefit from understanding U.S. contract law. This book notes several important areas where U.S. contract law differs from contract law in other countries.

Note to Professors: There is a Teacher's Manual accessible online for instructors adopting this textbook. It contains answers to the "Applying What You Learned" exercises, discussion points for the "Reflection Prompts" and additional exercises and teaching suggestions. Please see https://www.e-elgar.com/the-fundamentals-of-contract-law-and-clauses-companion-site.

Part II

A roadmap to a contract

What is a contract? Contract scholars and philosophers have pondered this question for years. This book does not. This book leaves aside the difficult theoretical and philosophical questions and focuses on the practical. Part II explains what a contract is in the most literal sense, by looking at the purpose of contracts and contract clauses, outlining the anatomy of a contract, and providing a brief overview of the substantive law governing contracts.

1

The purpose of a contract and contract clauses

A written contract serves several purposes. It memorializes the agreement between the parties. It sets forth the rights, remedies, and performance obligations of each party. But a contract is not merely a finished product – it is also a planning instrument. The negotiation and drafting of terms enable the parties to better understand what each expects to get from the transaction or relationship. The process of capturing these expectations and transforming them into contract terms helps clarify and solidify them.

A contract is more than the end result of a negotiation process – it is the process itself. Words and conduct during the negotiating and drafting process are often considered by the parties to be part of their agreement, even if not embodied in the words of the contract.

Contracts have a deterrent role. While they are often at the center of litigation disputes, contracts are more often used to *avoid* litigation. Misunderstandings or disputes between parties are often resolved by one party pointing out a relevant provision of the contract to the other party. Typically, this is not done to show that the party is "right," but that its request is reasonable and in accordance with their original understanding.

In other words, a contract enables parties to assert rights, but also helps keep the peace. It encourages parties to discuss their expectations during the negotiation process and encourages them to resolve their differences after a transaction has been initiated without resorting to litigation.

One or both parties may consider the contract to be a breathing document, meaning that even written terms may be subject to adjustment provided that the parties are acting in good faith. Production delays, market occurrences, and other unexpected events may result in one party seeking changes to the contract. This may be especially true where a U.S. company is negotiating with a foreign company with different cultural, business, and legal norms governing contracts.[1]

There are different types of contract clauses. Clauses containing individualized terms are specific to a transaction and are typically negotiated by the parties. These include pricing terms and the description of goods and services. There are also clauses relating to the background laws of the transaction. When parties enter into a contract, they do so against an existing legal background. The business terms that they negotiate are not the only terms that apply to the contract. The contract operates within an existing legal framework which can be filled with traps for the unwary. For example, if the transaction involves the sale of goods, a background law is the Uniform Commercial Code. If the contract is a patent license, a background law is patent law. It is important for lawyers and businesspeople to understand what the background laws and default rules are for a particular transaction. Parties to a contract can change much of the law that governs a contract but they can't do that if they don't know what that law is. More than one background law may apply to a given transaction. Of course, the background law of contracts is always relevant to a contract. [2]

Generally, there are three types of clauses that relate to background rules. The first type of clause changes the default rules of the background law. The default rules are those rules that govern the transaction unless the parties agree otherwise in their contract. The parties can erase, restrict, or expand what their rights are under default law by putting it in their contract. It is important for a contracting party (and the contracting party's lawyer) to *know the default rules so that the party knows what he or she is giving up or granting*. For example, consequential damages are available under the Uniform Commercial Code; however, these damages may be limited or excluded by agreement of the parties. If you know the default rules, you are aware of the value of what you are giving up (or getting). Knowledge of the default rules can strengthen your negotiating position.

The second type of clause conforms to mandatory rules of the background law. Mandatory rules require contracting parties to abide by them and the

1 In China, for example, the signing of a contract often merely marks the existence of a relationship and the commencement of negotiations. *See* Patricia Pattison & Daniel Herron, *The Mountains are High and the Emperor is Far Away: Sanctity of Contract in China*, 40 Am. Bus. L. J. 459, 460 (2003); *see also* Nancy S. Kim, *A Dynamic Approach to Contract Disputes*, 84 Neb. L. Rev. 506, 531–539 (2005) (discussing the ways that cultural and linguistic differences may affect contractual relations).

2 This doesn't mean it will be the *only* background law – in fact, other background law will almost certainly also apply and it's important to understand that other background law. It is beyond the scope of *any* single book to cover the background laws relevant to all contracts.

parties can't contract out of those rules. For example, if Sue and Bob enter into an employment relationship, they can't agree that Sue will not report Bob's wages to the Internal Revenue Service or that she will pay him less than the minimum wage. It is important for a contracting party (and the contracting party's lawyer) to know the mandatory rules to avoid engaging in illegal or otherwise unlawful activity.

The third type of clause reflects definitions that determine whether and what law applies to the transaction. For example, in a nondisclosure agreement, the parties will typically define what information will be protected under the agreement. The background law of trade secrets typically defines a trade secret as "confidential information" that gives businesses a "competitive advantage." Accordingly, the parties will define information that they wish to protect in their agreement as information that gives them a "competitive advantage." It is important to know the definitional background law in order to draft the agreement so that it falls within the scope of that law or, alternatively, falls outside the scope of that law.

An understanding of a contract requires more than an understanding of the meaning of the words it contains. Similarly, good contract drafting requires more than knowledge of stylistic rules and conventions – it requires a solid understanding of the specific transaction, the intent and the motivations of the parties, and the background laws.

Note: This book focuses primarily on the background law of contracts. This book also discusses the Uniform Commercial Code ("UCC"). Article 2 of the UCC governs transactions involving the sale of goods. "Goods" are defined as "moveable" things, other than money or securities and does not include real property, rights in intellectual property or services. A transaction may involve both sales of goods and services. In these hybrid transactions, most courts will look at the predominant purpose of the transaction (i.e. whether it is primarily to provide goods or services) to determine whether the UCC applies. Most of the provisions of the UCC have been adopted by most states. The UCC is the default law governing sales transactions but the parties to a contract may modify or negate many of its provisions by express language in their contract. It is important to remember that for most transactions, other background laws will also apply.

2

The anatomy of a contract

The basic format of a contract typically includes the following: a preamble, recital or background, the main body of the agreement, the miscellaneous or "boilerplate" provisions, the ending, and the signature block.

The preamble states the parties' name and address, the name of the agreement and the effective date.

Example clause

This Master Purchase Agreement is entered into on [date] (the "Effective Date") between Rondo Inc., an Illinois corporation having its principal office at [address], and Gerato Systems, Inc., a New York corporation having its principal office at [address].

Troubleshooting: It is a good idea to verify the name of the party with whom you are entering into the contract to ensure that the correct party is named. A corporation may have different subsidiaries and divisions so be sure to check that the party you intend to contract with is the one named in the contract.

The recitals or background describe the contract and provide some context. The paragraph containing the recitals begins with the term "whereas," and ends with words indicating the parties' agreement.

Example clause

Whereas, Company wishes to appoint Reseller, on a non-exclusive basis and only within the Territory defined herein, for the marketing and systems integration of Licensed Software and the provision of certain services related to such marketing efforts;
Whereas, Reseller wishes to accept such appointment under the terms of this agreement;
Now, therefore, the parties agree as follows:

The use of "whereas" is not necessary and the background can be drafted in modern English, as follows:

Example clause

1. Corporation A is the owner of the Softex System. Corporation B desires to license the Softex System.
2. Corporation A is also the owner of the Vortex System. Corporation B is the exclusive licensee of the Vortex System.
3. The parties wish to enter into one agreement for the licensing of both the Softex System and the Vortex System.

   Accordingly, the parties agree as follows:

The recitals or background generally are not binding but may be used by a court in order to determine the intent of the parties or to assist in the interpretation of the contract.[1]

Caveat: One party may be "estopped" or prevented from denying a recited fact if the other party detrimentally and in good faith relies upon the truthfulness of the recitals.[2] Recitals may be useful to help the parties themselves understand the background and context of a transaction at a later date (if, for example, the individuals who negotiated the agreement on behalf of the company are no longer at the company or the agreement is assigned to another company).

1 Francis v. Francis, 285 P.3d 707, 712–713 (Okla. Civ. App. Div. 2012) ("Generally recitals in a contract will not control the operative clauses of the contract unless the latter are ambiguous, but they may be looked to in determining the proper construction of the contract and the parties' intention."); Khan v. BDO Seidman, LLP, 935 N.E.2d 1174, 1194 (Ill. App. 4th Dist. 2010) ("[A] preamble or recital is often an aid to the construction of a written instrument" (citation omitted)); Captiva Lake Investments, LLC v. Ameristructure, Inc., 436 S.W.3d 619, 625 (Mo. App. E.D. 2014) ("Recitals are not strictly a part of the contract because they do not impose contractual duties on the parties . . . Missouri courts look to the recitals to determine the intent of the parties only when the operative language is ambiguous, uncertain or indefinite."); Country Community Timberlake Village, L.P. v. HMW Special Utility Dist. Of Harris, 438 S.W. 661, 669 (Tex. App. – Houston (1st Dist) 2014) ("Recitals in a contract do not control the operative clauses of the contract unless the latter are ambiguous."); Hagene v. Derek Polling Const., 902 N.E. 1269, 1274 (Ill. App. 5th Dist. 2009) ("The contract recitals create a context through which the operational portion of the contract can be better understood, because they indicate the relevant circumstances to its execution.").

2 GGS Co., Ltd. v. Masuda, 919 P.2d 1008, 1015 (Hawai'I App. 1996) ("A recital of fact in an integrated agreement is evidence of the fact [recited] and its weight depends on the circumstances . . . Moreover, 'in some circumstances a recital may embody a representation of fact by one party to the other, and the party making such a representation may be barred by estoppel from showing the truth contrary to the representation after another has relied on the representation.'") (Citing RESTATEMENT (SECOND) OF CONTRACTS §218 comment c (1979)). Please note that all references to RESTATEMENT (SECOND) OF CONTRACTS (1979) will be simply "RESTATEMENT (SECOND) CONTRACTS").

The main body of the agreement sets forth the legal obligations of the parties and constitutes the bulk of the contract. This is where the parties will define terms, outline their obligations and any conditions to those obligations, set forth payment terms, and provide representations and warranties.

The miscellaneous provisions contain standard contract clauses that govern many different types of contracts. These provisions include choice of law and choice of forum clauses, assignment clauses, severability clauses, and construction provisions. These clauses are often referred to as "boilerplate" because they appear standard and are rarely the result of negotiation between non-lawyers. Lawyers, however, should understand and carefully review these provisions. As this book explains, these provisions affect the rights and obligations of the parties to the contract and it is important to understand their significance.

Example clause

Choice of Law and Forum. The laws of the State of New York, U.S.A., excluding its conflict of laws rules, govern all matters arising out of or relating to this Agreement. If the parties have a controversy, dispute or difference arising out of this Agreement, either party may initiate litigation only in the U.S. District Court for the Southern District of New York or, if such court lacks subject matter jurisdiction, in the Supreme Court of the State of New York in and for New York County.

Example clause

Severability. If any provision of this Agreement is determined to be illegal or otherwise unenforceable, then the remaining provisions remain in full force and effect.

The Agreement may also contain an ending or some closing language which, like the recitals, indicates the parties' intent to create a binding agreement.

Example clause

By and through the signatures affixed below of their duly authorized agents, the parties hereby execute this Contract which shall become effective on the date of the last signature.

Reflection Prompt: What is the meaning of the words "By and through the signatures affixed below"? Could the clause be rewritten in modern English? *Should* it be?

Note: Many of the Reflection Prompts ask you to compare two Example Clauses. Sometimes the difference between the clauses will be stylistic only, but often there will be substantive differences. These substantive differences may be based upon the doctrine or they may be based upon business considerations. The reader should consider whether altering the language aids in understanding the clause, whether it changes the substantive meaning, and whether it changes the parties' *perception* of the clause. The Example Clauses are not "model" clauses in terms of substance or style. Rather, the purpose of the Example Clauses is to provide useful examples for illustrating the relevant doctrinal concept or application. The Example Clauses demonstrate that there are many ways to draft a clause and drafters should consider the effect of adding, deleting, or modifying contract language.

Immediately following the ending is a signature block:

Example

[Company 1]	[Company 2]
By: ____________________	By: ____________________
Name: ____________________	Name: ____________________
Title: ____________________	Title: ____________________
Date: ____________________	Date: ____________________

Troubleshooting: It is important that you have the correct party sign the agreement. An officer of a company should never sign a company agreement with just her name, like this:

Incorrect!

By: Jane Smith
Jane Smith

Jane Smith may be personally liable for signing her name on the signature line without indicating that she is signing *on behalf of* the company. It should be clearly indicated that the company is the signatory and that the individual signing is merely the agent for the company. She must also list the full correct name of her company.[3] The correct way for Jane Smith to sign the agreement is by clearly indicating that she is signing on behalf of the company, like this:

Example

Smith, Inc.
By: Jane Smith
Name: Jane Smith
Title: Chief Executive Officer

Not all contracts contain every section mentioned above. Many contracts do not contain recitals or a background. Many do not contain an ending. Apart from the recitals and the ending, however, most contracts follow the basic format outlined in this chapter.

3 G.W. Andersen Construction Co. v. Mars Sales, 164 Cal. App. 3d 326, 210 Cal. Rptr. 409 (1985) (finding that the co-owner of a corporation could be held individually liable on contract which he intended to sign in his capacity as agent for corporation); African Bio-Botanica, Inc. v. Leiner, 264 N.J. Super. 359, 362, 624 A.2d 1003, 1005 (1993) (In order to be shielded from personal liability, defendant must affirmatively disclose that she was acting as an agent for corporation); *see also* RESTATEMENT (SECOND) AGENCY, §§ 321–322 (2000).

3

A very brief overview of contract law

A contract must be (1) properly formed and (2) legally enforceable. If there is a validly formed and legally enforceable contract, the parties must perform their obligations under the contract. If a party fails to perform her obligations, the other party may sue for breach of contract. The breaching party may claim a defense or excuse for not performing. If no defense or excuse applies, the court must determine what the injured party's remedy is, meaning it must decide what the breaching party should do because of her failure to perform. In most cases, that party has to pay damages (money). In some cases, the injured party may ask the court for equitable relief which may mean specific performance (where the court orders the breaching party to do what was promised under the contract) or an injunction (where the court orders the party to refrain from doing something). These four aspects of contract law – proper formation, contract defenses, breach, and remedy – are discussed in further detail below.

Contracts are governed by state law. The law of contracts has developed over the years through cases decided by judges but also through legislation. The cases and the statutes vary in some key respects from state to state. This book provides general principles of contract law that are common in most of the 50 states and notes where there is a split in authority among states. The book also comments where U.S. contract law may differ significantly from the law in other countries.

Caveat: It is beyond the scope of any single book – including this one – to address *every* aspect of contract law in every state and every country. As the statutes and case law may vary depending on the jurisdiction, you must research the laws in the specific country or state governing a particular contract. Furthermore, as previously noted, contract law is not the only relevant law governing the enforceability of a contract.

Each of the four aspects of contract law (formation, defense, breach, and remedy) requires courts to interpret the meaning of words and deeds.

Interpretation issues pervade contract cases and affect how courts apply doctrinal rules. Accordingly, this chapter concludes with a summary of common rules of interpretation and construction.

3.1 Proper formation

"Properly formed" means that the contract reflects an offer, acceptance, consideration, and mutual assent. In a commercial setting, offer and acceptance typically means that the parties had agreed to terms that were specific and definite enough that they knew what they were supposed to do under the contract (another way to look at it is to ask whether a judge could determine what the parties are supposed to do by reading the contract). Consideration means that a party was motivated to do something or to agree to do something in exchange for what the other party agreed to do. Mutual assent means that the parties shared the same understanding regarding the subject matter of the contract.

Let's use the following example to illustrate: Sam offers to sell Barbara his used blue bike for $50. Barbara agrees to buy it for that amount. The offer must be specific and definite enough that Barbara understands that Sam is serious about selling his blue bike. If Sam said something like, "If I were to offer you my bike for $50, would you take it?" that would not constitute an offer since it is not clear that he intends to sell his bike for $50. He might just be thinking about it and not ready, willing, and able to do it. Since his query is not an offer, Barbara's reply of, "Sure, I would!" would not constitute an acceptance. If, however, Sam said, "I'm selling my bike for $50. Do you want to buy it?" that would likely be considered an offer since it indicates that he is ready, willing and able to sell his bike for that price. If Barbara says, "I'll buy it!" before Sam has walked away or indicated that he has changed his mind, she has accepted his offer. The consideration is the promise of money ($50) in exchange for the promise of a bike. There is mutual assent if they are referring to the same bike. If, however, Sam has *two* blue bikes in different condition, and he was referring to one and Barbara to the other, mutual assent is lacking.

Caveat: There are different formation requirements in different countries, which is important to remember if you are conducting business with a company outside of the United States. Civil law countries, such as Germany, typically do not have the requirement of consideration. Scottish contract law does not require consideration. In some countries, such as England and New Zealand, there is a requirement that the parties intend to create legal relations. In those countries, parties to a commercial or business contract are presumed to have intended to create legal relations; however, agreements between friends and family members are typically not binding because the parties are generally found to lack the requisite intent to create legal relations.

3.2 Contract enforceability

In some cases, a party can escape a contract even though there was an offer that was accepted in a timely manner. One of the parties may lack legal capacity because of insanity or infancy (meaning that he or she was younger than the minimum age legally required in that state to enter into a contract, which in most states is 18 years of age). A contract may not be enforced against the party lacking legal capacity.

In addition, the Statute of Frauds requires certain contracts to be in writing. Contracts for the sale of real property, marital contracts, guaranty agreements, contracts for the sale of goods $500 or more, and contracts which by their terms cannot be completed within a year must all be in writing. Please keep in mind that a state may, by legislation, require that other contracts be in writing or that certain provisions be separately initialed, in a particular format or font size, and/or contain specific language.

Caveat: Because this book is only a source of general information, it does not address every legislative provision requiring contracts to be in a specific form. The occasional references to such provisions are for purposes of illustration only. It is imperative that you research the law in the jurisdiction that governs the agreement.

There are other defenses to contract formation, such as unconscionability and mistake. Many people confuse mistake with a lack of mutual assent, (also known as a misunderstanding). In the example of the sale of the blue bike, a misunderstanding would involve the wrong bike; a mistake would involve the price of the bike or a feature of the bike. The defenses are discussed in more detail later in this book. For now, just remember that a party is not always obligated to go through with a contract even if it was properly formed (although it will be harder to get out of a properly formed contract than one that was never formed in the first place).

3.3 Contract performance and breach

If a contract has been properly formed and there are no available contract defenses, the parties must perform pursuant to the terms of the contract. If one party doesn't perform her contractual obligations, that party has breached. The breach can be *material* or *minor,* meaning it can be a big deal or not such a big deal.

It makes a difference whether the breach is material or minor. A material breach excuses the non-breaching party from having to do what she was supposed to do under the contract – and allows her to sue the breaching party. On the other hand, a minor breach does *not* excuse the non-breaching party from her contractual obligations, although she may sue for damages arising from the minor breach.

3.4 Remedies (what can one party do when the other party has breached the contract?)

Generally speaking, there are two types of remedies for breach of contract: damages and equitable relief.

Damages refer to money the non-breaching party should get because the breaching party didn't do what she was supposed to do under the contract. There are different ways to measure how much money the non-breaching party should get. The most common measure is called the expectation measure, which means damages are measured by what the non-breaching party expected to get from the contract. For example, let's say that Barbara enters into a written contract with Sam where she agrees to buy a car for $12,000 from him. (The contract is signed so it satisfies the Statute of Frauds, which requires contracts for sales of goods $500 or more to be in writing). Sam breaches the contract when he later refuses to sell the car to Barbara despite their properly formed, legally enforceable, written contract. Barbara buys a similar car from Ann for $15,000. Barbara's expectation damages are $3,000, which is how much more Barbara has to pay for the same car because of Sam's breach.

In addition, if there are expenses related to the transaction with Ann that would not have been part of her transaction with Sam, Barbara may be able to recover them. Those additional expenses are referred to as incidental expenses, and include shipping and storage costs that she would not have incurred if Sam had kept his end of the deal. There may also be consequential expenses. For example, Barbara might have had a contract to resell the same car at a mark-up to Tom but is no longer able to do that because she has no car to resell or because by the time she bought the car from Ann, Tom had already bought another car. In order to be recoverable, consequential damages need to be foreseeable, meaning, in this case, that Sam knew that Barbara was buying the car to resell to someone else.

In some cases, a party may ask for reliance or restitution instead of expectation damages. Reliance damages refer to the money that the non-breaching party spent because of the contract. If, for example, Barbara made a down payment or prepaid garage space for her expected new car, she could seek those costs as reliance damages. Restitution refers to any benefit that Barbara conferred upon Sam as part of the contract. If, for example, she gave him a deposit, the return of that money would constitute restitution.

A party may seek restitution even where there is no enforceable contract. For example, if a party is excused from performance, either party may seek restitution for any benefit conferred, such as any payments made to the other party, even though there is no "breach" because there is no contract.

Instead of damages, a party may seek equitable relief, which is either specific performance or an injunction. Specific performance is when a court orders the breaching party to perform its contractual obligations. It is typically granted in cases where damages (i.e. money) would not satisfy the non-breaching party because of the nature of the transaction, the difficulty of calculating damages, or the uniqueness of the goods involved. Injunctive relief is when the non-breaching party wants the court to order the breaching party *not* to do something (unlike specific performance, where the party is ordered to *do* something). For example, a party may seek an injunction to stop the other party from working for a competitor in violation of a non-compete clause in an employment agreement.

3.5 Construction and interpretation

The preceding provides a brief summary of how the law determines the important phases of a contract, from formation to performance (or breach), and remedy. But each phase depends upon interpretation. For example, a properly formed contract requires offer and acceptance, but determining whether there is an offer and/or acceptance requires interpreting the words and conduct of the parties. Interpretation touches every part of contract law. Many contract disputes involve some type of disagreement regarding the meaning of a word or action. Interpretation involves determining or explaining the meaning of the words. Construction of a contract involves determining the legal effect of the words that are used or how to interpret them. In most jurisdictions, contract construction and interpretation are usually questions of law that are resolved by a court.[1]

1 Monitronics Int'l, Inc. v. Veasley, 323 Ga. App. 126, 746 S.E.2d 793, 2013 Ga. App. LEXIS 657, 2013 WL 3659757 (Court of Appeals, Georgia, July 16, 2013); Fisher v. Revell, 343 S.W.3d 776, 779 (C.A. Tenn., Sept.

A court should interpret a contract's provisions according to the intent of the parties and in light of the purpose of the contract.[2] This does not mean exactly what it may seem. Contract law adopts an objective standard of interpretation, meaning that most courts evaluate the intent of the parties based upon the plain meaning of their words and actions from the standpoint of a "reasonable person" rather than the actual parties. What matters is not the unexpressed, inner thoughts and beliefs of the parties (their subjective intent), but what they said and did (their manifested intent).[3]

Disagreements over interpretation are at the heart of most contract disputes. Often – but not always – these disputes involve the meaning of clauses contained in written contracts. Many courts adhere to the traditional plain meaning rule or four corners rule and examine the "plain and ordinary meaning" of the written words as contained within the four corners of the document.[4] This means that if the terms are unambiguous, the courts must enforce the agreement as written without considering extrinsic evidence (meaning evidence outside of the written agreement).[5] Courts may consider trade usage (evidence of a usage, practice, or custom that is observed with regularity in a particular trade),[6] course of performance (meaning the way the parties have performed under the contract) and course of dealing (meaning past dealings between the parties) to resolve an ambiguity.

30, 2009) ("The interpretation of a written contract is a matter of law and not of fact."); U.S.B. Acquisition Co., Inc. v. Stamm, 660 So. 2d 1075, 1079 (Fla. App. 4th Dist. 1995) ("Construction of contractual language is usually a matter of law for the court").

2 Allmand v. Pavletic, 292 S.W. 3d 618, 630 (Tenn. 2009) (citing Allstate Ins. Co. v. Watson, 195 S.W. 3d 609, 611 (Tenn. 2006) ("A cardinal rule of contractual interpretation is to ascertain and give effect to the intent of the parties."); NuStar Energy, L.P. v. Diamond Offshore Co., 402 S.W.3d 461, 465 (Tex. App. Houston – [14th Dist.], 2013) ("When interpreting a contract, our primary concern is to ascertain and give effect to the written expression of the parties' intent").

3 NuStar Energy, L.P. v. Diamond Offshore Co., 402 S.W.3d 461, 466 (Tex. App. Houston [14th Dist.], 2013) ("The parties' intent is governed by what is written in the contract, not by what one side contends they intended but failed to say."); Salehi v. Surfside III Condominium Owners Assn., 200 Cal. App. 4th 1146, 1159 (2011) ("Evidence of the undisclosed subjective intent of the parties is irrelevant to determining the meaning of contractual language . . . It is the outward expression of the agreement, rather than a party's unexpressed intention, which the court will enforce.") (citing Winete v. Price, 4 Cal. App. 4th 1159, 1165–66) (1992).

4 Dick Broadcasting Co., Inc. of Tennessee v. Oak Ridge FM, Inc., 395 S.W.3d 653, 659 (2013) ("We initially determine the parties' intent by examining the plain and ordinary meaning of the written words that are "contained within the four corners of the contract"; 84 Lumber Co. v. Smith, 356 S.W. 3d 380, 383 (Tenn. 2011) (citing Kiser v. Wolfe, 353 S.W. 3d 741, 747 (Tenn. 2011)).

5 NuStar Energy, L.P. v. Diamond Offshore Co., 402 S.W.3d 461, 466 (Texas. App. Houston [14th Dist.] June 11, 2013).

6 *See* Uniform Commercial Code (hereafter "UCC") §1-205(1) (2007); RESTATEMENT (SECOND) CONTRACTS §222.

Other courts adopt a more contextual approach and permit relevant extrinsic evidence to determine the circumstances in which the agreement was made in order to determine the intent of the parties.[7] The Restatement Second of Contracts[8] and the Uniform Commercial Code[9] assume the parties intended to include trade usage, past dealings, and course of performance unless they are expressly excluded in the agreement.

While technically not a rule of construction, the parol evidence rule determines what may be the subject of interpretation.[10] The parol evidence rule excludes evidence of a prior oral or written agreement or contemporaneous oral agreement to alter or supplement the terms of a later written contract if that later written contract was intended by the parties to be an integration (a final, complete and exclusive agreement regarding the transaction).[11] An issue often arises whether the parties intended the writing to be a "final, complete and exclusive" agreement regarding the transaction. To avoid later disputes regarding whether the writing is a final, complete, and exclusive agreement, the parties may include a merger or integration clause which states that the present agreement integrates or merges all prior understandings between the parties, thus signaling that the parol evidence rule should apply.

Example clause

This Agreement is the complete, final and exclusive agreement between the parties and supersedes all prior or contemporaneous agreements or understanding, written or oral, regarding its subject matter. No additional terms, conditions, representations or understandings are binding unless in writing signed by both parties.

Courts may, however, disregard such a clause if it appears to have been non-negotiated and unintended.[12]

---

7 RESTATEMENT (SECOND) CONTRACTS, §212(1); Regional Steel Corporation v. Liberty Surplus Insurance Corporation, 226 Cal. App. 4th 1377, 1389 (2014) (noting that the "context in which a term appears is critical").

8 RESTATEMENT (SECOND) CONTRACTS §§221–223.

9 UCC § 2-202(a); RESTATEMENT (SECOND) CONTRACTS §202.

10 RESTATEMENT (SECOND), CONTRACTS §213, cmt. A. (describing the parol evidence rule as being, not a "rule of interpretation; it defines the subject matter of interpretation").

11 *See* MARGARET N. KNIFFIN, CORBIN ON CONTRACTS, INTERPRETATION OF CONTRACTS, Vol. 5, §24.11 (1998) (noting that interpretation of a contract is distinct from the application of the parol evidence rule).

12 Denny's Restaurants, Inc. v. Security Union Title Ins. Co., 71 Wash. App. 194, 203 (1993) (stating that "boilerplate integration clauses are inoperative if they are false; parties to a contract are not bound by incorrect statements of fact."); *see also* Israel v. Chabra, 12 N.Y.3d 158, 163 (2009) (noting that "[u]nder the common

Please note that the UCC allows even final agreements to be supplemented by course of dealing, course of performance, or usage of trade[13] unless "carefully negated."[14]

Example clause

Merger; Negation of Course of Performance and Trade Usage. The parties intend this Agreement to be the final, complete, exclusive and fully integrated statement of their agreement. It is the intent of the parties to negate the effect of trade usage, course of performance and prior dealings in the construction and interpretation of this agreement. No evidence of trade usage, course of performance or course of prior dealings between the parties shall be relevant to qualify, supplement or explain any of its terms.

Example clause

No Trade Usage or Course of Dealing. The provisions of this Agreement may not be explained, altered, supplemented or qualified through evidence of trade usage or prior course of dealing.

Reflection Prompt: What is the difference between the two Example Clauses above? Which one do you prefer and why?

An integration clause typically also includes a no-oral modification or NOM clause, which permits modifications only in a writing signed by both parties. The parol evidence rule does not bar later modifications. Courts may not enforce NOM clauses if evidence of the oral modification is clear and convincing and the modification is supported by consideration.[15] (Remember that if the agreement as modified falls within the Statute of Frauds, it must be

law, a contractual 'no oral modification' clause was not enforceable because contracting parties were viewed as being able to waive such a clause, thereby orally amending their written agreement").

13 UCC §2-202 (A final agreement "may not be contradicted . . . but may be explained or supplemented (a) by course of performance, course of dealing, or usage of trade").

14 UCC §2-202, Cmt. 2; Columbia Nitrogen Corporation v. Royster Company 451 F.2d 3, 9–10 (4th Cir. 1971) (where the contract did not expressly state that trade usage cannot be used to explain or supplement the terms, it should be admitted to interpret the contract); Heggblade-Margueleas-Tenneco, Inc. v. Sunshine Biscuit, Inc., 131 Cal. Rptr. 183, 188 (Cal. App. 5th Dist. 1976) ("Since the contracts in question are silent about the applicability of the usage and custom, evidence of such usage and custom was admissible to explain the meaning of the quantity figures").

15 Barinaga v. JP Morgan Chase & Co., 749 F. Supp. 2d 1164, 1173 (D. Or. 2010) ("Oregon courts allow the oral modification of a written contract containing an express no-oral modification clause . . . . However, to be binding, the terms of an oral modification of a written contract must be established by clear and convincing evidence and must be supported by consideration").

in writing). A few states have legislation expressly permitting NOM clauses.[16] The UCC expressly allows NOM clauses,[17] however, the clause may be waived by subsequent performance.[18]

Example clause

This Agreement is the entire agreement between the parties and supersedes all prior understandings and agreements between the parties, whether oral or written. This Agreement may be amended only in a written document, signed by both parties.

Example clause

This Agreement and Exhibits attached hereto and incorporated herein constitute the entire, final, complete and exclusive agreement between the parties and supersede all previous agreements or representations, oral or written, relating to this Agreement. This Agreement may not be modified or amended except in a writing signed by a duly authorized representative of each party.

Reflection Prompt: Which clause is better drafted? How would you redraft each clause?

If the terms are ambiguous (meaning susceptible of more than one reasonable meaning),[19] courts apply rules of construction to help determine the

---

16 *See* NY GENERAL OBLIGATIONS LAW §15-301(1) ("A written agreement or other written instrument which contains a provision to the effect that it cannot be changed orally, cannot be changed by an executory agreement unless such executory agreement is in writing and signed by the party against whom enforcement of the change is sought or by his agent."); Cal. Civ. Code §1698(c) ("Unless the contract expressly provides, a contract in writing may be modified by an oral agreement supported by new consideration."); Fanucchi & Limi Farms v. United Agri Products, 414 F.3d 1075, 1081 (9th Cir. 2005) ("Section 1698(c) allows oral modification of a written contract only if the written contract does not provide otherwise"); *compare* Cal. Civ. Code §1698(b) ("A contract in writing may be modified by an oral agreement to the extent that the oral agreement is executed by the parties").

17 UCC §2-209(2). *See also* Stalloy Metals, Inc. v. Kennametal, Inc., 983 N.E.2d 823, 831 (Ohio App. 11 Dist. 2012) (finding that no-oral modification clause was binding and evidence of oral conversation to modify terms was not allowed).

18 UCC §2-208(4). *See also* Allapatttah Services, Inc. v. Exxon Corp., 61 F. Supp. 2d 1308, 1316 (S.D. Fla. 1999) (noting that "the UCC does not rigidly enforce clauses which preclude modification in the absence of a writing assented by both parties . . . Parties to a contract with an express term disclaiming the efficacy of a modification unless in writing can waive such an express term through their subsequent performance").

19 Fisher v. Revell, 343 S.W.3d 776, 780 (Tenn, Ct. App. Sept. 30, 2009) ("Contractual language is ambiguous when it is susceptible to more than one interpretation and reasonably intelligent persons could come to different conclusions as to the meaning of the contract").

intent of the parties.[20] The following rules of construction typically apply when there is an ambiguity or inconsistency in the terms of a contract:

1. As a general matter, courts should interpret contract terms and their legal effects as a whole and in the context of their surrounding circumstances.[21]
2. If there are two ways to interpret a contract term, courts prefer the way that would result in a valid contract rather than one that is invalid or results in forfeiture.[22]
3. An effort should be made to harmonize the provisions so that none will be rendered meaningless.[23]
4. Specific terms are given more weight than more general provisions when there is an inconsistency between the two.[24]
5. When a contract term is susceptible of two different reasonable interpretations, courts may apply the rule of *contra proferentem* to construe the language against the party who drafted it.[25]
6. Separately negotiated or added terms are given more weight than terms that are not separately negotiated.[26]

Although the above are referred to as "rules," they are more maxims than mandatory rules. The overarching goal of courts in interpreting and construing contracts is to give effect to the intent of the parties without running afoul of policy considerations. Some courts refuse to apply the rule of *contra proferentem* where the agreement results from an arm's-length negotiation

---

20 Dick Broadcasting Co., Inc. of Tennessee v. Oak Ridge FM, Inc., 395 S.W.3d 653, 659 (2013) (noting that if the terms are ambiguous, other established rules of construction must be applied to determine the parties' intent).

21 KNIFFIN, *supra* n 11, at §24.21 (1998); *see also* Shorr Paper Products, Inc. v. Aurora Elevator, Inc., 198 Ill. App. 3d 9, 13 (May 30, 1990) ("In interpreting a contract, it is presumed that all provisions were intended for a purpose, and conflicting provisions will be reconciled if possible so as to give effect to all of the contract's provisions; Yazoo Properties v. Katz & Besthoff No. 284, Inc., 644 So. 2d 429, 434 (Miss. 1994) ("[A] contract should be read as a whole, giving meaning and effect to each provision in a manner which harmonizes with the other terms of the contract").

22 KNIFFIN, *supra* note 11, at 24.22; RESTATEMENT (SECOND) CONTRACTS, §203(a).

23 NuStar Energy, L.P. v. Diamond Offshore Co., 402 S.W.3d 461, 466 (Tex. App. Houston (14th Dist), June 11, 2013) ("We . . . examine the writing as a whole to harmonize and give effect to all of the contract's provisions").

24 KNIFFIN, *supra* note 11, at 24.23; RESTATEMENT (SECOND) CONTRACTS, §203(c).

25 Fisher v. Revell, 343 S.W. 776, 780 (CA, Tenn, Sept. 30, 2009) ("When an ambiguity is found in an insurance policy, it 'must be construed strongly against the insurer and in favor of the insured'" [citations omitted]. However, "[t]here must be two reasonable constructions of the language before the Court can find ambiguity and construe the policy toward the insured" [citations omitted]; U.S.B. Acquisition Co., Inc. v. Stamm, 660 So. 2d 1075, 1079 (Fla. App. 4th Dist. August 9, 1995) (To the extent any ambiguity existed, the contract must be construed against the party who drafted the instrument.); RESTATEMENT (SECOND) CONTRACTS §206.

26 RESTATEMENT (SECOND) CONTRACTS §203.

between sophisticated entities.[27] Accordingly, some agreements contain this clause:

Example clause

The parties have jointly participated in the negotiation and drafting of this Agreement and no ambiguity, omission or error shall be construed against any party for having drafted this Agreement. No presumption or burden of proof should be applied to favor or disfavor either party in the interpretation or construction of this agreement.

Courts, however, are not obligated to abide by this clause and may disregard it where there is no evidence the agreement was actually negotiated or where the party seeking to enforce the clause has engaged in wrongdoing, such as by intentionally introducing ambiguity into the contract.[28]

Now you have a basic understanding of what contract law is. But contract law is only part of the story. The law of contracts is, for the most part, a set of default rules that govern *unless* the parties have changed them in their contract. As you will see throughout this book, many of the provisions in a contract respond to or change these default rules of contract law.

CASE HIGHLIGHT

U.S.B. ACQUISITION COMPANY, INC. v. STAMM, 660 So. 2d 1075 (Fla. App. 4 Dist. 1995)

The Buyer/Appellant and Sellers/Appellees entered into an asset purchase agreement for the sale of a concrete manufacturing business. When it seemed as though the business was not going to be profitable – despite the Sellers' alleged rosy predictions to the contrary – the Buyer sued the Sellers, seeking rescission and alternatively, damages for breach of contract and fraud. At or before trial, the rescission and fraud counts were dropped.

The Buyer alleged that the Sellers intentionally misrepresented the capacity of the batch plant* it purchased and introduced evidence of pre-agreement representations, both

27 FabArc Steel Supply, Inc., v. Composite Const. Systems, Inc., 914 So. 2d 344, 360–362 (Ala. 2005) (concluding that the rule of *contra proferentem* should not control where both parties were sophisticated business entities and the contract was the result of arm's-length negotiations).

28 McMullin v. McMullin, 338 S.W.3d 315, 322 (Ky. App. 2011) (clause stating "no provision . . . shall be interpreted against any party because that party or their legal representative drafted the provisions hereof," did not control court's interpretation of contract where party intentionally introduced ambiguity into a contract).

CASE HIGHLIGHT *(continued)*

verbal and written, made by the Sellers regarding the capacity of the batch plant. The trial court held that evidence of pre-agreement representations concerning the batch plant were properly admissible to support a breach of contract claim because of what the trial court perceived to be the conflict between the following two provisions of the asset purchase agreement:

Paragraph 16 of the contract provided as follows:

> "All representations and covenants made by each party shall survive the closing for the benefit of the other party."

Paragraph 24 of the agreement contained the following language:

> "This is the parties' entire agreement and may not be modified except in writing signed by all the parties hereto."

. . .

The Sellers contended that the representations and covenants to which paragraph 16 referred, when construed with the integration language of paragraph 24, referred only to those representations and covenants contained in the asset purchase agreement and while admissible in support of the claim of fraud, could not be considered in support of the claim for breach of contract. The trial court, however, believed that the merger clause in paragraph 24 was negated by the survival clause in paragraph 16. The Court of Appeal disagreed with the trial court:

> "Every provision in a contract should be given meaning and effect and apparent inconsistencies reconciled if possible . . . If clauses in a contract appear to be repugnant to each other, they must be given such an interpretation and construction as will reconcile them if possible. . . . We think the proper construction of these two provisions is, as argued by the sellers below and here, that paragraph 16 means that the representations and covenants within the agreement itself survive the closing, and paragraph 24 is a merger clause which provides that the agreement as written constitutes the parties' entire agreement. Such an interpretation not only reconciles these two provisions but also recognize[s] a well-settled principle that representations made before or during the signing of a contract are presumed to have merged in the written agreement . . . Given the proper construction of paragraph 16, the evidence pertaining to pre-agreement representations made by or on behalf of the sellers, and to which their objections were overruled, would be in violation of the parol evidence rule to the extent that such extrinsic evidence was offered to add to the otherwise valid, complete and unambiguous written agreement. The buyer's fraud claim having been directed out, the parol evidence rule made inadmissible the pre-agreement representations . . . Absent that evidence, there was no basis upon which the jury could properly find a breach of the contract as it related to the batch plant. It was error for the court to deny the sellers' motion for directed verdict on this item."

* A batch plant is a mixing plant that produces or mixes batches of concrete.

Part III

Contract clauses and contract doctrine

Part III is divided into chapters which relate to different "phases" of a contract: formation, enforceability, performance and breach, parties other than the original parties to the contract, and remedies. Each chapter explains and illustrates how contract clauses can affect the application of doctrine and how doctrine can affect the application (or enforceability) of contract clauses.

4

Common contract clauses involving contract formation

In order for a contract to be enforceable, it must have been properly formed. This chapter explains how different contract clauses affect and are affected by the doctrinal concepts of consideration, offer and acceptance, and mutual assent.

Caveat: Please remember that there may also be specific requirements or formalities imposed by statute, such as a requirement that a contract be in writing or that certain provisions be initialed separately. In addition, the laws of other countries may require certain formalities which are not required in the U.S., such as an official seal or company stamp, in order to properly authenticate and form a contract.

4.1 Doctrinal concept: consideration

Principle: The formation of a contract requires consideration.

The contract doctrine of consideration refers to both a bargained-for exchange and the subject of the exchange. A bargained-for exchange means that a party is making a promise in order to get what the other party is promising or in order to get the other party to do something. It also refers to what is being exchanged.

For example, Jane promises to pay Mary $25 for Mary's coffee table and Mary agrees to sell her coffee table to Jane for $25. The requirement of consideration is fulfilled because Jane is making the promise to pay Mary $25 *in order* to receive Mary's coffee table. Mary is promising to sell Jane her coffee table because she wants the $25. There is a bargained-for exchange. The things being bargained for are "coffee table" and "money/$25."

Caveat: Equitable doctrines may make promises enforceable even without consideration. A donative promise (a promise to make a gift) which is not made as part of a bargained-for exchange may still be enforceable under the doctrine of promissory estoppel. If the promisor makes a promise that she knows or should know will induce the promisee to act in reliance on the promise to his detriment (detrimental reliance), the promise may be enforced to the extent justice requires.[1] In addition, a minority of jurisdictions follow the past consideration or moral obligation doctrine to enforce a promise to repay a material benefit previously received if enforcement is needed to prevent injustice.[2]

Generally, contract law permits anything to be the subject of a bargain as long as there is legal value. If Mary promised to give Jane her coffee table in exchange for Jane promising to be Mary's best friend, the exchange of promises would fail for lack of consideration. Why? Because a promise to be someone's best friend does not have legal value. If the subject matter of the contract has legal value, courts generally find consideration.

The subject matter of the bargain can be a benefit to the promisee or it can be a detriment to the promisor. This means that what the promisor promises can be something that improves the situation of the promisee (such as payment of money or delivery of a good), or it can be something that the promisor has to do (or refrain from doing) that she would otherwise have no obligation to do (or refrain from doing), even if the promisee is no better off as a result.

CLASSIC CASE

HAMER v. SIDWAY, 124 N.Y. 538 (1891)

Uncle promised his nephew $5,000 if he refrained from drinking, using tobacco, swearing, and playing cards or billiards for money until he became 21 years of age. The nephew did as agreed and after he turned 21, informed his uncle. In a letter, his uncle acknowledged that he owed his nephew the money, but said he would hold it for his nephew until the nephew felt ready to use it. Several years later, the uncle died without having paid the nephew the money. The uncle's executor claimed that the contract was without consideration and refused to pay. The court disagreed, stating that consideration may be a benefit to one party or a forbearance or detriment to the other party. Because the nephew restricted his lawful freedom of action and fully performed, it did not matter that the performance did not benefit the uncle.

1 RESTATEMENT (SECOND) CONTRACTS, §90.
2 RESTATEMENT (SECOND) CONTRACTS, §86.

Reflection Prompt: What are the reasons for the requirement of consideration and how do they affect this case?

The following clauses are examples of a statement of consideration, which is often found at the beginning of a contract as part of the recitals and before the body of the contract. It indicates that each party is making the promises in exchange for the promises made by the other.

Example clause

NOW, THEREFORE, in consideration of the mutual promises set forth in this Agreement, the parties agree to the following...

Example clause

NOW, THEREFORE, for the price and sum of Ten ($10.00) Dollars, cash in hand to us paid and other good and valuable considerations not herein mentioned, the receipt and sufficiency of all of which is hereby acknowledged...

Reflection Prompt: Examine the two Example Clauses above. What difference, if any, does it make to state a nominal sum and the words "the receipt and sufficiency of all of which is hereby acknowledged..."?

The recitals typically have no operative effect in that they don't require the parties to do anything, but that does not mean they serve no purpose. Remember that the parties involved in negotiating a contract may not be the same individuals who review the contract at a later date. The company may continue to be the "party" to the contract, but there may no longer be anyone who originally worked on the transaction at the company. Recitals provide background information to those who may not have worked on the transaction and are tasked with fulfilling its obligations at a later date. This is especially helpful if the transaction is unusual or non-standard for the company.

In addition, some courts will find that a recitation of consideration raises a rebuttable presumption of consideration.[3] Other courts find that the presumption is conclusive.[4] A court may take the recitals into account in

---

3 Estate of Fallon v. Fallon, 30 So. 3d 1281 (Miss. App., March 23, 2010) (deed that recited consideration "for the price and sum of Ten ($10.00) Dollars, cash in hand to us paid and other good and valuable considerations not herein mentioned, the receipt and sufficiency of all of which is hereby acknowledged" constituted a presumption of consideration that was not rebutted by the evidence). *Id.* at 1282.

4 Network Protection Services, LLC v. Fortinet, Inc., 2013 WL 4479336 (N.D. Cal).

interpreting or construing the contract.[5] For example, in one case, a court found that oral evidence that a conveyance was a gift was held ineffective to establish a gift as it contradicted recitals in the deed that consideration was paid.[6]

CASE HIGHLIGHT

NETWORK PROTECTION SCIENCES v. FORTINET, 2013 WL 4479336 (N.D. Cal 2013)

Network Protection Sciences (NPS) sued Fortinet for patent infringement. NPS had obtained the patent through an assignment agreement with a third party. One of the arguments made by Fortinet was that the assignment agreement was void for lack of consideration because NPS never paid for the patent. The assignment agreement stated that the patent was assigned "for good and valuable consideration, the receipt of which is hereby acknowledged." The court, applying Texas law, found:

> "This recital is conclusive. Even if no actual consideration were paid . . . NPS's agreement to be bound by the choice-of-law provision would be deemed adequate consideration."

Courts are more likely to uphold a mere recital of consideration where a transfer of property is involved. Courts typically will not invalidate a present grant of property for lack of consideration. Furthermore, the Restatement[7] provides that signed and delivered voluntary, written assignments are irrevocable. In other words, after you give a gift, you can't take it back by claiming you didn't receive consideration for it.

---

5 Burch v. Premier Homes, LLC, 199 Cal. App. 4th 730, 744 (Cal. App. 2d Dist. Div. 3, Sept. 28, 2011) (stating that where there is an apparent conflict between different clauses, the circumstances and the conditions and motives of the parties as shown by recitals should be taken in consideration).

6 Mahoney v. Mahoney, 103 S.W.2d 459, 461 (Tex. Civ. App. Feb. 5, 1937); In re Bishop's Estate, 209 Cal. App. 2d 48, 57–58, 25 Cal. Rptr. 763, 768–69 (Cal. App. 1962) (finding that recital that transfer effected was for "Ten Dollars and other valuable consideration" constituted a declaration by the grantor and competent evidence of the facts recited and dissipated any presumption that transfer was a gift).

7 RESTATEMENT (SECOND) CONTRACTS, §332(1), comment b.

CASE HIGHLIGHT

KELLER v. BASS PRO SHOPS, INC., 15 F.3d 122 (8th Cir. 1994)

Keller, the assignor of a patent, sought declaratory judgment that the assignment was void for lack of consideration. The assignment recited that it was made for "good and valuable consideration, the receipt and sufficiency of which are hereby acknowledged." The Court of Appeals for the Eighth Circuit, applying Arkansas law, held that Keller was estopped from challenging the assignment on the basis of lack of consideration because consideration was recited in the written instrument of assignment. It stated:

> "Under Arkansas law, recitation of consideration estops the grantor of the deed from claiming that it was executed without consideration . . . The purpose of such recitations is precisely to estop parties to the transaction from claiming that no consideration was received."

The court then went on to say that, in the alternative, the patent assignment was a "completed voluntary conveyance" and was therefore "not subject to attack for lack of consideration . . . A voluntary written assignment of a chose in action is irrevocable once the instrument is signed and delivered; consequently, it cannot later be set aside by the assignor for lack of consideration."

Troubleshooting: It generally doesn't hurt to include recitals, and it may save a contract from a claim of lack of consideration. Do not, however, *substitute* recitals or the statement of consideration for the consideration provisions in the agreement. The promises and performance obligations of the parties should be expressed in order to avoid later misunderstandings or disputes.

In some cases, however, the bargain may not be evident. For example, a guaranty may contain an obligation from the guarantor but it may not be clear what the guarantor is getting in return. In those cases, it's a good idea to include a recital of consideration because the exchange may not be evident.

Caveat: Although courts usually don't evaluate the contract terms to determine whether the consideration is adequate, there must in fact *be* consideration. In other words, the purported consideration must not be a sham. In some states, such as California, a written agreement is presumptive evidence of consideration.[8] Some courts may permit evidence which shows that

8 Cal. Civ. Code §1614 ("A written instrument is presumptive evidence of a consideration").

consideration was not paid[9] although other courts do not.[10] Jurisdictions may permit nominal consideration (i.e. a very small amount of money) or a recitation of consideration, to bind options and guaranties provided that certain requirements are met (such as the option or guaranty is in writing).[11] An option keeps an offer open for a specified period of time. A guaranty is a promise to pay for the debt of another.

Note: A recital of consideration will not bar the use of parol or extrinsic evidence to show fraud.[12]

CLASSIC CASE

DOUGHERTY v. SALT, 227 N.Y. 200 (1919)

In this Classic Case, the plaintiff sued his aunt's estate to recover on a promissory note that his aunt left him. After hearing from his guardian how her nephew was a "nice boy" and doing well in school, the aunt indicated she would like to help take care of her nephew and wrote a note for $3,000 which contained the words "for value received." The court noted that the words "for value received" raised an "inference of consideration." This inference, however, was overcome by the evidence. As the court noted:

> "This is a case where the testimony in disproof of value comes from the plaintiff's own witness, speaking at the plaintiff's instance. The transaction thus revealed admits of one interpretation and one only. The note was the voluntary and unenforceable promise of an executory gift."

Although most first-year casebooks use *Dougherty v. Salt* to illustrate that gratuitous promises are not binding, the case shows that words of consideration *do* have some effect, but that they may be overcome by evidence.

---

9 Sfreddo v. Sfreddo, 59 Va. App. 471, 720 S.E.2d 145, 154–56 (Va. App. Jan. 24, 2012) (stating that where no bargain actually occurred, the purported consideration is not in fact consideration).

10 Keller v. Bass Pro Shops, Inc., 15 F.3d 122 (8th Cir. 1994) (finding that assignor was estopped from challenging assignment on the basis of lack of consideration because consideration was recited in the written instrument of assignment and noting that "[t]he purpose of such recitations is precisely to estop parties to the transaction from claiming that no consideration was received.") *Id.* at 124.

11 Farrar v. Young, 158 W. Va. 977, 216 S.E.2d 575 (1975) (one dollar recited in deed is sufficient valuable consideration). Tyson v. McPhail Properties, 223 Ga.App. 683, 686(3); 478 S.E.2d 467 (1996) (recitation of $10 in option agreement signed under seal was sufficient to support agreement); *see also* RESTATEMENT (SECOND) CONTRACTS, 87 (1).

12 Hayes v. Sanger, 218 Ark. 716, 722–23, 239 S.W.2d 22, 25 (1951) (recital of consideration may estop grantor from alleging lack of consideration but may not be used to deny evidence of fraud or lack of volition on part of grantor).

Reflection Prompt: Would the result in *Dougherty v. Salt* have been different if the plaintiff's witness believed the note was given in exchange for continued good behavior from the nephew?

Caveat: The parol evidence rule and the four corners rule (which exclude a party from introducing evidence that the parties meant something other than what was written in the contract) do not prevent the admission of extrinsic evidence (meaning evidence outside the agreement) to resolve an *ambiguity*. If the agreement does not specify the nature of the consideration, but states only "for value received," a court may find an ambiguity that permits the admission of parol evidence to explain the specific nature of the consideration.[13]

CASE HIGHLIGHT

NASH v. TOWNSHIP INVESTMENTS, LLC, 320 Ga. App. 494 (2013)

Township loaned $475,151.93 to Metropolitan Land Development and Investment Corporation. Norman Nash, as Metropolitan's Chief Executive Officer, signed a promissory note to Township and also signed a personal guaranty. The note, signed in 2005, was renewed several times so that by September 2008, Metropolitan's indebtedness to Township exceeded $670,000. On September 8, 2008, Norman Nash and Norris Nash signed a promissory note (the "Note"). It stated:

> "For value received, the undersigned Norman J. Nash and Norris J. Nash (the "Borrowers") jointly and severally promise to pay to the order of Township Investments, LLC (the "Lender") the sum of Four Hundred Seventy eight Thousand, Eight Hundred Dollars ($478,800.00) together with interest from September 8, 2008 on the unpaid principal at the rate of Eight Percent (8%) per annum, compounded monthly."

The Nashes defaulted on the note and Township sued. The trial court granted summary judgment in favor of Township and the Nashes appealed.

The Nashes raised the affirmative defense that there was no consideration for the note. The testimony regarding the intent of the Nashes in signing the Note was disputed. Given this factual dispute, the Georgia Court of Appeals concluded that a genuine issue of material fact existed as to whether the borrowers received consideration and reversed the trial court's grant of summary judgment:

---

13 Nash v. Township Investments, LLC, 320 Ga. App. 494, 740 S.E.2d 236 (2013). *But see* Schron v. Troutman Saunders LLP, 20 N.Y.3d 430 (January 10, 2013) (recital of "other good and valuable consideration" in option agreement containing merger clause was not ambiguous and therefore extrinsic evidence was not permitted).

CASE HIGHLIGHT *(continued)*

"The terms of the note do not specify the nature of the consideration that the Nashes received in exchange for executing the note . . . Instead the Note states that it was given "[f]or value received." This recital is an ambiguity that, in light of the Nashes' defense, permits the admission of parol evidence regarding the specific nature of the consideration."

Troubleshooting: To avoid a dispute about whether consideration was received, the contract should contain express language regarding the specific nature of the consideration.

Example clause

Licensee shall pay the fees and royalties on Schedule 1 in exchange for the license granted to Licensee by Licensor in Section 2.

Example clause

In exchange for Company's obligation to pay Participant pursuant to Section 2.3, the Participant agrees as follows . . .

Reflection Prompt: What are the advantages and disadvantages to having the fees and royalties listed on an attachment or schedule to the agreement (as in the first Example Clause)? When would a party prefer to list consideration on an attachment rather than in the body of the agreement?

As the next Case Highlight explains, sometimes the parties may not want to reveal the consideration that was paid in a purchase document. They may use the language of "ten dollars and other valuable consideration," to establish that the contract is supported by consideration. The "ten dollars" or other sum sets forth a specific amount while the "other valuable consideration," language indicates a larger amount that is more than "nominal."[14]

14 Jarns Holding Inc. v. Huang, 2007 N.Y. Misc. LEXIS 6132 (Civil Court of the City of New York, July 23, 2007).

CASE HIGHLIGHT

JARNS HOLDINGS INC. v. HUANG, 2007 N.Y. Misc. LEXIS 6132, 238 N.Y.L.J. 37 (2007)

The petitioner purchased a building on March 21, 2002. At the time, the petitioner was aware of a master lease which had been given by its predecessor-in-interest to a third party. Subsequently, the master lease was extinguished and petitioner sought possession of the subject apartment. The respondent claimed that he entered into a sublease with the third party who held the master lease. The sublease provided that the third party leased the apartment to the respondent "on a long-term basis" and included a fixed monthly rental amount. The sublease was never recorded. The petitioner argued that it was a subsequent purchaser for valuable consideration and in good faith and that the sublease was void against it as it did not have actual or constructive notice of it.

Under N.Y. law, the sublease must be recorded in order to be valid against the petitioner provided the petitioner was a subsequent purchaser in good faith and for valuable consideration. The respondent argued that the petitioner was not a good faith purchaser for valuable consideration because the deed petitioner received contained a recital of consideration for only "Ten Dollars and other valuable consideration." Respondent argued that this was clearly not a "fair equivalence" for the property conveyed.

The court disagreed:

"In contract law, the phrasing of consideration as 'Ten Dollars and other valuable consideration' or 'One Dollar and other valuable consideration' are very common ways to recite consideration in a contract for the sale of real property. The 'valuable consideration' portion of the recital creates a presumption of consideration . . . However, this sort of recital by itself is insufficient to support a promise, so a specific amount is added to the recital, and such a nominal sum is called a 'peppercorn' . . . This type of recital of consideration signifies the fulfillment of adequate consideration by listing a specific amount to be paid, and goes on to include a general phrasing of consideration, 'and other valuable consideration', which belies a much larger sum that ultimately proves the consideration to be adequate.

Peppercorns are commonly used because buyers, for various sound business reasons, do not wish to publicly disclose in the purchase instrument exactly what they paid for a particular piece of real property, or other asset. As there must be a specific amount paid in a contract for it to be valid, the 'Ten Dollars' serves as that nominal sum, or the 'peppercorn'. The 'other valuable consideration' is the language that masks the larger sum, and is what makes the consideration 'adequate' as relative to the thing being purchased . . . Proof that a purchaser paid valuable consideration for a deed constitutes prima facie evidence that the purchase was in good faith and would remain sufficient unless overcome by other proof . . . Petitioner states it has, and can present to the court, proof of the substantial consideration it paid for the subject building. It has not done so yet. If it does, and provided respondent does not present convincing evidence to the contrary (not done as yet), the Court will find that pursuant to Real Property Law §291, petitioner is a subsequent purchaser in good faith and for valuable consideration who recorded first."

Caveat: Typically, courts do not consider the adequacy of consideration for purposes of contract formation but an imbalance in the values exchanged may indicate a sham or nominal consideration, or that the transaction was invalid on the grounds of fraud, mistake, misrepresentation, duress, or some other invalidating cause.[15] Furthermore, adequate, valuable or fair consideration may be required for certain transactions under state law[16] or to protect the rights of subsequent transferees. For example, a general rule in property law is that a bona fide purchaser for value cuts off the rights of prior assignees or purchasers who have failed to record the prior transaction.[17] In other words, a subsequent purchaser without notice cuts off the rights of a prior purchaser who has failed to properly record its interests only if that subsequent purchaser in fact paid valuable consideration and was not a donee or other gratuitous transferee.[18]

The word "consideration" or "exchange" is not required:

---

15 ALLAN FARNSWORTH, CONTRACTS, 3rd ed. §2.11 (". . . a seller promises to sell a farm in return for the buyer's promise to pay a dollar or the buyer's actual payment of a dollar. Is the seller's promise supported by consideration? To say that it is would not mean that the promise is necessarily enforceable. The imbalance in the exchange might still be used to support a showing, for example, of misrepresentation or duress by the buyer, of joking or mistake by the seller, of the seller's mental incompetency, or of the unconscionability of the bargain.") FARNSWORTH 3rd edition at 71 (1999). Farnsworth further notes that such transactions typically arise in the context of "disguised gratuitous promises." *Id.*

16 *See,* for example, N.Y. CLS Dr. & Cr. §273 (2014). ("Every conveyance made and every obligation incurred by a person who is or will be thereby rendered insolvent is fraudulent as to creditors without regard to his actual intent if the conveyance is made or the obligation is incurred without a fair consideration.") NY CLS Dr & Cr. §272 (2014) defines "fair consideration" as follows:

"Fair consideration is given for property, or obligation.

a. When in exchange for such property, or obligation, as a fair equivalent therefor, and in good faith, property is conveyed or an antecedent debt is satisfied, or

b. When such property, or obligation is received in good faith to secure a present advance or antecedent debt in amount not disproportionately small as compared with the value of the property, or obligation obtained."

See also Berndt v. Berndt, 192 Misc 57, 79 N.Y.S.2d 143 (1948) (no "fair consideration" under N.Y. CLS Dr. & Cr. §273 where property had fair market value of $7,000 and recital in deed was for $1.00 paid).

17 In the Case Highlight, Jarns Holdings Inc. v. Huang, the court considered whether ten dollars constituted "valuable consideration" because the New York statute governing recording of conveyances stated that unrecorded conveyances are void against any subsequent purchaser in good faith and for a valuable consideration. N.Y. CLS Real P. §291; *see also* 35 U.S.C. §261 ("Applications for patent, patents, or any interest therein, shall be assignable by law by an instrument in writing . . . An assignment, grant or conveyance shall be void as against any subsequent purchaser or mortgagee for a valuable consideration, without notice, unless it is recorded in the Patent and Trademark Office within three months from its date or prior to the date or such subsequent purchase or mortgage").

18 Filmtec Corporation v. Allied Signal, Inc. and UOP, Inc., 939 F.2d 1568 (Fed. Cir. 1991) ("Both the common law rule and the statute contemplate that the subsequent purchaser be exactly that – a transferee who pays valuable consideration, and is without notice of the prior transfer . . . the requirement is that the subsequent purchaser, in order to cut off the rights of the prior purchaser, must be more than a donee or other gratuitous transferee. There must be in fact valuable consideration paid so that the subsequent purchaser can, as a matter of law, claim record reliance as a premise upon which the purchase was made.") *Id.* at 1574.

Example clause

Company shall pay Partner a referral fee of three percent (3%) based upon the net revenue recognized from the licensing of Company products paid to Company from the referral account obtained by Partner.

Example clause

Licensee shall pay the Licensor a royalty of 3% per Product sold or used by Licensee or Licensee's customers.

Reflection Prompt: Compare the language in the two Example Clauses above. Which clause contains more precise language? How would the referral fee be calculated (and what does "net revenue recognized" mean)? If you were representing Partner, would you request any changes to the language in the first Example Clause? Why? Does the language in the second Example Clause create an ambiguity?

Even though consideration is typically *money* exchanged for a product or service, it doesn't have to be money. It can be an exchange of services or products or the opportunity to do something (or refrain from doing something).

Example clause

In exchange for my participation in the production of *Sea Buoys,* I agree to the following terms and conditions . . .

Caveat: Generally, be wary of "at will" provisions. These provisions contain the words "at will" or "at any time." A contract containing a "modification at will" provision means that it may be modified by one party at any time. If a party may change a term "at will" then a court may find that the party's promise is illusory and that the party is not truly obligated or committed to the term.

Example clause

Company may change the terms of this Agreement at any time without notice.

Another common "at will" provision is a "termination at will" provision.

Example clause

Company may terminate Consultant with or without cause and with or without notice.

Example clause

Either party may terminate this Agreement at any time without notice.

"Termination at will" provisions are fairly common in distributorship agreements. If one party has the unlimited right to cancel or terminate for any reason, the contract may be void for lack of mutuality.[19] Most courts, however, are moving in the direction of finding that the implied covenant of good faith and fair dealing constrains the discretion of the party with the power to terminate the contract.

Furthermore, if there is an express notice period, even a short one, most courts will *not* find the agreement to be illusory.[20]

Example clause

Either party may terminate this Agreement at any time upon thirty days' notice.

The clause above is *not* illusory because there is a notice requirement. Because each party is obligated to abide by the contract for at least 30 days, the contract is not illusory.

Employment contracts typically contain "at will" provisions.

19 Miami Coca-Cola Bottling Co. v. Orange Crush, 296 F. 693 (C.C.A. 5th Cir. 1924) (agreement where manufacturer could cancel license at any time was void for lack of mutuality).

20 Alpha Distributing Co. of California, Inc. v. Jack Daniel, 454 F.2d 442 (1972) (finding that distributorship that lasted more than ten years was terminable upon reasonable notice and that three months constituted reasonable notice). Some courts, however, do not require notice of termination where the distributorship is terminable at will. *See* Kraftco Corp. v. Kolbus, 1 Ill. App. 3d 635, 274 N.E.2d 153 (1971); Dunn v. Goebel Brewing Co., 357 Mich. 693, 99 N.W.2d 380 (1959) (defendant has contractual right to terminate agreement at will).

Example clause

Both parties acknowledge that Company or Employee may terminate Employee's employment with Company at any time for any reason, including no reason at all, and that Company may demote or discipline Employee or alter the terms of Employee's employment at any time in its discretion, with or without cause, notwithstanding anything to the contrary contained in or arising from any handbook, statements, policies, or practices of Company relating to the employment, discipline, or termination of its employees.

As a matter of policy, people should not be forced to work together if they are incompatible. On the other hand, courts recognize that there is usually a power imbalance in employment situations, with the employer in a much stronger position than the employee. Courts generally enforce "at will" employment contracts provided the employer acts in good faith.[21] Good faith is an abstract concept but generally means that the employer is acting honestly. In other words, an employer who fires a sales person who has just closed a big deal to avoid paying commission is not acting in good faith. An employer also cannot fire someone for a discriminatory reason, such as finding out the employee is of a particular religious faith.

In addition, satisfaction clauses such as the following raise the issue of consideration because one of the parties has the power to reject the other party's performance.

Example clause

Contractor shall perform the work as specified in the Statement of Work and subject to the Company's satisfaction and approval.

The Company in the Example Clause above has the discretion to determine whether the work is satisfactory. Nevertheless, most courts would find the clause is *not* illusory because the Company must exercise its discretionary authority in good faith or in a commercially reasonable manner.[22] The

21 O'Connor v. Hayes Body Corp., 258 Mich. 280, 242 N.W. 233 (1932) (employment agreement for no definite term was terminable at will by either party); Kelley v. City of Mesa, 873 F. Supp. 320, 329, 3 AD Cas. 983 (D. Ariz 1994) (Arizona recognizes implied covenant of good faith and fair dealing in employment "at will" situations but that does not create duty to terminate employee only for good cause); Caton v. Leach Corp., 896 F.2d 939, 946 (5th Cir. 1990) (noting that California's implied covenant of good faith and fair dealing does not obliterate right to "at will" termination of employment expressly embodied in written contract).

22 Mattei v. Hopper, 51 Cal. 2d 119, 330 P.2d 625, 627 (1958); Western Hills, Oregon, Ltd. v. Pfau, 265 Or. 137, 143, 508 P.2d 201, 208 (1973) (noting that satisfaction clauses generally fall into two categories, those

Company is thus bound to the contract by its obligation to act reasonably or in good faith, depending upon the nature of the work. If evaluating the work requires personal judgment, then the Company can reject the Contractor's work in good faith. If, however, the work can be evaluated using an objective measure, then the Company can reject it only if the work fails to conform to that objective measure. Some contract clauses expressly put the requirement to act in good faith and/or in a reasonable manner in the contract. For example:

Example clause

Contractor shall perform the work as specified in the Statement of Work and subject to the Company's satisfaction and approval. Company agrees to act in good faith and in a timely and commercially reasonable manner in approving the work.

Caveat: Beware that even careful drafting may not transform the standard applicable to the satisfaction clause. Most courts will impose a commercially reasonable standard if objective criteria can be applied.

A party's discretionary authority may be of concern in purchase or supplier agreements. If, for example, the agreement states that one party must supply goods to the other party, but does not require the other party to purchase goods and does not otherwise restrict that party's ability to purchase from other suppliers, a court may find the agreement is illusory and unenforceable.

UCC §2-306 expressly recognizes requirements and output contracts and imposes a duty of good faith on the parties. Requirements contracts require the buyer to purchase all of a specified good only from the supplier who promises to supply the same over a period of time. Output contracts require the supplier to sell all of her output of agreed-upon goods to the buyer who agrees to purchase the same. Although the buyer does not agree to purchase, and the seller does not agree to produce, a specified quantity of goods, the UCC requires that the parties exercise their obligations in good faith.

Caveat: If the contract restricts both parties in *some way*, courts will generally find consideration. This restriction may be one that limits the parties from entering into a similar transaction with other parties, such as an exclusivity requirement.

---

involving taste, fancy or personal judgment, which requires the party act in good faith, and those which involve utility, fitness or value, which requires the party act reasonably).

A potential pitfall involving consideration is when the parties modify or change the terms of the agreement. Although the Restatement (in certain circumstances)[23] and the UCC permit modifications without consideration,[24] most jurisdictions require new consideration in order to make a modification binding. Therefore, the parties must agree to a new bargain, such as an additional payment or service, in exchange for whatever is being modified.

An accord is an agreement to discharge an existing disputed claim. An accord needs consideration in order to be enforceable. A different performance or settlement of a good faith dispute would constitute sufficient consideration. The accord is satisfied when the agreement is performed.

CLASSIC CASE

FOAKES v. BEER, 9 App. Cas. 605 (1884)

Foakes owed Beer £2,090.19s. The parties entered into an agreement which provided that if Beer forgave the interest on his debt, Foakes would pay Beer £500 of his debt immediately and the remainder of the principal in installments. Beer later brought suit against Foakes for the interest, alleging that any agreement to forgive interest was without consideration since Foakes, by paying Beer as promised, was only doing what he already had a legal obligation to do. The court ruled in Beer's favor, upholding the principle that "payment of a lesser sum on the day cannot be any satisfaction of the whole, because it appears to the judges that by no possibility a lesser sum can be a satisfaction to the plaintiff of a greater sum."

Reflection Prompt: If Foakes had agreed to deliver a box of homemade cookies with every payment to Beer, would the accord have been enforceable?

"Modification at will" provisions, such as the following, are common in digital agreements on websites.

Example clause

Company reserves the right to modify or discontinue, at any time and from time to time, the Services or any part of the Services, with or without notice.

---

23 RESTATEMENT (SECOND) CONTRACTS permits modifications without consideration if the modification is "fair and equitable in view of circumstances not anticipated by the parties when the contract was made." *Id.* at §89.

24 UNIFORM COMMERCIAL CODE, §2-209(1).

As more companies conduct business electronically and through their websites, parties should realize the impact of these digital contracts on their transactions *and* on their negotiated contracts. While some courts would invalidate a contract containing a "modification at will" provision, surprisingly, several have enforced them where the provision was contained in a company's "terms of use" on its website and the user continued to use the website after having received notice of the modified terms.[25]

CASE HIGHLIGHT

VERNON v. QWEST COMMUNICATIONS INTERN., INC., 857 F.Supp. 2d 1135 (D. Colo. 2012)

Plaintiffs were subscribers to Qwest's Internet service who challenged a $200 early termination fee. Qwest filed a motion to compel arbitration pursuant to its Subscriber Agreement. One of the arguments raised by plaintiffs was that the arbitration clause was illusory because Section 4 of the agreement stated that Qwest may:

"(a) *at any time, effective upon posting to* www.quest.com/legal *or any written legal notice to you, including e-mail*: (i) stop offering the Service and/or rental Equipment, (ii) modify the Service and/or any of the terms and conditions of this Agreement . . . Please check such website and your e-mail regularly for changes.

(b) *upon 30 days notice to you*: . . . (ii) change this Agreement or the Service in a way that directly results in a material and adverse economic impact to you. Qwest may reduce the foregoing notice period where commercially reasonable and/or if such increase is based upon Regulatory Activity.

Your continued use of the Service and/or Equipment constitutes acceptance of those changes. You must immediately stop using the Service and Equipment and cancel your Service if you do not agree to the changes. Any changes or other terms you make to this Agreement or propose in any other documents, written or electronic, are void."

The court found that the arbitration provision was enforceable under Colorado law because each party had made promises under the Subscriber Agreement. Therefore, "even if that particular clause [Section 4] lacks mutuality" the court found the arbitration provision was not illusory.

25 *See*, for example, Vernon v. Qwest Communications International, Inc., 857 F. Supp. 2d 1135, 1153–1156 (D. Colo. 2012) (upholding "modification at will" provision); *but see* Harris v. Blockbuster, Inc., 622 F. Supp. 2d 396, at 399 (N.D. Tex. 2009) (striking down "modification at will" provision as illusory); *In re Zappos.com, Inc., Customer Data Security Breach Litigation* 2012 WL 4466660 at *5 (D. Nev.) ("Most federal courts that have considered this issue have held that if a party retains the unilateral, unrestricted right to terminate the arbitration agreement, it is illusory and unenforceable, especially where there is no obligation to receive consent from, or even notify the other parties to the contract.").

Other courts have reached a different conclusion and found "modification at will" clauses to be unenforceable, such as in the following case.

CASE HIGHLIGHT

IN RE ZAPPOS.COM, INC., CUSTOMER DATA SEC. BREACH, 893 F.Supp. 2d 1058 (D. Nev. 2012)

Plaintiffs sued Zappos, an online retailer of shoes, after a security breach that resulted in the theft of their personal information from Zappos' servers. Zappos moved to compel arbitration pursuant to its online agreement. Zappos' Terms of Use stated:

> "We reserve the right to change this Site and these terms and conditions at any time. ACCESSING, BROWSING OR OTHERWISE USING THE SITE INDICATES YOUR AGREEMENT TO ALL THE TERMS AND CONDITIONS IN THIS AGREEMENT, SO PLEASE READ THIS AGREEMENT CAREFULLY BEFORE PROCEEDING" (emphasis in original).

Plaintiffs argued that because the Terms of Use granted Zappos the unilateral right to revise the arbitration clause, the contract was illusory and therefore, unenforceable. The court agreed, denying Zappos' motion to compel arbitration and finding

> "[E]ven if Plaintiffs could be said to have consented to the terms, the Terms of Use constitutes an illusory contract because it allows Zappos to avoid arbitration by unilaterally changing the Terms at any time while binding any consumer to mandatory arbitration in Las Vegas, Nevada."

Caveat: A "modification at will" provision provides an example of "greedy drafting" which may hurt the drafter. By inserting such a provision, the drafter intends to preserve the right to change terms at will, leaving it unconstrained by the contract. While this may seem like a good idea, a court may find that the term renders the contract void for lack of mutuality. In other words, the party with the ability to change terms at will is not actually bound by the contract and so the contract lacks consideration. A contract without consideration is *void*. This leaves the company without any contract at all because *none of the provisions are enforceable if the contract has not been validly formed*!

Finally, in the employment context, some courts have held that a noncompete agreement entered into after an employee has started work is validly formed only if there is independent consideration, such as additional compensation or a "bonus". Courts are split regarding whether continued employment constitutes consideration for the new agreement.[26]

As previously noted, many contracts specifically state that modifications need to be in writing. These clauses are referred to as "NOM" or "no oral modification" clauses. The UCC permits such provisions, meaning that if the contract contains a NOM clause, modifications must be in writing. (A court, however, may find that a party has "waived" the writing requirement.)[27] With respect to those contracts not governed by the UCC, many courts may refuse to enforce these clauses, thus permitting oral modifications.[28] There are, however, exceptions[29] and some states, such as New York, have enacted legislation permitting them.[30]

Example clause

This Agreement may not be modified or amended except in a writing signed by a duly authorized representative of either party.

Evidence of an oral modification is not excluded by the parol evidence rule because it is evidence of an agreement entered into *after* the written agreement was signed. The NOM clause, however, is usually included in an integration clause.

---

26 Labriola v. Pollard Group, 152 Wash. 2d 828 (2004) (continued employment of an "at will" employee did not serve as consideration in exchange for signing agreement not to compete); *but see contra* Centrol, Inc. v. Morrow, 489 N.W.2d 890 (1992) (finding signing of new non-competition agreements while already employed did not fail for lack of consideration).

27 UCC §2-209(4): "Although an attempt at modification or rescission does not satisfy the requirements of subsection (2) or (3) it can operate as a waiver".

28 City of Indianapolis v. Twin Lakes Enterprises, Inc., 568 N.E.2d 1073, 1084–85 (Ind. App. 1 Dist. 1991) (stating that a contract providing that modifications must be in writing may "nevertheless be modified orally").

29 Regions Equipment Finance Corp. v. AT 2400, Official Number 530775, 640 F.3d 124, 128 (5th Cir. 2011) (noting that while the traditional common law rule is that no oral modification clauses are unenforceable, the rule is not always followed); Martinsville Nylon Employees Council Corp. v. N.L.R.B., 969 F.2d 1263, 1267 (D.C. Cir. 1992) (noting that "in modern times, the common law rule has been discarded in broad areas and criticizing the common law rule because it "denies to all contracting parties, no matter how sophisticated, the ability to decide for themselves whether to restrict the manner in which their agreement may be modified").

30 *See* N.Y. Gen. Oblig. L. §15-301(1) ("A written agreement . . . which contains a provision to the effect that it cannot be changed orally, cannot be changed by an executory agreement unless such executory agreement is in writing and signed by the party against whom enforcement of the change is sought or by his agent); Cal. Civ. Code §1698(c) ("Unless the contract otherwise expressly provides, a contract in writing may be modified by an oral agreement supported by new consideration. The statute of frauds is required to be satisfied if the contract as modified is within its provisions.").

Remember that oral modifications, like written ones, must be supported by consideration unless the transaction is governed by the UCC or a jurisdiction which does not require consideration for modifications.

Caveat: Remember that the Statute of Frauds requires that some contracts must be in writing. If the agreement as modified falls within the Statute of Frauds, the modification must be in writing.

Consideration includes price and payment terms. It also includes terms related to pricing, such as warranties or warranty disclaimers. A seller may want to include a clause that makes clear that warranty disclaimers were part of the consideration for the transaction.

Example clause

Basis of Bargain. Each party recognizes and agrees that the warranty disclaimers and liability and remedy limitations in this Agreement are material bargained for bases of this Agreement and that they have been taken into account in determining the consideration to be given by each party to enter into this Agreement.

4.2 Doctrinal concept: offer and acceptance

Principle: The formation of a contract requires offer and acceptance, which means that the parties must have a present intent to enter into an agreement.

In order for a contract to be formed, there must be an offer. An offer is an expression of present intent to enter into a contract, which means that the offeror is making clear a desire to enter into a contract immediately. The offer must contain terms definite and substantial enough that the promises and performances of the parties can be determined. The offer must be seasonably accepted, meaning that the offeree must accept within the time frame stated by the offer or, if no time frame is stated, within a reasonable time. The acceptance must also be unequivocal, and not subject to or conditioned upon any additional or different terms.[31] A conditional acceptance is not an effective acceptance but is instead a counteroffer. A counteroffer is both a rejection of the offer and a new offer which means that if the original offeror accepts the counteroffer, a contract is formed.

31 A conditional acceptance means that an offer has not been accepted. It should not be confused with conditions to performance in a contract. *See* Part III.C (2).

In first-year contracts classes, an example like the following is typically used to illustrate the concept of offer and acceptance:

"Dorothy Baum offers to sell to Betsy Rodriguez her car for $500. Betsy Rodriguez agrees to purchase Dorothy Baum's car for $500."

In the above scenario, Dorothy Baum is the offeror and Betsy Rodriguez is the offeree. In actual business transactions, however, the scenario is typically not so straightforward. In some cases, the offer may be in the form of an offer letter executed by only one party and then signed by the other to indicate acceptance. But in many business transactions, the contract is negotiated by both parties. Both parties are offerors and both parties are offerees.

Example clause

Cascade Range, Inc. and Dino, LLC agree as follows . . .

Caveat: Contracting can take different forms. While this book focuses on negotiated paper contracts which are signed, contracts can take other forms. With non-traditional contracting formats (also known as "wrap contracts"),[32] offer is typically in the form of reasonable notice that contract terms apply and acceptance take the form of a manifestation of assent after having an opportunity to reject. For example, a contract may be plastic-wrapped with a computer software disc, a form referred to as a shrinkwrap agreement. The offeree manifests assent and accepts the terms of the offer by opening the plastic wrap and using the software disc instead of rejecting the terms and returning the software disc to the place of purchase.[33] A clickwrap is a digital agreement to which the offeree manifests assent by clicking on an icon or button that indicates acceptance to the terms.[34]

In some cases, the parties may not be sure that they want to enter into the transaction but they want to explore the possibility. They may sign a letter of intent (also known as an "LOI") or memorandum of understanding (also known as an "MOU"). The parties may include or sign separately a term sheet,

32 *See*, for example, NANCY S. KIM, WRAP CONTRACTS: FOUNDATIONS AND RAMIFICATIONS 2–3 (2013) (referring to certain non-traditional forms as "wrap contracts").

33 *See* ProCD v. Zeidenberg, 86 F.3d 1447, 1452 (7th Cir. 1996).

34 For a more comprehensive discussion of offer and acceptance with wrap contracts and how they differ from traditional rules of offer and acceptance, *see* KIM, *supra* n. 32, at 93–126; *see also* Berkson v. Gogo, 2015 WL 1600755 at *15–18 (2015).

which outlines the basic terms of the deal.[35] The purpose of a term sheet is to put down on paper the deal points to determine whether the parties want to enter into the deal before they are committed to it. Although the parties do not intend to be bound to the transaction as a result of these documents, they may intend for certain provisions to be binding. These provisions may include confidentiality obligations and/or an obligation to negotiate the underlying transaction in good faith. The parties should clearly specify which provisions they intend to be binding and which provisions they intend to be non-binding.

Troubleshooting: If the parties do not draft the letter of intent to clearly indicate that it is non-binding, a court may find that it creates binding obligations. In some cases, even where a court found a letter of intent to be non-binding, it held that the parties had an obligation to negotiate in good faith.[36] The parties themselves may create an obligation to negotiate in good faith either expressly or through their actions.[37]

CASE HIGHLIGHT

SIGA TECHNOLOGIES, INC. v. PHARMATHENE, INC., 67 A.3d 330 (Del. 2013)

SIGA owned ST-246, an anti-viral drug for the treatment of smallpox. The efficacy of the drug was uncertain when SIGA, encountering financial difficulties, entered into discussions with PharmAthene about a possible collaboration. The parties eventually agreed to outline the terms of a license agreement. The two page license agreement term sheet ("LATS") stated the parties intended to "establish a partnership to further develop and commercialize [ST-246] for the treatment of [s]mallpox and orthopox-related infections and to develop other orthopox virus therapeutics." It also contained terms relating to covered patents, licenses, license fees, and royalties. The term sheet was not signed and contained a footer on each page that stated "Non Binding Terms." Subsequently, PharmAthene decided that it preferred a merger instead of a license agreement with SIGA. The parties drafted a merger term sheet that included the following provision:

35 Please do not confuse a letter of intent with a letter of agreement. The parties intend for the latter to be binding.

36 Weigel Broadcasting v. TV-49, 2006 WL 3486861 (N.D. Ill. Nov. 29, 2006).

37 SIGA Technologies, Inc. v. PharmAthene, Inc., 67 A.3d 330 (Del. 2013); Gregory J. Marsden and George J. Siedel, *A Comparative Law Perspective on Legal Limitations of Negotiating Power: Is BATNA Legal?* (draft on file with author) (explaining how even sophisticated negotiators may be trapped by an agreement to negotiate in good faith with the consequences of having to pay expectation damages).

CASE HIGHLIGHT *(continued)*

> "SIGA and PharmAthene will negotiate the terms of a definitive License Agreement in accordance with the terms set forth in the Term Sheet . . . attached on Schedule 1 hereto. The License Agreement will be executed simultaneously with the Definitive [Merger] Agreement and will become effective only upon the termination of the Definitive Merger Agreement."

The LATS was attached as an exhibit to the merger term sheet. On March 10, the parties signed a merger letter of intent and attached the merger term sheet and the LATS.

On March 20, 2006, the parties entered into a Bridge Loan Agreement where PharmAthene loaned SIGA $3million for expenses relating to the merger and for costs related to developing ST-246. It contemplated that the parties might not ultimately agree on either a merger or license agreement; however, it also stated the following in Section 2.3:

> "Upon any termination of the Merger Term Sheet . . . termination of the Definitive Agreement relating to the Merger, or if a Definitive Agreement is not executed . . ., SIGA and PharmAthene will negotiate in good faith with the intention of executing a definitive License Agreement in accordance with the terms set forth in the License Agreement Term Sheet . . . and [SIGA] agrees for a period of 90 days during which the definitive license agreement is under negotiation, it shall not, directly or indirectly, initiate discussions or engage in negotiations with any corporations, partnership, person or other entity or group concerning any Competing Transaction without the prior written consent of the other party or notice from the other party that it desires to terminate discussions hereunder."

On June 8, 2006, the parties signed the Merger Agreement, which contained a Section 12.3 which was nearly identical to Section 2.3 of the Bridge Loan Agreement and provided that if the merger was terminated, the parties agreed to negotiate in good faith to enter into a license agreement with the terms of the LATS. Section 13.3 also stated that the parties must use their "best efforts to take such actions as may be necessary or reasonably requested by the other parties hereto to carry out and consummate the transactions contemplated by this Agreement."

SIGA terminated the Merger Agreement and soon thereafter announced that it had received a $16.5 million NIH grant and that ST-246 provided 100 percent protection against smallpox in a primate trial. SIGA subsequently proposed different economic terms from those contained in the LATS. When PharmAthene objected, SIGA argued that the LATS was not binding because of the "Non-Binding Terms" footer. PharmAthene filed suit. The Vice Chancellor of the Court of Chancery entered judgment in favor of PharmAthene and SIGA appealed. The Supreme Court of Delaware found that "[t]he express contractual language in the Bridge Loan and Merger Agreements obligated the parties to 'negotiate in good faith with the intention of executing a definitive License Agreement in accordance with the terms set forth in the LATS.'" The court stated that this meant the parties had to

CASE HIGHLIGHT *(continued)*

negotiate in good faith a license agreement with economic terms "substantially similar" to the terms of the LATS:

> "Although the LATS itself is not signed and contains a footer on each page stating 'Non Binding Terms,' the record supports the Vice Chancellor's factual conclusion that 'incorporation of the LATS into the Bridge Loan and Merger Agreements reflects an intent on the part of both parties to negotiate toward a license agreement with economic terms substantially similar to the terms of the LATS if the merger was not consummated.'"

The court concluded that SIGA breached its contractual obligations under both the Merger Agreement and the Bridge Loan Agreement.

Reflection Prompt: What facts suggest that SIGA had not acted to negotiate in good faith?

Parties who do not intend to create binding obligations should use express language to make that clear:

Example clause

This is a non-binding letter of intent which is intended to facilitate negotiation and preparation of the Agreement which will embody the final understanding between the parties. Except for the obligation of confidentiality set forth in section 3.2, this letter of intent does not create legally binding obligations of the parties.

Example clause

Neither party will be legally bound or have any rights under this letter of intent as a result of discussions between the parties or their lawyers or the preparation of any draft documents. Either party may discontinue or terminate discussions at any time without incurring any liability to the other party. Each party acknowledges that nothing herein restricts the other party from entering into negotiations of any kind with any other party.

Reflection Prompt: What are the differences between the two Example Clauses above? Under what circumstances might a party prefer the first Example Clause? Under what circumstances might a party prefer the second Example Clause?

Caveat: Remember that most agreements do not need to be in writing in order to be binding. The parties should be aware that their words and actions may create an oral agreement. Furthermore, even though a promise may not amount to an offer, a promisee may still be permitted to recover under the doctrine of promissory estoppel.[38]

Troubleshooting: Offer and acceptance may become an issue where the contract terms are not definite enough to make clear what the obligations of the parties are. This can be the result of vague language but it can also be the result of not using the present tense. For example, the following is inadequate to express a present intent:

Example of an ineffective clause

Dorothy Baum will sell to Betsy Rodriguez her car for $500. Betsy Rodriguez will agree to purchase Dorothy Baum's car for $500.

An assignment of intellectual property rights should be in the present tense in order to be effective. For example, the following is *incorrect.*

Incorrect!

Contractor will assign all right, title and interest in and to the Work as defined above.

The above is the *incorrect* way to draft an assignment. Although it may be grammatically accurate to put the assignment in the future tense because the work has not yet been created, it is incorrect from a legal standpoint. The assignment must be in the present tense in order to make it a present assignment.

38 *See*, for example, Hoffman v. Red Owl Stores, Inc., 26 Wis. 2d 683, 698 (1965) (promise giving rise to the cause of action does not have to be so comprehensive as to meet the requirements of an offer for a contract); RESTATEMENT (SECOND) CONTRACTS, §90(1).

Example clause

Contractor hereby assigns all right, title and interest in and to the Work.

A failure to put the clause in the present tense may lead a court to find that the Contractor has not yet made the assignment and that something further must happen before legal title is transferred.[39] As the following Case Highlight indicates, this may have significant ramifications.

CASE HIGHLIGHT

BOARD OF TRUSTEES OF THE LELAND STANFORD JUNIOR UNIVERSITY v. ROCHE MOLECULAR SYSTEMS, INC., 583 F.3d 832 (Fed. Cir. 2009) (aff'd 131 S.Ct. 2188 (2011))

Stanford University sued Roche Molecular Systems, a manufacturer of HIV detection kits for patent infringement. Roche claimed that Stanford lacked standing because Roche had ownership interests in the relevant patents. The technology related to the patents was developed by researchers at Stanford and Cetus, a research company. (Roche eventually purchased Cetus's business related to this research, including its agreements). One of the researchers, Mark Holodniy, signed an agreement with Stanford University which stated: "I agree to assign or confirm in writing to Stanford . . . right title and interest" in any inventions. Holodniy also conducted research at Cetus and signed an agreement stating: "I will assign and do hereby assign to CETUS, my right, title, and interest in each of the ideas, inventions and improvements." The United States Court of Appeals for the Federal Circuit found that the contract language "agree to assign" reflects a "mere promise to assign rights in the future, not an immediate transfer of expectant interests," so that Stanford did not immediately gain title to Holodniy's inventions, although it may have gained certain equitable rights against Holodniy. By contrast, the language "do hereby assign" contained in the Cetus agreement did effect a present assignment of Holodniy's future inventions so that Cetus immediately gained title to Holodniy's inventions.

39 Board of Trustees of the Leland Stanford Junior University v. Roche Molecular Systems, Inc., 583 F.3d 832 (Fed. Cir. 2009), aff'd 131 S.Ct. 2188 (2011).

An offer creates in the offeree the power of acceptance meaning that the offeree has the power to create a binding contract by accepting. The offeree's power of acceptance may be terminated if the offeror revokes the offer prior to the offeree's acceptance. The offeree's power of acceptance may also be terminated by rejecting the offer. Once rejected, the offeree cannot later accept unless the offeree had paid for an option to keep the offer only. As previously noted, even nominal consideration suffices for an option contract.[40] Part performance[41] or reliance[42] may create an option contract, meaning that the offer may be irrevocable at least for a period of time if the promise has partially performed or detrimentally relied upon the promise.

The offer may specify a particular mode or method of acceptance and an acceptance must comply with the terms of the offer.[43] An offer that invites acceptance by performance is called an offer for a unilateral contract. An offer that invites acceptance by a return promise is called an offer for a bilateral contract. If the offeror does not specify how to accept (by return promise or performance) or the manner or mode of acceptance, both the Restatement and the UCC permit acceptance either by promise or by performance[44] and in "any manner . . . and any medium reasonable in the circumstances."[45] A late acceptance is not in compliance with the terms of the offer. An offer that sets a specific time for acceptance lapses upon the expiration of that time so that a late acceptance does not result in contract formation.[46]

A counteroffer is both a rejection of an offer (which terminates the offeree's power of acceptance) and an offer (which creates in the original offeror the power of acceptance). A late acceptance creates a counteroffer which must be accepted in order to form a contract.[47]

40 RESTATEMENT (SECOND) CONTRACTS, §87(1).
41 RESTATEMENT (SECOND) CONTRACTS, §45(1).
42 RESTATEMENT (SECOND) CONTRACTS, §87(2).
43 RESTATEMENT (SECOND) CONTRACTS, §60.
44 RESTATEMENT (SECOND) CONTRACTS, §32; UCC §2-206((1)b).
45 RESTATEMENT (SECOND) CONTRACTS, §31(2); UCC §2-206((1)a).
46 RESTATEMENT (SECOND) CONTRACTS, §41(1).
47 Ruggerio v. Dynamic Elec. Sys. Inc., 2012 WL 3043102, at *10 (E.D.N.Y. July 25, 2012) (noting that "a late acceptance creates a counteroffer, which must in turn be accepted by the original offeror to create a contract.") *See also* RESTATEMENT (SECOND) CONTRACTS, §70, cmt. a (late or defective acceptance has the "effect of a counter-offer").

CASE HIGHLIGHT

RUGGERIO v. DYNAMIC ELEC. SYS. INC., 2012 WL 3043102, 2012 U.S. Dist. LEXIS 103940 (E.D.N.Y. July 25, 2012)

Defendant sent a Letter Agreement and a Release to plaintiff. The Letter Agreement stated:

> "you are eligible to receive the severance benefits described in this letter ("Letter Agreement") if you will sign and return the Letter Agreement *and* Attachment A ("Release") to me by March 19, 2011 and do not revoke your acceptance." (emphasis in original)

Plaintiff signed the Release on April 6, 2011, more than two weeks after the deadline in the Letter Agreement and never signed the Letter Agreement. In a letter dated June 13, 2011, plaintiff wrote to defendants stating that she did not consider the Letter Agreement and Release binding. In a letter dated July 11, 2011, defendants mailed a check to plaintiff allegedly representing the settlement amount. The plaintiff rejected the check and repeated that she considered the Release "null and void."

The court agreed, noting that the Letter Agreement provided a specific method of acceptance and that it was "undisputed that plaintiff never signed the Letter Agreement and did not sign the Release until April 6, 2011. Thus, plaintiff's acceptance was late and defective." Plaintiff's late and defective acceptance constituted a counteroffer which was never accepted by defendants. The attempted July payment by defendants could not constitute acceptance because it occurred several weeks after plaintiff had already revoked her counteroffer.

If the transaction involves the sale of goods and the transaction is conducted using one or more forms, special rules apply under UCC § 2-207.[48] Many companies conduct business using form contracts, and the exchange of contracting

48 UCC §2-207: "Additional Terms in Acceptance or Confirmation

(1) A definite and seasonable expression of acceptance or a written confirmation which is sent within a reasonable time operates as an acceptance even though it states terms additional to or different from those offered or agreed upon, unless acceptance is expressly made conditional on assent to the additional or different terms.

(2) The additional terms are to be construed as proposals for addition to the contract. Between merchants such terms become part of the contract unless:
   (a) the offer expressly limits acceptance to the terms of the offer;
   (b) they materially alter it; or
   (c) notification of objection to them has already been given or is given within a reasonable time after notice of them is received.

(3) Conduct by both parties which recognizes the existence of a contract is sufficient to establish a contract for sale although the writings of the parties do not otherwise establish a contract. In such case the terms of the particular contract consist of those terms on which the writings of the parties agree, together with any supplementary terms incorporated under any other provisions of this Act."

forms has been referred to as the "Battle of the Forms," as each party tries to prevail through the use of its form. Recall that under common law rules of offer and acceptance, an acceptance must be definite and unequivocal. A purported acceptance that stated different or additional terms was a counteroffer. If the parties proceeded with the transaction after an exchange of forms, the terms of the last form would govern under the common law. §2-207 addresses the Battle of the Forms situation and changes the common law.

In order to be effective under §2-207, an acceptance must be "definite and seasonable" meaning that the acceptance must be clear and unequivocal and communicated in a timely manner. What happens if the acceptance, though definite and reasonable, contains terms that are not contained in the offer? The acceptance is effective even if it contains terms that are "additional to or different from" the terms on the form containing the offer unless the acceptance is "expressly made conditional on assent to the additional or different terms." If the acceptance is not expressly made conditional on assent to the additional or different terms, then what happens next depends upon whether the parties are both merchants. It may be helpful to proceed step by step through §2-207 with the help of the flow chart in Figure 4.1.

Assume that Buyer is interested in buying some chairs from Seller. Buyer sends Seller a purchase order for 100 chairs at $10.50/chair. The following outlines what happens in different scenarios:

(1) Seller sends Buyer a sales acknowledgment form which states that it will sell the chairs for $11/chair. Seller has *not* made a "definite" acceptance but has instead made a counteroffer.

(2) Instead of (1), assume Seller sends Buyer a sales acknowledgment form which states:

"The acceptance of Buyer's order is expressly made conditional on Buyer's assent to the terms and conditions set forth herein."

Seller has not accepted Buyer's purchase order but has made a counter offer. Buyer must specifically and affirmatively agree to the Seller's terms in order for the terms to govern.[49] Note how the language in Seller's form tracks the language of UCC §2-207(1).

---

49 *See* PCS Nitrogen Fertilizer, L.P. v. Christy Refractories, L.L.C., 225 F.3d 974, 980 (8th Cir. 2000) (noting that "mere acceptance of and payment for goods does not constitute acceptance of all the terms in the seller's counter-offer" but that "specific and affirmative assent" is necessary).

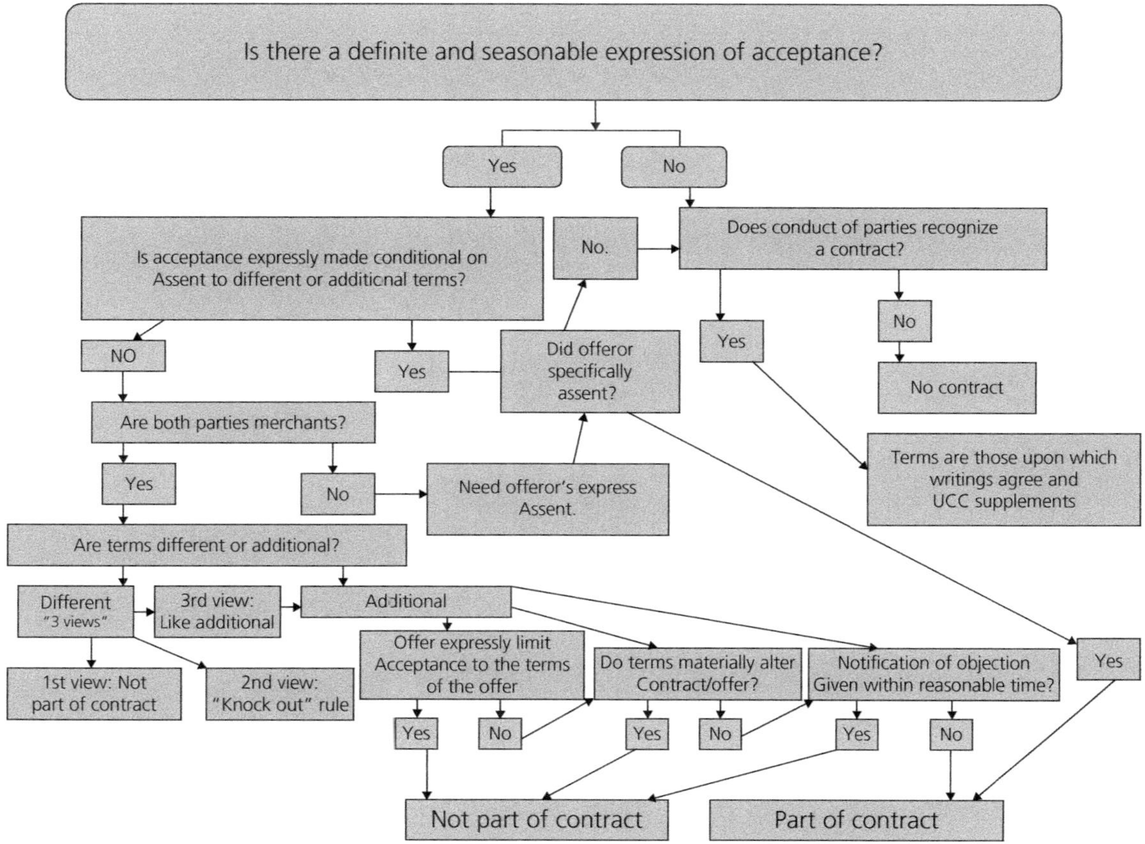

Figure 4.1 What terms govern in a "Battle of the Forms" situation under UCC §2-207?

(a) If, after sending the sales acknowledgment form, the Seller ships the chairs and Buyer pays for them without specifically agreeing to Seller's terms, then under §2-207(3), their conduct manifests the existence of a contract. The contract terms are the price and quantity agreed upon and UCC gap filler terms supplement.[50]

(3) Instead of (1) or (2), assume Seller sends Buyer a sales acknowledgment form which contains the following language:

"All requests for returns or refunds must be made in writing within thirty days and sent to the address on the top of this form."

Buyer's purchase order contained no language about what to do in the event of returns or refunds.

(a) Is the language a material alteration of Buyer's form? A material alteration means that the additional language creates an unfair surprise or a hardship for Buyer. Examples of a material alteration include limitations of liability, warranty disclaimers, and forum selection clauses. A requirement of written notice such as that contained on the Seller's form, on the other hand, is standard and so unlikely to be considered a material alteration.

(b) What if Buyer's purchase order contained the following language?

> "This purchase order expressly limits acceptance to its terms and conditions, and notification of objection to any different or additional terms in any response to this offer from the Seller is hereby given."

If Buyer's purchase order contained the above language, then Seller's additional terms are not part of the contract because the purchase order "expressly limits acceptance" to the terms of the offer and "notification of objection" has been given – even though the additional terms don't materially alter the offer. Again, note that the language in the form (this time, Buyer's form contract) mirrors the language in UCC §2-207(2).

(4) Instead of (1)–(3), assume Seller sends Buyer a sales acknowledgment form which includes a warranty disclaimer. These provisions materially alter the offer and do not become part of the contract.[51]

---

50 UCC gap filler terms are UCC provisions that provide default terms which apply to a transaction unless the parties have agreed to other terms. They generally consist of §§2-301 to 2-319 of the UCC and include warranty, price and delivery terms.

51 *See* Southeastern Adhesives Co. v. Funder America, Inc., 366 S.E.2d 505, 508 (1988) (finding warranty

(5) Instead of (1)–(4), assume that Buyer's purchase order contains a provision that requires that all disputes be subject to arbitration before the International Chamber of Commerce in Vienna, Austria. Seller's sales acknowledgment form contains a provision stating that all disputes must be brought in the federal and/or state courts in Chicago, Illinois. (Assume that Seller's form did not state that acceptance was expressly made conditional on assent to its terms). Which dispute resolution terms govern?

(a) Under the "knock out" rule, which is the majority view, the conflicting terms knock themselves out so that neither party's dispute resolution terms become part of the contract.[52]

In international transactions for the sale of goods, it may be the United Nations Convention on the International Sale of Goods ("CISG") and not the UCC which governs the transaction. The CISG applies if the parties have their place of business in different nation states and those nation states have ratified the CISG, or if the parties chose to have their contract governed by the CISG. The United States is a member of the CISG, and so are many other countries although notably, the United Kingdom is not. The CISG treats "Battle of the Forms" situations differently from the UCC. Under Article 19(1) of the CISG, a Seller's reply (to a purchase order/offer) which contains additional terms is a counteroffer.[53] If Buyer accepts the goods, then Buyer accepts the Seller's terms.

Troubleshooting: The parties may opt out of the CISG[54] but the language must specifically do so as courts have held that the general choice of law clause does not exclude the application of the CISG.[55] The parties may opt out of the CISG by including a clause like the following in their contract:

disclaimers to be ineffective as they materially altered offer); UCC 2-207, Cmt. 4 (citing disclaimers of standard warranties as that of merchantability or fitness for particular purposes as examples of clauses that would normally "materially alter" the contract).

52 This hypothetical is based upon Flender Corp. v. Tippins, Intern., Inc., 830 A.2d 1279 (Pa. 2003). In that case, the court refused to compel arbitration as neither dispute resolution provisions was part of the contract. Presumably then, the claim could be brought in any court with jurisdiction. In that case, the suit was brought in Pennsylvania, where the defendant was located.

53 CISG Article 19.

54 CISG Article 6.

55 *See* Kurt M. Saunders and Leondard Rymsza, *Contract Formation and Performance Under the UCC and CISG: A Comparative Case Study*, 32 J. of Legal Studies 1–46 (2015).

Example clause

Unless otherwise required by applicable law, this Agreement and any action related thereto will be governed and interpreted by and under the laws of the State of Utah without giving effect to any conflicts of law principles that provide for the application of the law of another jurisdiction. The United Nations Convention on Contracts for the International Sale of Goods does not apply to this Agreement. Any claim, dispute, or action arising, directly or indirectly, from this Agreement shall be litigated in the state or federal courts located in Salt Lake County, Utah and the parties irrevocably consent to the personal jurisdiction of such courts.

Example clause

The parties hereby exclude application of the United Nations Convention on the International Sale of Goods (CISG) to any transaction under this contract. Any dispute arising under this contract will be governed by the laws of the State of California, United States of America, excluding its conflict of laws. Any dispute arising under this contract shall be subject to the exclusive jurisdiction of the state of California or a United States federal court located in the State of California. The Seller waives any and all objections that it might otherwise have as to personal jurisdiction and venue in these exclusive tribunals.

APPLYING WHAT YOU LEARNED

Contract clauses involving contract formation

Bernardo Buyer, a real estate developer, was interested in purchasing and developing a ten-acre parcel of Samuel Seller's property. In order to split the parcel and develop the property, county permits were required but the Seller did not want to obtain those permits himself. Buyer and Seller entered into an agreement which provided for Seller to sell the ten-acre parcel for $500,000 by September 2006 if Buyer decided to purchase the property after Buyer sought the county approvals and permits at Buyer's expense. The Agreement contained certain "Contingencies," including the following in Paragraph 7:

"7. It is the intent of Buyer that the time period from execution of this contract until the closing of escrow is the time that will be needed in order to be successful in developing this project. It is expressly understood that the Buyer may, at its absolute and sole discretion during this period, elect not to continue in this transaction and this purchase contract will become null and void."

1. Do you see any problems with Paragraph 7 of this Agreement? If you were representing Buyer, what could you do to avoid any potential problems?

2. Assume that Buyer has spent thousands of dollars to obtain the necessary county approvals when Seller decides he does not want to sell the property. Buyer seeks specific performance of the agreement. Will Buyer prevail? What arguments might Buyer make?

4.3 Doctrinal concept: mutual assent

Principle: The parties must share the same understanding of what they are agreeing to as judged by their words or acts (meaning assent is determined objectively by what they say and how they act, not what they subjectively believed or meant by their words and deeds).

While parties to a commercial transaction may reach agreement on the general subject matter of the contract, they may disagree on important terms. If essential terms are omitted, a court may find a lack of mutual assent.

Troubleshooting: A potential area of concern is where one party believes a term has one meaning, and the other party believes it has another. If the term is important, one party may claim a lack of mutual assent. Not surprisingly, many contracts contain a "definitions" section. These defined terms are intended to ensure that the parties mean the same thing when they refer to a particular term.

Example clause

"Software" – "Software" mean Botsys' Level 1 software in object code format order by ConSystems but not including any updates."

Caveat: Pay special attention to defined terms that you might mistake for generic terms elsewhere in the contract. Assume that the agreement between Botsys and ConSystems contained the following warranty provision:

"Botsys warrants that for a period of ninety (90) days from the delivery of Software, the Software, if properly used by ConSystems, shall operate in conformity with the Documentation for such Software."

ConSystems might mistakenly believe that the warranty includes updates to the Software but the defined meaning of "Software" does not include updates. This might also affect other provisions, such as the indemnification provision if, for example, Botsys only indemnifies ConSystems for claims brought for using the "Software" and the claim is based upon the use of an update.

5

Contract clauses and contract enforceability

There are different reasons why a contract may be unenforceable even though the basic ingredients of contract formation (offer, acceptance, consideration, and mutual assent) exist. Contract defenses are set forth in different doctrinal categories, such as fraud, duress, unconscionability, and mistake. The parties may include a provision that addresses several doctrinal concepts that share the same underlying principle.

5.1 Doctrinal concepts: duress, undue influence, and unconscionability

Principle: A party must enter into an agreement voluntarily and of his or her own free will.

An essential ingredient to a valid contract is that the parties freely consented. A contract is basically private law created by two individuals. In our democratic, free market society, judicial intervention into a private agreement is justified only if each party voluntarily entered into the agreement. If a party was forced to enter into the contract, the justification for contract enforcement by the court disappears.

The concepts of voluntariness and free will, however, are abstract and in a society where people have different levels of power and money, it can be difficult to determine whether someone actually consented to something. How much pressure is too much pressure? Duress, undue influence and unconscionability all involve situations where one of the parties argues that he or she did not really want to agree to the contract but was pressured to do so. Duress requires the highest level of pressure or coercion. In most jurisdictions, there must be some sort of threat which makes it clear that the party seeking to escape the contract felt as though he or she had no choice but to agree to the contract terms. In a commercial setting, that usually means that the other party failed to act in good faith and used hardball tactics that exceeded what was socially acceptable. Undue influence involves an abuse of power where one party was unfairly persuaded or exploited by someone with whom he or she had a close or confidential relationship. This would include an unscrupulous attorney persuading a client to make her the beneficiary of the client's will. No threat is required because of the nature of the relationship. Unconscionability does not require a threat or a special relationship but it does require unfairness. Unconscionability has both a procedural and substantive element.[1] It usually requires a finding that the terms are unfair and favor one party (substantive unconscionability) and that the manner in which the transaction was entered into was unfair (procedural unconscionability). Generally, unconscionability is a "sliding scale," meaning that the more substantively oppressive the terms, the less evidence is required of procedural unconscionability and vice versa.[2] If a court finds a contract or clause to be unconscionable, it may refuse to enforce the clause or the contract or it may limit the application of the clause to avoid an unconscionable result.[3]

CLASSIC CASE

WILLIAMS v. WALKER-THOMAS FURNITURE CO., 350 F.2d 445 (D.C. Cir. 1965)

Williams purchased several household items from Walker-Thomas. The payments were to be made in installments and the terms of each purchase were contained in a printed-form contract which provided that title would remain in the furniture company until the total of all the monthly payments made equaled the stated value of the item. In the event of a default in the payment of any monthly installment, Walker-Thomas could repossess the item. The printed-form contract contained the following provision:

> "the amount of each periodical installment payment to be made by [purchaser] to the Company under this present lease shall be inclusive of and not in addition to the amount of each installment payment to be made by [purchaser] under such prior leases, bills or accounts; and all payments now and hereafter made by [purchaser] shall be credited pro rata on all outstanding leases, bills and accounts due the Company by [purchaser] at the time each such payment is made."

The effect of the provision was to keep a balance due on every purchased item until the balance on all items, whenever purchased, was fully paid.

1 Carmona v. Lincoln Millennium Car Wash, Inc., 226 Cal. App. 4th 74 (2014).
2 Armendariz v. Foundation Health Psychcare Services, Inc., 24 Cal. 4th 83 at 114 (2004).
3 *Id.* (citing Cal. Civ. Code. §1650.5, subd. (a)).

CLASSIC CASE *(continued)*

The court stated:

"Unconscionability has generally been recognized to include an absence of meaningful choice on the part of one of the parties together with contract terms which are unreasonably favorable to the other party. Whether a meaningful choice is present in a particular case can only be determined by consideration of all the circumstances surrounding the transaction. In many cases the meaningfulness of the choice is negated by a gross inequality of bargaining power. The manner in which the contract was entered into is also relevant to this consideration. Did each party to the contract, considering his obvious education or lack of it, have a reasonable opportunity to understand the terms of the contract, or were the important terms hidden in a maze of fine print and minimized by deceptive sales practices? Ordinarily, one who signs an agreement without full knowledge of its terms might be held to assume the risk that he has entered a one-sided bargain. But when a party of little bargaining power, and hence little real choice, signs a commercially unreasonable contract with little or no knowledge of its terms, it is hardly likely that his consent, or even an objective manifestation of his consent, was ever given to all the terms. In such a case the usual rule that the terms of the agreement are not to be questioned should be abandoned and the court should consider whether the terms of the contract are so unfair that enforcement should be withheld.

In determining reasonableness or fairness, the primary concern must be with the terms of the contract considered in light of the circumstances existing when the contract was made."

The court remanded to the trial court for further proceedings.

Arbitration clauses[4] may trigger an unconscionability analysis where the clauses are one-sided.[5] The following case provides an example of an agreement which a court found unconscionable. Note how the unconscionability analysis hinges upon one provision, yet that provision affects the operation of the entire agreement. As the case demonstrates, a court may choose not to sever an unconscionable provision even if doing so would save the rest of the agreement. The case also provides a useful example of how legislation may affect a court's analysis of the enforceability of a contract.

4 An arbitration clause requires a party to submit to a private hearing rather than permitting the party to file a claim in a court of law.

5 Arnold v. United Companies Lending Corp., 204 W.Va. 229, 511 S.E.2d 854 (1998) (finding arbitration agreement with nonreciprocal obligations unconscionable); Carmona v. Lincoln Millenium Car Wash, 226 Cal. App. 4th 74 (2014) (one-sided arbitration clause unconscionable); Caplin Enters. v. Arrington, 2014 MISS. LEXIS 232 (May 8, 2014) (arbitration agreement unconscionable where defendant check cashing business could pursue "all" judicial remedies while plaintiffs had to submit claims to arbitration).

CASE HIGHLIGHT

CARMONA v. LINCOLN MILLENIUM CAR WASH, INC., 226 Cal. App. 4th 74 (2014)

Plaintiffs were employed by defendant car wash companies and brought a class action against them for wage and hour violations. Each plaintiff had signed an employment agreement which contained the following clauses:

> "Settlement by Arbitration
> Any dispute under or out of or regarding any aspect of employee's employment, including its information, or any act which would violate any provision in this employment contract, shall be resolved exclusively through final and binding arbitration by an experienced licensed [sic] to practice law in California and selected in accordance with the expedited Employment Dispute rules of the American Arbitration Association in effect at the time of such dispute, pursuant to the Federal Arbitration Act. Judgment will be on any award by arbitrator's by [sic] in any court having jurisdiction."

. . .

> "Confidential Information
> "I acknowledge that I have been informed that it is the policy of the Employee to maintain as secret and confidential all information relating to [the car wash] and my employment.
>
> "I agree and understand that any problems or concerns with anything related to my at will employment with [sic] be discussed with management and ownership so it can be resolved before any information is divulged to any persons, firms, corporations, media agency, governmental entities or agencies, other entities [sic]."

. . .

The agreement also contained a subagreement entitled "Confidentiality Agreement," which stated:

> "*Confidential Information.* Employee acknowledges that he/she has learned and will learn Confidential Information, as defined herein, relating to the business conducted by [the car wash]. Employee agrees that he/she will not, except in the normal and proper course of his/her duties, disclose or enable anyone else to disclose or use, either during the Employment Term or subsequent thereto for the applicable period of, any such Confidential Information without prior written approval from [the car wash].
>
> "'Confidential Information' shall include, but not [be] limited to, the following types of information, both existing and contemplated, and regarding [the car wash]; corporate information, including contractual licensing arrangements, plans, strategies, tactics, policies, resolutions,

CASE HIGHLIGHT *(continued)*

> patent applications and any litigation or negotiations; marketing information, including sales or product plans, strategies, tactics, methods, customers, prospects, or market research data; financial information, including costs and performance data, debt arrangements, equity structure, investors and holdings; operational formulae, control and inspection practices and background information suppliers; technical information, including machinery, designs, drawings and specifications; and personnel information, including personnel lists, resumes [sic], pay rates, personnel data, organizational structure and performance evaluations."

. . .

The subagreement also stated the following:

> "*Enforceability*. The Employee understands that [the car wash]'s position is highly dependent on the Confidential Information. . . . Any disclosure or breach of this Agreement will cause immediate, irreparable harm to [the car wash]. THAT IS TO INCLUDE any information shared with other employees of the company. Any breach or threatened breach of this Agreement, therefore may be present [sic] to either a court or binding arbitrator for enforcement by both injunction and damages. In the event that [the car wash] institutes litigation or arbitration seeking enforcement of this Agreement, [the car wash] shall be entitled to recover reasonable attorney fees and costs incurred in such litigation or arbitration."

. . .

The arbitration clause and the confidentiality clause had been translated into Spanish but no part of the confidentiality subagreement, including the enforceability clause, had been translated into Spanish. The native language of the plaintiffs was Spanish and they could not read English. Each plaintiff testified that he thought the employment agreement was a work application that had to be signed in the form presented to him, that the agreement was not explained to him and that he did not understand he was waiving his rights.

First, the court explained that the "arbitration agreement" included the clause entitled "Settlement by Arbitration," as well as the provisions in the subagreement that pertained to dispute resolution procedures. The court, citing both Cal. Civ. Code §1641 ("The whole of a contract is to be taken together, so as to give effect to every party, if reasonably practicable, each clause helping to interpret the other") and §1642 ("Several contracts relating to the same matters, between the same parties, and made as parts of substantially one transaction, are to be taken together"), noted that despite the clauses being under separate headings, they should be read in conjunction to ascertain the "entire" arbitration agreement.

The court found the agreement to arbitrate unconscionable. It noted that procedural unconscionability depends upon whether there is oppression or surprise due to unequal bargaining power. The court stated:

> "Oppression arises from an inequality of bargaining power, when one party has no real power to negotiate or a meaningful choice. Surprise occurs when the allegedly unconscionable provision is hidden. Here, we have both oppression and surprise."

CASE HIGHLIGHT *(continued)*

The agreement to arbitration was procedurally unconscionable because it was an "adhesion contract," which was presented on a non-negotiable basis by the car wash companies who were in a superior bargaining position to the employees who were seeking a job. There was no evidence that the employees had an opportunity to negotiate the terms. The defendants did not provide the applicable rules of the American Arbitration Association, did not explain what the agreement meant, and gave plaintiffs insufficient time to review the agreement. The court stated that what elevated this case to a "high degree" of procedural unconscionability was the enforceability clause, which was left untranslated in Spanish.

The court noted that given the high degree of procedural unconscionability, "even a low degree of substantive unconscionability could render the arbitration agreement unconscionable." The court, however, found that the level of substantive unconscionability was not particularly low. As made clear by the enforceability clause, the arbitration required arbitration for only the employees, who were the weaker party in terms of bargaining power. The employer, on the other hand, had the option of choosing court or arbitration.

In addition, attorneys' fees were available only to the employers. The employers argued that a CA statute, Civ. Code §1717, rendered the one-sided attorneys' fees provision mutual. Cal. Civ. Code §1717 states that a contract provision which gives one party the right to attorneys' fees will also apply to the other if it is the prevailing party. The court rejected this argument as "flawed logic" as that statute was intended to prevent the application of substantively unconscionable attorneys' fee provisions – not save them from being found unconscionable.

The court also found that the arbitration agreement lacked mutuality because it presumed "immediate, irreparable harm" to the defendants but does not state a similar presumption of harm to employees.

Finally, the court found the provision which required the employees to discuss any problems with the defendants before divulging that information to anyone else lacked mutuality because the employer had no similar obligation to discuss concerns with employees first. The result would be that the employer would have a "free peek" at any case the employee might bring against them.

The defendants also argued that the trial court abused its discretion by not severing the unconscionable provisions while still preserving the agreement to arbitrate in the arbitration clause. The court disagreed, stating that the existence of multiple unconscionable provisions demonstrated a systemic lack of mutuality and therefore, the trial court did not abuse its discretion.

The terms "mutuality," "mutuality of obligation," and "mutuality of consideration" confuse students, practitioners, and even judges.[6] It's better to focus on the effect that a lack of mutuality has. Was there valid consideration – did *both* parties make a binding commitment? If the promise of one party was illusory and did not actually bind that party, then the contract lacks consideration and was not validly formed.

The issue of contract formation is distinct from that of contract enforceability. Are the provisions lopsided? Do they favor one party more than the other? That's not a problem with formation as long as there is valid consideration. Remember, the things being exchanged do not have to be of equal value – the bargain doesn't have to be "fair" in order for it to constitute consideration. Fairness, however, may affect whether the contract is enforceable.

CLASSIC CASE

BATSAKIS v. DEMOTSIS, 226 S.W.2d 673 (1949)

Demotsis was in dire financial circumstances in Greece during World War II, although she had money and property in the United States. Batsakis agreed to lend to Demotsis 500,000 drachmae which at the time, had the value of approximately $25.00 in U.S. money. In return, Demotsis executed a note that stated that she had received from Batsakis $2,000 in U.S. money and that she promised to return the money to him after the war ended or before, if possible. The court found that "[m]ere inadequacy of consideration will not void a contract . . . Defendant got exactly what she contracted for according to her own testimony."

The court awarded Batsakis the $2,000 with interest.

In order to be validly formed, a contract must be supported by consideration. This means that each party to a contract must be bound or committed in some way but it does not mean that they must be bound or committed *in the same way*.[7]

6 Dan Ryan Builders, Inc. v. Nelson, 230 W.Va. 281 (2012). In answering in the negative the question of whether W. Virginia law requires that an arbitration provision be supported by mutual consideration when the contract is supported by adequate consideration, the Supreme Court of W. Virginia noted that the "federal district court previously determined that the arbitration provision was not enforceable because it lacked mutuality of obligation" and "mutuality of consideration." *Id.*

7 *Id.* at 289 ("So long as the overall contract is supported by sufficient consideration, there is no requirement of consideration for each promise within the contract, or of 'mutuality of obligation,' in order for a contract to be formed").

For example, assume Retailer enters into a contract to purchase as many tee shirts as she wants from Manufacturer for $5/shirt but makes no commitment to purchase any minimum quantity of shirts from Manufacturer, and is not limited in any other way (i.e. Retailer has not agreed to purchase exclusively or even primarily from Manufacturer). Retailer has not actually made a commitment although Manufacturer has. If Retailer orders shirts from Manufacturer, Manufacturer would have to supply them at $5/each. This contract lacks consideration. Although $5 for a shirt constitutes consideration, Retailer is not actually committed to paying that $5, although Manufacturer is committed to supplying shirts *if* Retailer places an order. Because Retailer's promise is illusory, the contract is not binding.

Retailer's obligations, however, do not have to be the same or symmetrical to Manufacturer's obligations. Retailer, for example, may be able to terminate the agreement upon 10 days' notice while Manufacturer must give Retailer a year's notice. While the terms may be lopsided, that does not mean the contract lacks consideration.

While the obligations agreed to by both parties need not be symmetrical in order for a contract to be validly formed, it may affect whether the contract will be *enforced*. (Remember that formation of a contract is not the same thing as enforceability of a contract. A properly formed contract may still be invalid or unenforceable.) A court may consider whether a provision is so unfair as to be unconscionable.[8] In the example where Retailer may terminate the agreement upon 10 days' notice while Manufacturer must give a year's notice, it is probably not unconscionable. There may be a legitimate business reason for the lopsidedness of the clause – it may be difficult for Retailer to find another Manufacturer on short notice, for example. Furthermore, there must be some evidence of procedural unconscionability.

---

8 *Id.* at 289 ("Mutuality of obligation is not a factor to consider in the formation of a contract. Mutuality of obligation is, however, a factor for a court to consider when assessing whether a contract (or provision therein) is unconscionable. In other words, a provision in a contract that lacks mutuality – that is, an obligation that could be called unilateral, unbalanced, or non-reciprocal – may lead a court to find the provision is so lop-sided and unfair that, as a matter of equity, the provision should not be enforced"). *See also* Carmona v. Lincoln Millenium Car Wash, Inc., 226 Cal. App. 4th 74 (2014) (striking down arbitration clause that required employee to submit to arbitration but not employer); Caplin Enters. v. Arrington, 2014 Miss. LEXIS 232 ("[T]he arbitration clause in the new version of the contract, which permitted Zippy Check to pursue judicial remedies while relegating the plaintiffs' claims to arbitration, is . . . clearly oppressive and substantively unconscionable"). *Id.* at *17–18.

The parties to a contract often include a clause to indicate that they entered into the transaction or relationship voluntarily or that they had legal advice, such as the following:

Example clause

Independent Review. Each party warrants and represents that it has carefully read this Agreement, that it executes this Agreement with full knowledge of the contents of this Agreement, the legal consequences hereof, and any and all rights which each may have with respect to one another, that it has had the opportunity to receive independent legal advice with respect to the matters set forth in this Agreement and with respect to the rights and asserted rights arising out of such matters, and that it is entering into this Agreement of its own free will.

Example clause

Each party represents that she or he has sought and obtained independent legal advice from counsel of his or her own selection and the respective legal rights and obligations and the practical and legal effects of this Agreement have been fully explained to each of the parties by his or her respective legal counsel. Each party acknowledges that this Agreement is fair and not the result of any fraud, duress, coercion, or undue influence exercised by the other party or by any other person or persons. Each party represents that he or she clearly understands and assents to all the provisions of this Agreement and is signing this Agreement freely and voluntarily.

Such a clause is intended to negate a later claim of duress, undue influence, or unconscionability. A court may still invalidate the agreement despite the inclusion of such a provision if there is evidence of duress, undue influence, or unconscionability but it may make it harder to prove such claims.

Caveat: Some state statutes require that a party waiving certain rights be represented by legal counsel.[9]

9 For example, in California, a contract that provides for attorneys' fees is construed as applying to the entire contract *unless* each party was represented by counsel and such representation is specified in the contract. Cal. Civ. Code §1717.

5.2 Doctrinal concepts: illegality, invalidity, and subsequent changes in the law

Principle: A party may be excused from performance if the subject matter of the contract is not legal or if performance would be against public policy.

While parties may create their own private law, their private law does not supersede laws that govern society. An agreement to commit a crime is obviously invalid and no court is going to enforce it. If Wanda hires Pepper to rob a bank in return for $10,000, and they sign a written agreement, there is offer, acceptance, consideration, and mutual assent. But if Wanda refuses to pay Pepper after Pepper robs the bank, Pepper will not be able to sue Wanda in court for the $10,000. The illegal nature of their agreement takes it out of the realm of judicial enforcement. These agreements are invalid *ab initio*, meaning they are invalid at the time they are formed.

There is, however, a more typical scenario in commercial transactions and that is where the contract or contract provision was legal at the time the parties signed it, but subsequently became illegal or unenforceable because something happened. That "something" may be the passage of legislation or a court decision that renders a formerly legal provision unenforceable. This might require that the parties terminate the contract immediately or it may mean that one or more provisions are unenforceable but that performance can continue. A court will not construe a contract so that it is modified by subsequent changes in the law unless the language clearly indicates that the parties so intended.

For example, the parties might agree to enter into a contract to construct a ten-story building but legislation is subsequently passed making it illegal to construct any building over nine stories. A court will not force construction because the legislation trumps the private agreement between the parties.

Troubleshooting: The parties may indicate in their agreement whether they intend to be bound by subsequent changes in the law. The intent of the parties to be bound by subsequent changes in the law must be clearly expressed.

Example clause

The Agreement is subject to the Condominium Act as defined in Section 12 and the provisions of the Condominium Act are hereby incorporated as the same may be from time to time amended.

Example clause

The parties agree to be bound by the relevant provisions of the Federal and State Statutes and Municipal Ordinances and Regulations as amended and supplemented. In the event that said laws are amended or revised then the Entity shall be subject to the new legislation.

A contract or provision will be found invalid if it is against public policy or state law. Courts tend to scrutinize certain types of clauses, such as non-compete clauses, arbitration clauses, jury trial waivers, forum selection clauses, choice of law clauses, liquidated damages clauses, exculpatory clauses, and limitations of liability.

A forum selection clause states that the parties agree to submit to the personal jurisdiction of the courts of a particular forum (meaning place, such as state, county, or district). Here is an example:

Example clause

All actions and proceedings arising out of or relating to this Agreement shall be brought and heard in New York state or federal court sitting in Nassau County in the State of New York and the parties hereby irrevocably consent to the exclusive jurisdiction of such courts in any action or proceeding and irrevocably waive the defense of inconvenient forum to the maintenance of such action or proceeding.

Historically, courts found forum selection clauses to be against public policy and unenforceable but that view is rapidly changing.[10] Today, most courts evaluating the validity of these clauses will enforce them – and so decline jurisdiction – if the parties freely and expressly agreed to the clause, the clause is unambiguous, and if the selected forum's laws do not conflict with a

10 *See* M/S Bremen v. Zapata Off-Shore Co., 407 U.S. 1, 10–11, 92 S.Ct. 1913 (1972) ("Forum selection clauses have historically not been favored by American courts. Many courts, federal and state, have declined to enforce such clauses on the ground that they were 'contrary to public policy,' or that their effect was to 'oust the jurisdiction' of the court").

fundamental policy of the state where the suit was initially brought.[11] Some states, such New York,[12] have statutes which expressly permit these clauses. A federal statute also permits these clauses.[13]

A choice of law clause differs from a forum selection clause but is often contained in the same paragraph. A choice of law clause states that the parties have selected the law of a particular jurisdiction (state and/or country) to govern the contract. The following provides an example of such a clause:

Example clause

Governing law. This Agreement will be governed by and construed in accordance with the laws of the state of New York without giving effect to any conflict of laws provisions.

In most jurisdictions, the validity of a choice of law clause is a threshold question that is determined not under the law specified in the clause, but under the relevant forum's choice of law rules governing such clauses.[14] If the court

11 *See*, for example, *id.* at 3–5 (finding forum selection clauses presumptively enforceable); Falk & Fish, L.L.P. v. Pinkston's Lawnmower and Equipment, Inc., 317 S.W.3d 523 (2010) (Although, forum selection clauses are generally enforceable unless enforcement would be unreasonable, the clause is overreaching or the product of fraud, or enforcement would contravene a strong public policy of the state – in the case before it, the forum selection clause in an attorney representation letter was not clear on its face and so client did not consent to personal jurisdiction in Texas). *Id.* at 527–530; Cagle v. Mathers Family Trust, 295 P.3d 460 (2013) ("The vast majority of cases, including every Colorado court of appeals case decided since *Bremen* treats forum selection clauses as presumptively enforceable.") *Id.* at 464.

12 NY CPLR §501. Contractual provisions fixing venue – "Subject to the provisions of subdivision two of §510, written agreement fixing place of trial, made before an action is commenced, shall be enforced upon a motion for change of place of trial"; NY CPLR §510. Grounds for change of place of trial – "The court, upon motion, may change the place of trial of an action where: 1. the county designated for that purpose is not a proper county; or 2. there is reason to believe that an impartial trial cannot be had in the proper county; or 3. the convenience of material witnesses and the ends of justice will be promoted by the change"; Grey v. Colonial Home Improvement Co., Inc., 57 Misc. 2d 321 (1967) (Even though plaintiff may not have understood the meaning and importance of the clause in the contract stipulating venue, she is bound by the terms thereof") *id.* at 322.

13 28 U.S.C.A. §1404. Change of venue – "(a) For the convenience of parties and witnesses, in the interest of justice, a district court may transfer any civil action to any district or division where it might have been brought or to any district or division to which all parties have consented"; Atlantic Marine Construction Company, Inc. v. U.S. Dist. Court for Western Dist. of Texas, 134 S.Ct. 568, 581 (2013) ("When the parties have agreed to a valid forum-selection clause, a district court should ordinarily transfer the case to the forum specified in the clause. Only under extraordinary circumstances unrelated to the convenience of the parties should a §1404(a) motion be denied").

14 *See* Dessert Beauty Inc. v. Platinum Funding Corp., 519 F. Supp. 2d 410, 419 (S.D.N.Y. 2007); Finance One Public Co., Ltd. v. Lehman Bros. Special Financing, Inc., 414 F.3d 325 (2nd Cir. 2005) ("Determining which jurisdiction's law governs the scope of a valid choice-of-law clause is not a simple matter. On the one hand, once a court finds that a contractual choice-of-law clause is valid, the law selected in the clause dictates how the contract's provisions should be interpreted, and so arguably that laws should also dictate how the choice-of-law clause – which is itself one of the contract's provisions – should be interpreted . . . More commonly, however, courts consider the scope of a contractual choice-of-law clause to be a threshold question like the clause's validity.") *Id.* at 333.

finds the clause is valid, the law selected in the clause applies to the construction of the contract.[15] In some jurisdictions, the choice of law clause does not apply to tort claims while in most jurisdictions, it depends on whether the clause is clearly drafted to include tort and/or extra-contractual claims.[16] The following is an example of a "narrow" choice of law clause, which specifies the state law that will be used only to construe a contract:

Example clause

This Agreement shall be construed under the laws of the State of California.

A "broad" choice of law clause states that a particular state's law will govern all matters arising from the agreement.[17] Courts are split on whether the use of "construed and governed" together will make the clause broad,[18] such as the following:

Example clause

This Agreement shall be construed and governed by the laws of the State of California.

If the parties want their choice of law clause to govern *all* disputes (not just the construction of the contract), they should use language that makes that clear. The following are examples:

15 *Id.* at 419.

16 *Id.* (noting that, under New York law, "tort claims are outside the scope of contractual choice-of-law provisions that specify what law governs constructions of the terms of the contract."); *see also* Finance One Public Co. Ltd. v. Lehman Bros. Special Financing, Inc., 414 F.3d 325 (2nd Cir. 2005); Caton v. Leach Corp., 896 F.2d 939, 944 (5th Cir. 1990) (noting choice of law clauses may be "narrow" or "broad" and finding that a narrowly drafted choice of law clause does not address the general rights and liabilities of the parties and thus does not apply to a claim for restitution under quantum meruit or tort claims).

17 For more discussion of choice of law clauses, *see* Timothy Murray, *Drafting Choice of Law Clauses,* available at http://www.mhandl.com/content/draftingchoiceoflawclauses.

18 *See* Panthera Rail Car LLC v. Kasgro Rail Corp., 985 F. Supp. 2d 677, 691 (W.D. Pa. 2013) (noting that "whether contractual choice-of-law clauses govern torts that later arise related to the contractual relationship . . . is an unsettled question"). In Panthera, the court found that Minnesota law governed only breach of contract claim and not tort claim where clause stated, "This Lease shall be governed by and construed in accordance with the laws of the State of Minnesota." *Id.* at 696. *But see* Moses v. Business Bard Exp., Inc., 929 F.2d 1131, 1139–40 (6th Cir. 1991) (finding that clause stating, "This Franchise and License Agreement and the construction thereof shall be governed by the laws of the state of Michigan" referred to more than construction of the agreement and applied to claims of fraud and misrepresentation). In Baumgardner v. Bimbo Food Bakeries Distributions, Inc., 697 F. Supp. 2d 801 (N.D. Ohio 2010), the choice of law clause stated: "The validity, interpretation and performance of this Agreement shall be controlled by and construed in accordance with the laws of New York." The court found that New York law governed both the contract and tort claims. *Id.* at 806.

Example clause

The laws of the State of California (without giving effect to its conflict of laws principles) shall govern, construe, and enforce all of the rights and duties of the parties arising from or relating in any way to the subject matter of this contract.

Example clause

Any and all matters in dispute between the parties arising from or relating to this Agreement including without limitation any claim of fraud, misrepresentation, or any other alleged tort or violation of the contract, shall be construed, governed and enforced in accordance with the laws of the State of California (without giving effect to any conflict of laws principles) regardless of the legal theory upon which such dispute is asserted.

As with forum selection clauses, a court may decline to apply the choice of law clause if (a) the chosen state has no substantial relationship to the parties or the transaction and there is no other reasonable basis for the parties' choice or (b) to protect a fundamental state policy.[19] For example, if the choice of law clause designates a state that has a different policy regarding the enforceability of non-compete agreements, in a dispute involving a non-compete agreement, a court may decline to give effect to the choice of law clause.[20]

CASE HIGHLIGHT

BRACK v. OMNI LOAN CO., LTD., 164 Cal. App. 4th 1312 (2008)

Omni, a Nevada corporation with its principal place of business in Las Vegas, Nevada, provided consumer loans to members of the military. In 1997, Omni tried to obtain permission from the Commissioner of Corporations to make loans in California to nonresident members of the military without complying with the requirements of the Finance Lenders

19 RESTATEMENT (SECOND) CONFLICT OF LAWS, §187. *See also* Turford v. Underwood, 952 S.W.2d 641 (1997) (finding employment contract addendum containing covenant not to compete was governed by Texas law even though it contained a Michigan choice of law provision because Texas has a "materially greater interest" in the enforceability of employment agreements in Texas than does Michigan.") *Id.* at 643.

20 Benchmark Medical Holdings, Inc. v. Barnes, 328 F. Supp. 2d 1236, 1242 (M.D. Ala. 2004) (Due to the state of Alabama's fundamental public policy against non-competition agreements, court applied Alabama law despite Pennsylvania governing law clause).

CASE HIGHLIGHT *(continued)*

Law, a California law regulating lenders and brokers of consumer and commercial loans. The Commissioner declined to grant Omni's request. Nevertheless, Omni opened a loan office in California. Omni's borrowers in California were nonresident members of the military who agreed to repay their loans (in amounts typically ranging from between $900 to $1,800) by allowing deductions from their military paychecks. They also provided Omni with a security interest in personal property.

Joshua Brack was a nonresident member of the military stationed at Camp Pendleton in San Diego County. His loan agreement charged an interest rate of 34.89 percent per annum for his loan and included a prepaid finance charge and a charge for property insurance. His loan was also secured by personal property. The loan agreement contained a choice of law provision that stated:

> "You agree that this loan contract is subject to Nevada State law."

Brack repaid his loan and then filed a class action lawsuit against Omni alleging violations of the Finance Lenders Law and other California consumer laws. Omni asserted that the loan agreement was governed by the law of Nevada.

The trial court found that Nevada had a substantial relationship to the loan agreements because Omni was incorporated in Nevada and the loans were approved there. It also determined that California had no fundamental interest in the loan transactions. The Court of Appeal disagreed:

> "To be fundamental within the meaning of Restatement section 187, a policy must be a substantial one . . . The relative significance of a particular policy or statutory scheme can be determined by considering whether parties may, by agreement, avoid the policy or statutory requirement."

After analyzing the policies set forth in the relevant section, the court stated:

"[T]he requirements of the Finance Lenders Law are matters of fundamental public policy which cannot be waived by way of agreement between the parties . . . .

Application of the choice-of-law provision in the Omni loan agreements would undermine the fundamental policy expressed in the Finance Lenders Law . . . The choice of law provisions in Omni's loan agreements immunized Omni's activities in this state from this entire regulatory scheme and thereby conflicted with it in a substantial manner."

The court then concluded that California's interest in enforcing its law was greater than Nevada's interest in enforcing its laws:

> "Here, application of Nevada law would deprive a substantial segment of the borrowing public in this state of the substantive and regulatory protection California affords all of its other consumers. Nevada on the other hand has no policy which prevents lenders from subjecting themselves to the regulatory authority of other states. That is to say, nothing in Nevada law prevented Omni from fully complying with California law. Rather, Nevada's interest in applying its law is limited to its more general interest in enforcing the provisions of contracts made by one of its

CASE HIGHLIGHT *(continued)*

citizens. Given these circumstances, application of Nevada law would impair California's regulatory interests to a far greater extent than application of California law would impair Nevada's interests . . . In sum, although there was a reasonable basis for selecting Nevada law in the loan agreements, its application here conflicted with a fundamental policy of this state in circumstances in which California has a greater interest than Nevada. Hence the choice-of-law provisions of Omni's loan agreements are not enforceable here."

A pre-dispute jury trial waiver means that the parties agree to opt out of a jury trial; not that they have opted out of a court trial. An arbitration clause means that the parties have opted for an alternative to the judicial system.[21] Although both pre-dispute jury trial waivers and arbitration clauses result in the parties foregoing a jury trial, they are treated differently in some jurisdictions as arbitration is viewed as conserving judicial resources while pre-dispute jury trial waivers are not. In California[22] and Georgia,[23] pre-dispute jury trial waivers are unenforceable. Even in jurisdictions that find them enforceable, courts may scrutinize the terms closely to be sure that the parties knowingly and voluntarily waived their rights. Arbitration clauses, on the other hand, are expressly authorized by many state statutes (including California and Georgia)[24] and the Federal Arbitration Act.[25]

The applicability of an arbitration clause depends upon formation (whether a valid agreement to arbitration exists) and scope (whether the claim at issue is subject to the clause).

21 Woodside Homes of California, Inc. v. Superior Court, 47 Cal. Rptr. 3d, 683, 687 (2006) ("[A]rbitration . . . conserves judicial resources far more than the selection of a court trial over a jury trial. It therefore is rational for the Legislature to promote the use of arbitration and reference hearings by permitting predispute agreements, while not according the same advantage to jury trial waivers").

22 Grafton Partners, L.P. v. Superior Court, 36 Cal. 4th 944 (2005) (holding that pre-dispute jury trial waiver was unenforceable); In re County of Orange, 784 F.3d 520, 532 (9th Cir. 2015) ("California law holds, as a matter of public policy, that a litigant cannot waive its right to a jury trial by entering into a contract that contains a pre-dispute jury trial waiver clause").

23 Bank South, N.A. v. Howard, 264 Ga. 339 (1994) (finding unenforceable provision in guaranty waiving right to jury trial).

24 California Code of Civil Procedure §1281 ("A written agreement to submit to arbitration an existing controversy or a controversy thereafter arising is valid, enforceable and irrevocable, save upon such grounds as exist for the revocation of any contract."); Ga. Code Ann., §9-9-3 ("A written agreement to submit any existing controversy to arbitration or a provision in a written contract to submit any controversy thereafter arising is enforceable without regard to the justiciable character of the controversy and confers jurisdiction on the courts of the state to enforce it and to enter judgment on an award).

25 9 U.S.C. §2.

CASE HIGHLIGHT

KIRBY HIGHLAND LAKES SURGERY CENTER, L.L.P. v. KIRBY, 183 S.W.3d 891 (Tex. App. – Austin, 2006)

Dr. Edward Kirby, who operated an outpatient surgical center with his wife, Helen Kirby, entered into a Partnership Agreement with several other doctors. The Partnership also executed a Purchase and Sale Agreement with the Kirbys where it would purchase the assets of Dr. Kirby's outpatient surgical center. After a dispute over fees, the Kirbys later sued the Partnership for breach of contract under the Purchase and Sale Agreement. The Purchase and Sale Agreement did not contain an arbitration clause but explicitly required Dr. Kirby to execute the Partnership Agreement. The Partnership Agreement contained an arbitration clause that stated that all "disputes or controversies arising under or related to this Agreement shall be arbitrated." The Partnership moved to compel arbitration of Kirbys' claims, which the district court denied. The Partnership appealed.

The Court of Appeals of Texas stated that while Texas law governs whether a valid arbitration clause exists, the "scope of a valid arbitration clause . . . is governed by federal law." The court noted that doubts concerning the scope of coverage of arbitration should be resolved in favor of arbitration and stated:

> "The Partnership Agreement's arbitration clause embraces '[a]ll disputes or controversies arising under or related to this Agreement,' terminology that federal courts applying the [Federal Arbitration Act] have termed 'extremely broad' and 'capable of expansive reach' [citations omitted]. Such 'related to' language, in contrast to narrower phrases like 'arising out of,' extends to 'all disputes between the parties having a significant relationship to the contract regardless of the label attached to the dispute' or that 'touch' matters covered by the contract containing the arbitration provisions . . . However 'related to' does not mean unlimited in scope . . . For instance, such language is not as broad as 'any and all disputes between' the parties [citations omitted]."

The court found that the Kirbys' claims were "related to" the Partnership Agreement and subject to the arbitration clause.

Troubleshooting: Clauses that are likely to prompt judicial scrutiny because they raise public policy concerns should be drafted in a conspicuous manner to show that the parties knowingly agreed to the clause. You may even wish to have the affected party separately initial such a clause. In particular, waivers and releases of liability raise concerns regarding fairness and many states have statutes which necessitate careful drafting that makes clear that the parties intended the provision. On the other hand, the releasing party should be careful not to release the other party from unintended claims. For example, an employee signing a release to a workers' compensation claim should be careful not to inadvertently release the employer from liability for a sexual discrimination claim.[26]

For the party receiving the benefit of the release, specific reference to legislation may be wise even if it is not expressly required. For example, Cal. Civ. Code §1542 states that a "general release does not extend to claims which the creditor does not know or suspect to exist in his or her favor at the time of executing the release, which if known by him or her must have materially affected his or her settlement with the debtor." Consequently, a release to be governed by California law should expressly waive claims, both known and unknown, if that is what the parties intend and it should expressly reference Cal. Civ. Code §1542.[27]

Example clause

WAIVER AND RELEASE. In consideration of the severance benefits, additional health benefits and other consideration provided to me by Company, I hereby completely release and forever discharge Company and any affiliated and parent companies and their officers, directors, agents, and employees from any claims, rights, demands, actions, or obligations known or unknown, suspected or unsuspected, which I may now have, have ever had, or may in the future have (exclusive of any workers compensation matter) regarding my employment, benefits, and separation from Company including any and all claims under state or federal employment laws and regulations.

WAIVER OF CAL. CIVIL CODE SECTION 1542. It is understood and agreed that I hereby EXPRESSLY WAIVE all rights under Section 1542 of the California Civil Code, which provides as follows:

26 *See* Jefferson v. California Dept. of Youth Authority, 28 Cal. 4th 299 (2002) (finding that release signed to settle a worker's compensation claim which discharged employer "from all claims and causes of action, whether now known or ascertained, or which may hereafter arise or develop as a result of the [claimed] injury" also covered sex discrimination claim).

27 Perez v. Uline, 157 Cal. App. 4th 953, 958–59 (2007) ("upholding an agreement that did not specifically refer to California Civil Code §1542 although 'it might have been more comprehensive to have a reference' to the section in the release").

> CAL. CIV. CODE §1542 Certain Claims Not Affected by General Release. A GENERAL RELEASE DOES NOT EXTEND TO CLAIMS WHICH THE CREDITOR DOES NOT KNOW OR SUSPECT TO EXIST IN HIS FAVOR AT THE TIME OF EXECUTING THE RELEASE, WHICH IF KNOWN BY HIM MUST HAVE MATERIALLY AFFECTED HIS SETTLEMENT WITH DEBTOR.

It is particularly important to refrain from greedy drafting where non-compete or non-solicitation clauses are involved. In California, a non-competition agreement or contractual clause is void[28] unless it is agreed to in connection with the sale of a business[29] or the dissolution of a partnership or a disassociation of a partner from the partnership.[30] Furthermore, forcing an employee to sign an employment agreement containing a term or condition that the employer knows is prohibited by law may constitute a criminal misdemeanor![31] Most courts will scrutinize a non-compete clause to determine whether it is reasonable.

Upon a finding of invalidity, a court has several options. A court may invalidate the entire agreement or it may invalidate only the relevant provision. Some jurisdictions, however, will not "blue pencil" (strike out lines) of a clause.[32]

---

28 Cal. Business & Professions Code §16600 ("Except as provided in this chapter, every contract by which anyone is restrained from engaging in a lawful profession, trade, or business of any kind is to that extent void."); Dowell v. Biosense Webster, Inc., 179 Cal. App. 4th 564, 573–575 (2009) (finding noncompete and nonsolicitation clause in employment agreement which forbade former employees for a period of 18 months from rendering services to a competitor to be against California public policy).

29 Cal. Business & Professions Code §16601 – Sale of goodwill of business or ownership interest in or operating assets of business entity or division or subsidiary thereof; agreement not to compete ("Any person who sells the goodwill of a business . . . . may agree with the buyer to refrain from carrying on a similar business within a specified geographic area in which the business so sold . . . so long as the buyer . . . carries on a like business therein").

30 Cal. Business & Professions Code §16602.

31 Cal. Labor Code §432.5 – Unlawful terms and conditions – provides that "[n]o employer, agent, manager, superintendent, or officer thereof, shall require any employee or applicant for employment to agree, in writing, to any term or condition which is known by such employer, or agent, manager, superintendent, or officer thereof to be prohibited by law"). Cal. Labor Code §433 states that "[a]ny person violating this article is guilty of a misdemeanor").

32 Allied Informatics, Inc. v. Yeruva, 554 S.E.2d 550, 553 (C.A. of Georgia, August 28, 2001) ("Restrictive covenants ancillary to employment contracts are subject to strict scrutiny and cannot be blue-penciled").

CASE HIGHLIGHT

ALLIED INFORMATICS, INC. v. YERUVA, 554 S.E.2d 550 (C.A. of Georgia, August 28, 2001)

Yeruva entered into an employment agreement with Allied Informatics, Inc. which contained the following non-solicitation clause:

> "6. SOLICITATION
> EMPLOYEE agrees that he/she will not directly or indirectly solicit employment or enter into a contractual agreement with any Client/Firm, where he/she was assigned to work, for a period of one year after the last working day of the assignment. If the employee violates this term, employee shall owe an amount of $10,000.00 (Ten thousand dollars) to Allied as liquidated damages for time and money spent for recru[i]ting, loss of use and marketing of employee services."

The court found that the provision was over-broad because it did not limit the type of business the employee is prohibited from doing with the employer's clients:

> "The terms 'employment' and 'contractual agreement' are not limited in the agreement and could encompass work that has nothing to do with the type of work that Yeruva did while he was employed with Allied . . . Such a provision is not reasonably necessary to protect the interests of Allied and is therefore overbroad and unenforceable."

If the parties want the court to invalidate only part of the agreement, rather than the entirety, it should include a severability clause.

Example clause

If any provision of this Agreement is held invalid or unenforceable, in whole or in part, under any statute or rule of law, such invalidity or unenforceability shall not affect the remaining provisions hereof, which shall remain in full force and effect.

The rule of severability holds that if an illegal clause can be severed from the contract without defeating the primary purpose of the agreement, the agreement may survive.[33] Some courts may find that the

33 Dawson v. Godammer, 295 Wis. 2d 728, 737 (2006).

absence of a severability clause indicates that the parties intended the contract to be entire and not severable and the entire agreement will be unenforceable.[34]

Caveat: As previously noted, some courts will not "blue pencil" (strike out individual lines) of a clause. Furthermore, a court may refuse to invalidate only specific provisions and may invalidate the entire agreement if it finds it is equitable to do so. A court is not required to abide by a severability clause.[35] However, given that the purpose of the court in a contract dispute is to enforce the intent of the parties, courts will generally honor a severability or savings clause unless doing so would render the agreement meaningless or violate public policy.

Troubleshooting: The parties should consider whether they want a severability clause to apply to all terms of the contract. There may be some terms that a party considers essential to the contract and that, if severed from the agreement, would undermine the bargain. For that reason, the parties may prefer a severability clause that expressly applies only to non-essential terms, such as the following:

Example clause

If any provision of this Agreement is determined to be invalid or unenforceable, in whole or in part, under any statute or rule of law, the remaining provisions of this Agreement remain in full force and effect if the essential terms and conditions of this Agreement for each party remain valid and enforceable.

The parties may specify which terms in the Agreement are considered essential, such as in the following:

34 Shaffer v. Royal Gate Dodge, Inc., 300 S.W.3d 556, 561 (Mo. Ct. App. 2009) ("The absence of a severability clause tends to indicate that a contract is entire and not severable").

35 City of Beaumont v. International Ass'n of Firefighters, Local Union No. 399, 241 S.W.3d 208, 216 (Tex. App. – Beaumont 2007) ("The existence of the severability clause in the contract does not change our conclusion that the clauses are mutually dependent promises").

Example clause

If any provision of this Agreement is determined to be invalid or unenforceable, in whole or in part, under any statute or rule of law, the remaining provisions of this Agreement remain in full force and effect if the essential terms and conditions of this Agreement for each party remain valid and enforceable. The parties agree that the essential terms and conditions of this Agreement include, but are not limited to, Section 4 of this Agreement and that if any of the provisions in Section 4 is found invalid or unenforceable, the remainder of this Agreement is not enforceable.

The parties may also state that the agreement will be modified as required to conform to changes in the law:

Example clause

The rules and regulations of the Federal Communications Commission govern the interpretation and enforcement of this Agreement. This Agreement is subject to modification if required by such rules and regulations.

In some cases, the transaction is not illegal on its face, but the parties are unable to perform because they fail to meet certain requirements, such as obtaining necessary licenses or permits. This book refers to this situation as one involving the "invalidity" of the agreement as the transaction itself is not illegal although performance by the parties, given their failure to meet certain requirements, would violate a law or ordinance. The parties may covenant or promise that each party is responsible for complying with laws necessary for performance.

Example clause

Each party shall at all times comply with all applicable laws, ordinances, rules, and regulations applicable to it. As applicable, each party shall give all required notices and shall procure and maintain all governmental permits, licenses, and inspections necessary for performance of this Agreement.

The agreement may also contain representations and/or warranties made by one or both of the parties. A representation is a statement regarding some fact or circumstance existing at the time it was made. A warranty is a promise that a representation or statement is true or will be true in the future. An agreement may require that one or both parties make certain representations and warranties to ensure that the transaction may be performed. For example, a party may warrant that it has the right to enter into the agreement and that doing so does not interfere with any other obligation it has to another party. A warranty is made at the time a contract is entered into by the parties. A representation is typically made in order to induce the other party to enter into the contract.

In many transactions, such as a large asset purchase, there is a period of time between the signing of the agreement and the "closing" of the transaction (when the money and the asset are transferred). During the "pre-closing" period of time, the buyer conducts due diligence, meaning it conducts an investigation or audit to make sure that there are no problems with its investment. Representations should be made in the present tense so they are effective at the time the contract is executed and during the pre-closing period. Representations may terminate after closing unless the parties specify otherwise in their agreement.

Example clause

All representations and covenants made by each party shall survive the Closing for the benefit of the other party.

Example clause

Sellers shall remake the representations and warranties in Section 3 as of the Closing Date (other than representations and warranties made specifically as to a certain date, in which case such representations and warranties shall be remade as of such certain date). The representations and warranties set forth in Section 8 shall survive indefinitely and all other representations and warranties in the Agreement shall survive the Closing for a period of six months.

Reflection Prompt: When would a party prefer the first Example Clause? When would a party prefer the second? Why?

Warranties and representations typically have different legal consequences[36]

36 The difference between representations and warranties was historically significant in insurance contracts: *See* Kizer v. Woodmen of the World, 180 SE 804, 807 (1935) (noting that the "difference between warranties and representations is often very vital. Construed as a warranty, the falsity of the statement amounts to an express breach of the contract, regardless of the good faith and honest purpose of the insured, and the statement does not have to be material, it has been held in some cases; construed as a representation, the falsity of the statement may render the contract voidable when it is shown to have been material to the risk and know-

although under the UCC a representation may create an express warranty.[37] The contract itself may treat the terms differently and cross-references in a contract may refer to one but not the other.

The difference between a representation and a warranty may be important when it comes to recovery. A showing of reliance is required to recover on a misrepresentation claim while reliance is not usually required to recover on a breach of warranty claim.[38] A breach of warranty does not invalidate the contract, but allows the injured party to recover damages. A false or fraudulent representation is grounds for a tort claim (such as negligent misrepresentation) and allows the injured party to rescind (undo) the transaction and recover all amounts paid. In some cases, a representation may operate as a condition which allows the injured party to avoid performance. For example, if Party Y learns during due diligence that Party X's representation that "Party X has obtained all necessary permits" is untrue, Party Y may be able to delay performance or even avoid the contract. Representations and warranties are typically made together:

---

ingly made."); City Bank & Trust Co. v. Comm'l Cas. Co., 176 So. 27, 30–31 (1937) ("The distinction between a representation and a warranty in an insurance contract is, that the former precedes and is not a party of the contract and need be only materially true, while the latter is part of the contract and must be strictly fulfilled, or the policy is void. Another difference between a warranty and a representation is that a warranty must be strictly true; a representation need only be substantially true. The falsity of a representation may render the contract voidable for fraud; but a noncompliance with a warranty is an express breach of contract" (citing 14 Ruling Case Law, p. 1026, §§206, 207, and 208).

37 UCC §2-313 (Express warranties are created by "affirmation of fact or promise" which "relates to the goods and becomes part of the basis of the bargain.") *See also* Goodwin v. Durant Bank & Trust Co., 952 P.2d 41, 43–44 (1998) (Bank represented model year of backhoe thus creating an express warranty).

38 Norcold, Inc. v. Gateway Supply Co., 798 N.E.2d 618, 623–24 (2003) (A decisive majority of courts that have considered this issue have reached the similar conclusion that reliance is not an element in a claim for breach of an express written warranty.") If the facts are not as warranted, a party can sue the party making the warranty for breach of contract. On the other hand, if a representation turns out not to be true, the other party typically must show that it relied upon the representation in entering into the transaction and that the representation was material. Deceitful or false misrepresentations are the basis of a claim of fraud. TINA L. STARK, DRAFTING CONTRACTS: HOW AND WHY LAWYERS DO WHAT THEY DO (2007) at 11–19; In re Nuttall, 201 F. 557, 560–561 (S.D.N.Y. 1912) ("a party can commit a legal fraud in a business transaction with another only by fraudulent misrepresentations of fact, or by such conduct or artifice for a fraudulent purpose as will mislead the other party"); Robert J. Johannes and Thomas A. Simonis, *Buyer's Pre-Closing Knowledge of Seller's Breach of Warranty*, 75 JUL Wis. Law. 18 (July 2002) (noting that "the majority of jurisdictions that have considered whether reliance is a required element of a cause of action for a breach of an express warranty in a sale of a business have concluded that reliance is not required") *id.* at 20; CBS, Inc. v. Ziff-Davis Pub. Co., 75 N.Y.2d 496 (1990) (holding that reliance on the truth of a warranted fact was not required for action based on breach of express warranty).

Example clause

Performer represents and warrants that he is not a party to any oral or written agreement that would prevent, limit or hinder the performance of any of his obligations hereunder.

Example clause

Author represents and warrants that the Work is the Author's original work and does not infringe upon any existing copyright or any rights of any third party and that Author's execution of this Agreement and the rights conveyed herein shall not interfere with, contradict, or contravene any agreement that Author has entered into with any third party.

Troubleshooting: If the parties are forced to terminate the entire transaction, there may be costs that have already been incurred. The parties should consider how costs should be allocated in such a situation. In particular, if the transaction involves a payment to one party, the parties may want to include a provision addressing whether those payments must be returned.

A warranty of authority states that a party has the power to sign the contract. While the concept of agency is typically not discussed in first-year contracts law courses, it is an important issue that may affect the validity of a contract. Companies enter into contracts every day, but obviously the company cannot itself sign contracts since it is not a physical person. It needs agents to act on its behalf.[39] An agent is someone who acts for or on behalf of another, referred to as the principal. Who has the authority to sign contracts on behalf of a company? The bylaws of a corporation may indicate which officers may sign contracts or the bylaws may permit the board of directors to, by resolution, authorize officers to sign contracts. Actual authority to sign the contract means the individual is authorized by the company (the principal) to sign the agreement.[40] Executive officers, such as the chief executive officer and the president, of a company typically have actual authority to sign contracts. Even if they do not, they have apparent authority. Apparent authority means that a reasonable third party would believe that the agent had authority to act on the principal's behalf.[41] Other employees may also have apparent authority depending upon their roles.[42] Some contracts contain a clause where each

39 RESTATEMENT (THIRD) OF AGENCY, §1.01 (1958).
40 RESTATEMENT (THIRD) OF AGENCY, §2.01.
41 RESTATEMENT (THIRD) OF AGENCY, §2.03.
42 Grand Trunk Western R. Co. v. H.W. Nelson Co., 116 F.2d 823, 834 (6th Cir. 1941) ("As a rule,

party expressly warrants that he or she is authorized to sign on behalf of the principal (i.e. the corporation).

Example clause

Warranty of Authority. Each person represents and warrants to the other that he or she is duly authorized and has legal capacity to execute and deliver this Agreement.

Example clause

The signatories hereto personally warrant that they have the right and power to enter into this Agreement and to bind the party for whom they are executing this Agreement.

The warranty of authority has particular relevance in the context of an employee (such as an officer of a company) signing on behalf of his or her employer. Under the principles of agency law, a principal must indemnify an agent for authorized acts. This means that in the above context, an employee of a company who is authorized by the company's management may sign a contract that binds the company. The company, and not the employee, will be liable to perform under the contract. If, however, the employee is *not* authorized to act on behalf of the company, the *employee may be personally liable* under the contract that he or she signed.

A company may want to be liable for statements made only by certain employees:

Example clause

No agent, employee or representative of Company other than Company's Chief Executive Officer, Chief Financial Officer and/or Chief Engineer has the authority to bind Company to any affirmation, representation, promise or warranty concerning the Equipment.

---

corporations like natural persons under agency contracts are bound only when the agent is either expressly or impliedly authorized to act for his principal, but in applying this rule it must be recognized that owing to the enormous scope of the business of present day corporations their activities are frequently divided into departments with managers or superintendents each of whom in such cases has the same relation to this department as has the general manager or superintendent to the general affairs of the corporation and the corporation is liable for the acts of the department managers or superintendents within the apparent scope of authority").

A party will have a difficult time convincing a court that it relied upon an oral representation or warranty by an unauthorized employee of the other party if the Agreement contains a clause like the following:

Example clause

No employee, agent, representative, or affiliate of COMPANY has authority to bind COMPANY to any oral representations or warranty concerning the Product. Any written representation or warranty not expressly contained in this Agreement will not be enforceable.

5.3 Doctrinal concepts: legal capacity (infancy, insanity, intoxication, and corporate nonexistence)

Principle: A party to a contract must have legal capacity to enter into it. A contract is voidable by a party who was not legally competent.

The law provides special protection for certain categories of people. A minor (under 18 years of age) lacks legal capacity, meaning that she or he generally cannot be bound to the terms of a contract and may disaffirm it.[43] (An adult transacting with a minor, however, cannot disaffirm the contract). There is an exception if the contract was for necessities ("necessaries"), such as food or housing. In addition, if a minor affirms the contract after reaching 18 years or fails to disaffirm the contract for a reasonable time after reaching the age of majority, the contract may be deemed ratified.[44]

In some jurisdictions, a fraudulent misrepresentation by the minor of his or her age means that the minor will not be able to disaffirm the contract.[45]

Some contracts contain a provision expressly stating that the signatory is an adult:

---

43 For further discussion on the infancy doctrine, *see* Cheryl B. Preston and Brandon T. Crowther, *Minor Restrictions: Adolescence Across Legal Disciplines, The Infancy Doctrine and the Restatement (Third) of Restitution and Unjust Enrichment*, 61 U. Kan. L. Rev. 343 (2012).

44 JOSEPH M. PERILLO, CONTRACTS, §8.3(a) (2014) ("[A]n infant may disaffirm contracts until a reasonable time after reaching majority. Failure to do so is a ratification.").

45 County Board of Education v. Hensley, 144 S.W. 63, 65 (1912) ("[W]hen an infant by reason of his personal appearance, family surroundings, and business activities, coupled with a misrepresentation or fraudulent concealment, leads one who deals with him in good faith, and not knowing that he is an infant, to believe that he is of age, he will be estopped from maintaining an action to avoid his executed contract").

Example clause

You represent and warrant that you are at least 18 years old and that all information you submit is accurate and truthful.

A company might also include a provision like the following:

Example clause

Individuals under the age of 18 must at all times use Company's services only in conjunction with and under the supervision of a parent or legal guardian who is at least 18 years of age.

Even if such a representation and warranty is ineffective because the signatory is a minor, it may help the company make a claim that it acted in good faith and/or with reasonable care. A contract might require that the child's legal guardian sign the contract on his or her behalf:

Example clause

I ____________________ state that I am the parent and legal guardian of ________________, a minor, age ________, who resides at ________________________. I hereby warrant that I am a legally competent adult and a parent or legally appointed guardian of the minor, and that I have every right to contract for the minor in the above regard. This agreement shall be binding upon the minor and me and our respective heirs, legal representatives and assigns.

Contracts entered into by mentally infirm parties may be disaffirmed by the incompetent party but not the other (legally competent) party.[46] A contract entered into by an intoxicated party may render a party legally incompetent, but only if the other party knew or should have known the intoxicated party lacked capacity.[47]

Finally, as noted in the discussion about agency, an employee of a company may be personally liable if he or she signs a contract on behalf of a non-existent corporation. A corporation does not exist if it has not been properly incorporated. If, for example, a founder of a company signs a lease prior to incorporating the company, the founder may be personally liable on

46 *Id.* at §§8.9–8.11.
47 *Id.* at §8.13; RESTATEMENT (SECOND) CONTRACTS §16.

the contract. Unless the contracting parties had originally agreed that the founder would not be liable, the founder will continue to be liable unless the corporation, the founder and the other party enter into a novation where all three parties agree to release the founder and have the corporation assume the liabilities under the contract.[48]

5.4 Doctrinal concept: basic assumption defenses (mutual mistake, unilateral mistake, impracticability, frustration of purpose)

Principle: A party may avoid her obligations under a contract where the party is ignorant of a fact that undermines her reason for entering into the contract, as long as she is not at fault for her lack of knowledge.

Basic assumption defenses include unilateral and mutual mistake, commercial impracticability, and frustration of purpose.

A mutual mistake is where both parties to the contract were wrong at the time they signed the contract in assuming an important fact (a mistake as to a "basic assumption").[49] That fact could be something having to do with the subject matter of the contract or even the environment. For example, assume that Developer Company enters into a contract to buy a building from RealEstate, Inc. in order to develop condominiums. Neither Developer Company nor Real Estate, Inc. is aware of an obscure ordinance that prohibits condominium developments on that city block. They have made a mistake as to a basic assumption of the transaction because they assumed that the building was suitable for developing into condominiums. That does not necessarily mean that Developer Company can get out of the agreement, however. It can only avoid the contract if it did not bear the risk of the mistake,[50] meaning that the issue had not been considered by it, it was not addressed in the contract, and it is not reasonable to make Developer Company responsible for

48 Beesley v. Hydrocarbon Separation, Inc., 358 S.W.3d 415, 423 (2012) ("When a promoter enters a contract on behalf of an unformed corporation, he is personally liable on the contract unless there is an agreement with the contracting party that the promoter is not liable. Absent such an agreement, a promoter is relieved of personal liability only when the corporation subsequently adopts the contract either expressly or by accepting its benefits.") After being properly incorporated, the corporation may subsequently assume liability for the contract by releasing the founder and adopting and ratifying the contract. *See* Hansen v. Fields Co., LLC, 763 S.E.2d 31, 34–35 ("While not initially liable for a promoter's contracts, a corporation may become liable for a promoter's preformation contract either through expressly ratifying the contract or through implicitly ratifying it by accepting its benefits with full knowledge of its terms."). *See* discussion of novation, Chapter 7.2.

49 RESTATEMENT (SECOND) CONTRACTS, §§151–154.

50 RESTATEMENT (SECOND) CONTRACTS, §154.

finding out about the ordinance. Developer Company should have checked with the city to make sure that it could use the building to develop condominiums. Unless it did some due diligence (and the ordinance was just so obscure that it could not have learned about it despite its diligence), a court is unlikely to allow Developer Company to avoid the contract on the basis of mutual mistake.

A unilateral mistake is similar to a mutual mistake except that only one party is mistaken about the important fact. In order to escape a contract where the mistake is unilateral (made by only one party), the mistaken party must demonstrate either that the other party was somehow at fault for the mistake (because she had caused the mistake or knew that the other party was mistaken) or enforcement of the contract would be unconscionable. Just like with mutual mistake, the mistaken party must not bear the risk of the mistake so if the mistaken party failed to do some basic investigation (either because it was supposed to under the contract or because it should have done so under the circumstances) then the mistaken party is out of luck.

Troubleshooting: In order to minimize the possibility of a mistake or a mistake defense, the parties can take several steps in their contract. The parties can incorporate representations and warranties. If both parties know that Developer Company is buying the building specifically for the purpose of building condominiums, Developer Company could seek a representation and/or warranty from RealEstate Inc. that the building is zoned for condominium development.

Example clause

Real Estate Inc., represents and warrants that the Property is zoned for Condominium Development as defined in Section 4.

If the fact represented is not true, the mistaken party can raise the defense of mutual mistake and claim that both parties were mistaken as to a basic assumption or raise the defense of unilateral mistake and claim that the other party knew of the mistake or was at fault. (It can also claim breach of warranty or misrepresentation).

On the other hand, the parties can include a statement that no representations were made regarding the condition of the property and this would undermine a later claim of mistake:

Example clause

Purchaser acknowledges and agrees that Real Estate Inc. makes no representation or warranty that the Property is zoned for Condominium Development as defined in Section 4.

Example clause

Representations. Buyer acknowledges that Real Estate Inc. has not made any representations or promises with respect to the Property except as expressly set forth in this Agreement and that Buyer has not relied upon any representations which are not written in this Agreement.

The parties can also expressly allocate the risk in their agreement, thus making one party "bear the risk" of any mistake:

Example clause

Buyer agrees to take the Property "as is" and with all faults and in the condition existing as of the close of escrow.

A quit claim deed only conveys the grantor's interest in property and does not provide a warranty of title. In other words, a quit claim deed allocates the risk of defective title to the Buyer.

Example clause

The Grantor hereby conveys, releases and quit claims all right, title, interest, claim and demand to the Grantee the property that has the legal description [set forth on Schedule A].

The parties can also indicate in the agreement that a party has *no* responsibility, such as:

Example clause

THE PARTIES ACKNOWLEDGE AND AGREE THAT SELLER HAS NO LIABILITY OR RESPONSIBILITY FOR THE REMOVAL OF ANY SUBSTANCE OR MATERIAL WHICH MAY BE POTENTIALLY INJURIOUS TO THE PUBLIC HEALTH OR WELFARE AND WHICH IS OR MAY BE LOCATED ON THE SUBJECT PROPERTY.

Caveat: The Example Clause above may be effective between the Buyer and the Seller, but the Seller may still be liable to third parties.

The remaining basic assumption defenses, impossibility, impracticability and frustration of purpose, are referred to as changed circumstances defenses. Like unilateral and mutual mistakes, they provide an excuse for getting out of a contract on the basis of a factual error. Unlike mistakes, however, the factual error occurs because something happens *after* the contract was formed. For example, in the above scenario, if the ordinance prohibiting condominium development was passed *after* the agreement had been entered into, then the proper defense would be a changed circumstances defense because the assumption that the building could be developed into a condo is *no longer* correct. Like mistakes, changed circumstances provide a defense only if it makes sense not to allocate the risk given the circumstances or the language of the contract.

Impossibility means that the changed circumstances made it impossible for the party seeking to avoid the contract to perform its obligations. In most cases, it is not impossible for a party to perform due to the changed circumstances, although it is very difficult and much more costly. Consequently, commercial impracticability provides a more common defense since the standard is lower – it doesn't have to be impossible to perform, although it does have to be impracticable (much more difficult and costly). With frustration of purpose, however, the circumstances haven't made performance more difficult; they have, however, destroyed the party's purpose or reason for entering into the contract. In the above example, if the ordinance was passed after the contract between Developer Co. and RealEstate Corp. was signed, Developer Co's performance – paying money for the building – is not made more difficult. Rather, Developer Co's purpose for buying the building (to build a condo) is destroyed.

A contract would not be worth much if one side could get out of it simply because he or she made factual errors or circumstances changed. Markets fluctuate, after all – it is the very reason many parties enter into contracts in the first place, to guard against market changes. Changed circumstances alone will not suffice to avoid one's contractual obligations. In order to excuse performance, the change must be one that fundamentally affects the deal between the parties – in the words of the Restatement Second of Contracts, it must be a *basic assumption* upon which the contract was made.[51] The change must also be one that the parties did not think was going to

51 RESTATEMENT (SECOND) CONTRACTS, §261.

happen.[52] An additional requirement is that it must not be fair to put the loss on the party seeking to avoid the contract because it was not his or her fault.[53]

Troubleshooting: As you might guess, parties may fear that a court may be either too lenient – or too rigid – about letting parties off the hook due to changed circumstances. Here, too, the parties can try to control the court's application of the doctrine by including a *force majeure* clause in their contract to outline what should happen in the event that forces outside their control occur. The following are examples of *force majeure* clauses.

Example clause

Except for an obligation to pay fees, neither party will be liable for failure to perform any of its obligations under this Agreement during any period in which such party cannot perform due to matters beyond their control, including, but not limited to, strike, fire, flood or other natural disaster, war or riot, provided that the delayed party immediately notifies the other party of such delay.

Example clause

A Party will be excused from a delay in performing, or a failure to perform, its obligations under this Agreement to the extent such delay or failure is caused by the occurrence of any contingency beyond the reasonable control, and without any fault, of such Party. In such event, the performance times shall be extended for a period of time equivalent to the time lost because of the excusable delay. However, if an excusable delay continues more than thirty (30) days, the Party not relying on the excusable delay may, at its option, terminate the affected Work Order(s) in whole or in part, upon notice to the other Party. In order to avail itself of the relief provided in this Section for an excusable delay, the Party must act with due diligence to remedy the cause of, or to mitigate or overcome, such delay or failure. For purposes of this Section, the phrase "due diligence" shall, at a minimum, require Contractor to maintain a contingency plan (and provide evidence of its current and periodic testing if requested by Client) for the continuation of business so that despite any disruption in Contractor's ability to fulfill its service obligations from any particular location or through the efforts of any particular individuals, Contractor will be able to fulfill its service obligations from an alternative/backup location.

52 *Id.*
53 *Id.*

As you can see, such clauses can be as general or specific as the parties want. Their purpose is to specify which circumstances warrant excuse or deferral of performance, and which do not. They also outline what the parties should do in the event of changed circumstances.

When the parties have addressed in their contract what conditions or circumstances excuse performance, courts may be less willing to find additional excuses.[54]

5.5 Doctrinal concepts: nondisclosure, misrepresentation, and fraud

Principle: A party may avoid its obligations under a contract if it relied upon the other party's false or misleading statements in entering into it.

While parties generally do not have a duty to negotiate a contract in good faith,[55] there are certain exceptions. Certain relationships or situations create a duty to disclose.[56] Even when there is no affirmative duty to disclose, a party cannot intentionally misrepresent facts to deceive or mislead the other party. In some cases, a material omission, or failure to disclose facts, amounts to a misrepresentation. A party relying upon a statement made by the other party should include it as a representation in the agreement.

Caveat: Contract law in other countries may impose a duty to negotiate in good faith. In France and Germany, for example, parties must negotiate contracts in good faith.

A party to a contract can avoid enforcement by raising a claim of fraud, misrepresentation, or nondisclosure. Assume the party seeking avoidance is

---

54 *See* Dills v. Town of Enfield, 557 A.2d 517, 525 (1989) ("Where, as in this case, sophisticated contracting parties have negotiated termination provisions, courts should be slow to invent additional ways to excuse performance").

55 After they enter into a contract, however, the parties have a duty to perform their obligations in good faith. Furthermore, the parties may themselves agree to negotiate in good faith. *See* SIGA Technologies, Inc. v. PharmAthene, Inc., 67 A.3d 330, 344 (2013) (finding that "an express contractual obligation to negotiate in good faith is binding on the contracting parties").

56 RSG, Inc. v. Sidump'r Trailer Co., 2011 U.S. Dist. LEXIS 2290 at *41–42 (D. Neb. Jan. 10, 2011) ("It is consistently recognized that one party to a business transaction is under a duty to exercise reasonable care to disclose facts basic to the transaction, if: 1) he knows that the other is about to enter into the transaction under a mistake as to those facts; and 2) he knows that the other party, because of the relationship between them, the customs of the trade or other objective circumstances, would reasonably expect a disclosure of those facts"); *see also* RESTATEMENT (SECOND) CONTRACTS, §161(d).

Party A and the party who has made the misrepresentation is Party B. Party A typically needs to argue the following:

1. reliance by Party A upon
2. a false
3. representation made
4. knowingly (or with reckless disregard as to its falsity) by Party B
5. upon which Party B intended Party A to rely, and
6. Party A was injured as a result of the misrepresentation.[57]

Example clause

Supplier represents that all Products are new and unused and do not contain used or repaired parts.

On the other hand, a party may wish to disclaim representations not expressly stated in the agreement to avoid a claim of negligent misrepresentation. The parties may also insert a "no reliance" clause such as the following:

Example clause

Each party represents and warrants that it is not relying on any representation by the other party, other than those set forth in, or incorporated by reference into, this Agreement. The parties expressly agree to this provision as part of their overall allocation of the risks and benefits of this Agreement.

Caveat: A court may still invalidate a contract despite a "no reliance" clause if there is evidence of fraud or if the party claiming fraud was not represented by counsel; however, as we have seen elsewhere, the existence of the language makes it harder for a party to claim that it was lied to or misled by the other party or that its reliance was reasonable.[58]

57 RSG, Inc. v. Sidump'r Trailer Co., 2011 U.S. Dist. LEXIS 2290 at *39–40 (D. Neb. Jan. 10, 2011) ("The elements of a claim for fraudulent misrepresentation under Nebraska law are: (1) that a representation was made; (2) that the representation was false; (3) that when made, the representation was known to be false or made recklessly without knowledge of its truth and as a positive assertion; (4) that the representation was made with the intention that the plaintiff should rely on it; (5) that the plaintiff did so rely on it; and (6) that the plaintiff suffered damage as a result").

58 RSG, Inc. v. Sidump'r Trailer Co., 2011 U.S. Dist. LEXIS 2290 at *49 (D. Neb. Jan. 10, 2011) ("Because the parties are sophisticated businessmen who were represented by competent and experienced counsel throughout the transaction, the 'no reliance' clause is enforceable with respect to the Buyer's breach of warranty claims. Accordingly, the court finds that it was not reasonable for the Buyer to rely on any oral or written representations outside of the Contract.") Note that a complaint alleging fraud is subject to heightened pleading stand-

5.6 Doctrinal concept: warranties under the UCC

Principle: The UCC contains specific provisions regarding warranties which are intended to reflect the reasonable expectations of buyers of goods. Warranties may be either express or implied.

A purchaser of goods has certain basic expectations about the nature or quality of the goods. Sometimes, a seller of goods may make certain promises about the product, either expressly or impliedly, which lead the purchaser to form these expectations.

The UCC states that a seller warrants good title in every contract for sale.[59] The warranty of title may be excluded or modified by specific language.[60] Courts have generally required that a disclaimer of the warranty of title use language that is precise and unambiguous.[61] Because the warranty of title is so basic, an effective disclaimer must clearly state that it pertains to the title the seller is purporting to transfer and not merely that it limits the seller's liability.

Example clause

Seller makes no warranty as to the title to the goods, and Buyer assumes all risks of non-ownership of the goods by Seller.[62]

By contrast, the following clauses were deemed *ineffective* to disclaim the warranty of title:

ards and must state with particularity the circumstances giving rise to the claim. The Federal Rules of Civil Procedure Rule 9 states: "In alleging fraud or mistake, a party must state with particularity the circumstances constituting fraud or mistake. Malice, intent, knowledge, or other conditions of a person's mind may be alleged generally."

59 UCC § 2-312.

60 UCC § 2-312(2).

61 Jones v. Linebaugh, 34 Mich. App. 305, 309–310 (1971) (bill of sale for car stated that seller sold and assigned all of seller's "right, title and interest" and that to the "best of [seller's] knowledge, there [was] no title in existence by way of registration with the State of Michigan or with any other State or with any Nation") *id.* at 309.

62 18 Am. Jur. Legal Forms 2d §253:825 (1974).

Example

All warranties pursuant to U.C.C.2–312 (warranty of title and against infringement) are hereby excluded from this transaction.
(Court found that the language was ineffective to disclaim warranty of title because it was similar to that which expresses how seller's liability will be limited, rather than what title seller purported to transfer.)[63]

Example

(Seller) . . . does hereby sell, assign, convey, transfer and deliver to Buyer any right, title and interest Seller may have in the following goods and chattels. . . . It is expressly understood and agreed that the Seller shall in nowise be deemed or held to be obligated, liable, or accountable upon or under guaranties [sic] or warranties, in any manner or form including, but not limited to, the implied warranties of title, merchantability, fitness for use or of quality.
(Court found that language did not disclaim warranty of title in the "specific" language required by UCC §2-312. The language was not a positive warning regarding the status of title and would be unlikely to "catch the eye of an unsophisticated buyer." In addition, language was couched in "negative terminology" and expressed "what the seller would be liable for rather than what the buyer is or is not receiving.")[64]

The seller may make express warranties by affirmatively making a factual statement or promise about a product or by sending a sample or model which becomes part of the basis of the bargain.[65] Most courts do not require reliance as an element in a claim for breach of an express written warranty.[66] Words such as "warrant" are not required.[67]

The UCC also imposes certain implied warranties. The implied warranty of fitness for a particular purpose applies where the seller knows or should know that the buyer plans to use the product for a particular purpose and knows or should know that the buyer is relying upon the seller's judgment.[68] The implied warranty of merchantability applies to sales by merchants[69] and

63 Moore v. Pro Team Corvette Sales, Inc., 152 Ohio App. 3d 71 (2002).
64 Sunseri v. RKO-Stanley Warner Theatres, Inc., 374 A.2d 1342, 1344–1345 (Pa. Super. Ct. 1977).
65 UCC §2-313.
66 *See* discussion Section 5.2, f.n. 38.
67 UCC §2-313.
68 UCC §2-315.
69 For definition of merchant, *see* UCC§2-104 (merchant is one who deals "in goods of the kind").

means that the goods being sold are of average quality, fit for the ordinary purposes for goods of that kind, properly packaged, and conform to any promises or affirmations of fact on the container.[70]

A seller may not disclaim an express warranty.[71] The parol evidence rule may, however, bar admission of oral statements if the court finds the parties intended the agreement to be an integrated, final agreement and if the agreement contains a statement that no express warranties were made.[72] In other words, a seller can't expressly make a statement about the product and then disown or disclaim that statement in the contract although the buyer may have a hard time proving the statement was made if it was made orally.[73] A merger clause and an express warranty disclaimer thus may effectively work to exclude an express warranty.[74]

CASE HIGHLIGHT

KING INDUSTRIES, INC. v. WORLDCO DATA SYSTEMS, INC., 736 F. Supp. 114 (E.D. Va. 1989)

The plaintiff, King Industries ("King") entered into two agreements: the first, a purchase agreement with defendant, Worldco Data Systems, Inc. ("Worldco") to purchase a computer system, and the second, a lease/purchase contract with defendant, Copelco Leasing Corporation ("Copelco") in order to finance the purchase of the computer system. King alleged that it had relied upon the defendants' skill and judgment in selecting a computer system and claimed that they breached express and implied warranties because the computer system was not fit for plaintiff's business needs.

The agreement between King and Worldco contained the following warranty disclaimer on the front page:

70 UCC §2-314.

71 UCC §2-313, cmt. 1.

72 King Industries, Inc. v. Worldco Data Systems, Inc., 736 F. Supp. 114 (E.D. Va. 1989) (noting that while the UCC disallows disclaimers of express warranties, the parol evidence rule bars oral statements that "contradict or vary the disclaimer of express warranties").

73 The Buyer may be able to introduce the evidence if an exception to the parol evidence rule, such as fraud or mistake, applies.

74 Hoffman v. Daimler Trucks North America, LLC, 940 F. Supp. 2d 347, 355 (W.D. Va. 2013) (finding that "any oral representation" made by the defendant that could become the basis for an express warranty "was disclaimed by the merger clause," which stated: "The front and back of this Order, along with other documents signed by Purchaser(s) in connection with this Order, comprise the entire agreement between the parties affecting this purchase. No oral agreements or understandings shall be binding").

CASE HIGHLIGHT *(continued)*

WDS MAKES NO WARRANTY OF ANY KIND, EXPRESS OR IMPLIED, INCLUDING WITHOUT LIMITATION WARRANTIES OF MERCHANTABILITY OR FITNESS FOR A PARTICULAR PURPOSE. (Capitalization in original)

The lease agreement between King and Copelco contained the following warranty disclaimer above the signature line:

LESSOR NEITHER BEING THE MANUFACTURER, SUPPLIER, NOR A DEALER IN THE EQUIPMENT, MAKES NO WARRANTY, EXPRESS OR IMPLIED, TO ANYONE, AS TO THE SUITABILITY, DURABILITY, DESIGN, CONDITION, CAPACITY, PERFORMANCE OR ANY OTHER ASPECT OF THE EQUIPMENT OR ITS MATERIAL OR WORKMANSHIP. LESSOR FURTHER DISCLAIMS ANY IMPLIED WARRANTIES OF ANY KIND WITH RESPECT TO THE EQUIPMENT INCLUDING THE WARRANTY OF MERCHANTABILITY AND FITNESS FOR USE OR PURPOSE. AS TO LESSOR AND ITS ASSIGNS, LESSEE LEASES THE EQUIPMENT "AS IS." (Capitalization in original)

The court found that the disclaimer of implied warranties was conspicuous and limited their liability for breach of implied warranties.

Next, the court addressed whether the defendants were liable for express warranties regarding the computer system. The court stated that even assuming that an express warranty was made, the issue was whether the disclaimers limited defendants' liability. The court stated that under UCC §2-316(1), a party cannot disclaim an express warranty:

"The effect of this section is that, 'If the factfinder determines that a seller's statement created an express warranty, words purportedly disclaiming that warranty will have no effect . . .' (citing 1 J. White & R. Summers, *Uniform Commercial Code*, §12-2 (3d ed. 1988).

Yet, the court noted that UCC §2-316(1) was subject to the provisions of UCC §2-202 on parol evidence and extrinsic evidence. The agreement between King and Worldco contained the following merger clause:

ALL TERMS AND CONDITIONS WRITTEN ON THE REVERSE SIDE HEREOF AND ON THE FACE HEREOF, INCLUDING SCHEDULE A HERETO, CONSTITUTE THE COMPLETE AND BINDING CONTRACT WHEN ACCEPTED BY WDS. THIS ORDER EXPRESSLY LIMITS ACCEPTANCE TO SUCH TERMS AND CONDITIONS PROPOSED BY THE BUYER ARE REJECTED. (Sic.) (Capitalization in original)

. . .

The court found that the parol evidence rule precluded the admission of oral statements that contradicted the terms of the written disclaimer:

> "[E]ven if the oral representations made by Worldco's representative became the 'basis of the bargain' and therefore constituted an express warranty, those oral statements would not be admissible to contradict or vary the disclaimer of express warranties clause contained in the integrated agreement between Worldco and plaintiff. This parol evidence would be admissible, however, in a properly pleaded fraud in the inducement claim."

CASE HIGHLIGHT *(continued)*

The leasing agreement between King and Copelco did not contain an integration clause but the court found that Copelco's liability was limited by the warranty disclaimer clause and the following language:

> "IF THE EQUIPMENT IS UNSATISFACTORY FOR ANY REASON, LESSEE SHALL MAKE CLAIM ON ACCOUNT THEREOF SOLELY AGAINST SUPPLIER, AND ANY OF SUPPLIER'S VENDORS." (Capitalization in original)

...

Finally, the court found no evidence of fraud and dismissed plaintiff's action with prejudice.

A seller may disclaim implied warranties as long as certain requirements are met.[75] First, the disclaimer must be conspicuous, meaning that it is written so that a "reasonable person" would have noticed it.[76] In determining

---

75

§2-316. Exclusion or Modification of Warranties.

(1) Words or conduct relevant to the creation of an express warranty and words or conduct tending to negate or limit warranty shall be construed wherever reasonable as consistent with each other; but subject to the provisions of this Article on parol or extrinsic evidence (Section 2-202) negation or limitation is inoperative to the extent that such construction is unreasonable.

(2) Subject to subsection (3), to exclude or modify the implied warranty of merchantability or any part of it the language must mention merchantability and in case of a writing must be conspicuous, and to exclude or modify any implied warranty of fitness the exclusion must be by a writing and conspicuous. Language to exclude all implied warranties of fitness is sufficient if it states, for example, that "There are no warranties which extend beyond the description on the face hereof."

(3) Notwithstanding subsection (2)

(a) unless the circumstances indicate otherwise, all implied warranties are excluded by expressions like "as is", "with all faults" or other language which in common understanding calls the buyer's attention to the exclusion of warranties and makes plain that there is no implied warranty; and

(b) when the buyer before entering into the contract has examined the goods or the sample or model as fully as he desired or has refused to examine the goods there is no implied warranty with regard to defects which an examination ought in the circumstances to have revealed to him; and

(c) an implied warranty can also be excluded or modified by course of dealing or course of performance or usage of trade.

(4) Remedies for breach of warranty can be limited in accordance with the provisions of this Article on liquidation or limitation of damages and on contractual modification of remedy (Sections 2-718 and 2-719).

76

§1-201. General Definitions.

...

(10) "Conspicuous", with reference to a term, means so written, displayed, or presented that a reasonable person against which it is to operate ought to have noticed it. Whether a term is "conspicuous" or not is a decision for the court. Conspicuous terms include the following: (A) a heading in capitals equal to or greater in size than the surrounding text, or in contrasting type, font, or color to the surrounding

conspicuousness, a court will consider factors such as the appearance of the disclaimer (including capitalization, bold font, color, underlined text, font size especially in relation to other wording), the location of the disclaimer within the document (whether it was on the same page or on the reverse of the document, whether the disclaimer paragraph was set apart from other provisions, whether it was marked with a caption or descriptive heading), and the disclaiming language itself (whether it used words such as "merchantability," "as is," or "with all faults," whether it was specific enough and unambiguous), and the relative sophistication of the parties.[77]

Caveat: The Magnuson-Moss Warranty Act, a federal law that governs warranties on consumer products, restricts a supplier's ability to modify or disclaim warranties.[78] State consumer statutes may also limit or prohibit warranty disclaimers.

CASE HIGHLIGHT

AMERICAN AERIAL SERVICES, INC. v. TEREX USA, LLC, 39 F. Supp. 3d 95 (D. Me. 2014)

Plaintiff American Aerial Services, Inc. ("Aerial") supplies cranes and labor for the construction of steel buildings. Aerial was interested in purchasing a crane manufactured by Terex. Aerial contacted Empire, one of Terex's authorized dealers, which emailed it information and attached a Terex advertising brochure which included the crane's specifications and information. On each page of the brochure was a disclaimer at the bottom which read, in small print, "[d]ata published herein is intended as a guide only and shall not be construed to warrant applicability for lifting purposes." On the back page of the brochure was the following language:

> "[t]he only warranty applicable to our equipment is the standard written warranty applicable to the particular product and sale, and Terex makes no other warranty, express or implied."

---

text of the same or lesser size; and (B) language in the body of a record or display in larger type than the surrounding text, or in contrasting type, font, or color to the surrounding text of the same size, or set off from surrounding text of the same size by symbols or other marks that call attention to the language.

See also Lumber Mutual Insurance Company v. Clarklift of Detroit, Inc., 224 Mich. App. 737, 739–744 (1997) (finding that "as is" disclaimer must be conspicuous so that a reasonable person would notice it).

77 UCC §1-201.

78 15 U.S.C.A. §2300 et. seq.

CASE HIGHLIGHT *(continued)*

Aerial subsequently sued Terex and Empire for, among other claims, breach of the implied warranty of merchantability. The defendants argued that the language on the back of the brochure disclaimed the implied warranty of merchantability. The court disagreed:

> "This language does not appear in capital letters; does not appear in type that is larger than the surrounding text; does not mention merchantability; and does not appear in a contrasting font or color compared to the surrounding text . . . There are no other marks that call attention to the quoted language. Therefore, I find that the quoted language on the back page of the Data Sheet is not conspicuous within the meaning of §2-316(2)."

The defendants also argued that the language on the back page excluded all implied warranties under §2-316(3)(a). The court again disagreed:

> "For a warranty exclusion to pass muster, the statute requires commonly used phrases such as 'with all faults,' or 'as is,' which, due to their widespread usage, are immediately recognized as disclaiming warranties even upon casual perusal by nonlawyers. *See* §2316(3)(a). That the drafters of the UCC also permitted a seller to exclude implied warranties with 'other language' left open the possibility that parties could use other terms not specified in the statute, but which convey the same meaning as 'with all faults' or 'as is.' The language on the back of the Data Sheet states simply that 'Terex makes no warranty, express or implied' [citation omitted]. Nothing about this statement could reasonably be said to constitute a term which 'calls the buyer's attention' to the attempted exclusion of all warranties in the same manner as the phrases 'as is' or 'with all faults,' and therefore, it does not satisfy §2-316(3)(a)."

In order to minimize disputes over the adequacy of the language, a drafter seeking to disclaim the warranty of merchantability should use language that is conspicuous and which mentions merchantability. In order to disclaim the implied warranty of fitness for a particular purpose, the disclaimer must be in writing, conspicuous and contain disclaiming language such as, "There are no warranties which extend beyond the description on the face hereof."[79]

79 *See* Las Vegas Metropolitan Police Dept. v. Harris Corp., M/A Com, Inc., 2015 WL 895054 (finding that warranty provision effectively disclaimed the warranty of merchantability and the warranty of fitness for a particular purpose because the heading was capitalized and underlined, the language was in all capitals and specifically mentioned merchantability and fitness). *Id.* at *9.

Example clause

THE WARRANTIES AND REMEDIES SET FORTH IN THIS SECTION CONSTITUTE THE ONLY WARRANTIES WITH RESPECT TO THE HARDWARE, SOFTWARE AND SERVICES AND THE OWNER'S EXCLUSIVE REMEDIES IN THE EVENT SUCH WARRANTIES ARE BREACHED. THEY ARE IN LIEU OF ALL OTHER WARRANTIES WHETHER WRITTEN, ORAL, EXPRESS, IMPLIED, OR STATUTORY INCLUDING, WITHOUT LIMITATION, THE WARRANTY OF MERCHANTABILITY AND THE WARRANTY OF FITNESS FOR A PARTICULAR PURPOSE.

Other language (such as an "as is" or "with all faults" clause) in circumstances which clearly indicate the exclusion of implied warranties are also effective.

Caveat: An "as is" clause is not effective to disclaim the warranty of title under the UCC.[80]

CASE HIGHLIGHT

WARD FARMS PARTNERSHIP v. ENERBASE CO-OP RESOURCES, 863 N.W.2d 868 (N.D. 2015)

Ward Farms Partnership purchased Enerbase's tractor for $19,000 at a third-party auction sale. The bidding card stated:

> "ALL ITEMS ARE SOLD AS IS, WHERE IS, WITHOUT GUARANTEE OF ANY KIND. The descriptions of items appearing in advertising prior to this auction are believed to be correct. Nevertheless, neither those descriptions nor any oral statements made by the Owner (or his agents or officers) or the Auctioneers (or his agents or officers) concerning any item shall be construed as a warranty, either expressed or implied." (Capitalization in original)

Michael Ward, a partner of Ward Farms, signed a bill of sale which stated:

> "All items sold As–Is, Where–Is . . . ALL SALES ARE FINAL." (Capitalization in original)

80 Rochester Equipment & Maintenance v. Roxbury Mountain Service, Inc., 68 A.D.3d 1803, 1804–1805 (2009) ("As is" clause in contract related to the condition and operability of vehicle rather than its title); Brokke v. Williams, 766 P.2d 1311, 1313 (1989) (fluorescent signs in pawn shop indicating that goods were sold "as is" was ineffective to disclaim warranty of title as warranty of title is not subject to disclaimers pertaining to fitness and merchantability).

CASE HIGHLIGHT *(continued)*

After the sale, Ward Farms discovered that the tractor required repairs estimated to cost $19,550 to $31,430. Ward Farms sued alleging fraud, misrepresentation, deceit, and breach of express and implied warranties.

Ward Farms alleged that it was told at the auction that the tractor was "field ready" and had been used recently to level roads. In addition, Michael Ward testified that when he visited Enerbase's shop several days prior to the auction, Enerbase's employees told him that the tractor had "been on the lot" and that they did not know of anything wrong with it. The lower court granted Enerbase's summary judgment motion to dismiss all the claims and Ward Farms appealed.

On appeal, the Supreme Court of North Dakota found that, even assuming the alleged statements were made by Enerbase, there was no actionable fraud. The statements that the tractor was "field ready" or "in good shape" were puffery because they were expressions of opinions which did not amount to fraud. Furthermore, the alleged statements that the tractor had been recently used and previously been for sale on Enerbase's lot did not constitute statements of material fact concerning the condition or value of the tractor which induced Ward Farms to purchase the tractor.

Ward Farms also argued that Enerbase breached the express and implied warranties of merchantability and that the statement that the tractor is "field ready" constituted a warranty. The court disagreed:

> "An expression regarding the value of the goods or a seller's opinion or commendation of the goods does not create a warranty . . . However, '[u]nless excluded or modified . . . a warranty that the goods shall be merchantable is implied in a contract for their sale if the seller is a merchant with respect to goods of that kind . . . [citations omitted].' The bill of sale, signed by Michael Ward, states in clear, conspicuous language: 'The undersigned, as purchaser, states that he has purchased at public auction the above listed items and therefore understands that they do not carry any warranty. All items sold As–Is, Where–Is . . . The undersigned acknowledges that he/she has read the foregoing statement . . . ALL SALES ARE FINAL' [capitalization in original]. We conclude the district court correctly determined the bill of sale fulfilled the requirements of N.D.C.C. §41–02–33(3)(a)*. . . Both the bidder contract and the bill of sale contained clear and conspicuous language disclaiming any warranties and stating all items are sold 'as is,' and Michael Ward admitted signing both documents. Ward Farms did not raise an issue of material fact regarding its breach of warranty claims. We conclude the district court did not err in granting Enerbase's summary judgment motion."

Finally, Ward Farms argued that the "as is" language gives rise to an unconscionable adhesion contract. The court disagreed, stating that North Dakota law expressly allows the sale of goods "as is." Furthermore, Michael Ward was an experienced farmer and attorney who understood that the tractor was being sold "as is." Accordingly, the contract was not unconscionable.

* N.D.C.C. §41–02–33(3)(a) is the equivalent of UCC §2-316

The UCC warranties are intended to reflect the reasonable expectations of the parties but may be disclaimed if certain conditions are met. Table 5.1 provides an overview of the UCC warranties and how they may be disclaimed.

Table 5.1 Overview of the UCC warranties and how they may be disclaimed

Type of warranty	What is it?	To whom does it apply?	How can you disclaim it?[81]
Warranty of Title (§2-312)	Warranty that title conveyed will be good and its transfer rightful	Any seller	Only by very precise and unambiguous language that makes clear that seller may not be conveying title; "as is" language is not sufficient
Implied Warranty of Merchantability (§2-314)	Warranty that goods will be merchantable (meaning goods will function and look the way most buyers expect them to look and function)	Merchants who regularly sell the type of good warranted (in other words, this is not a one-time sale of a good)	Must mention "merchantability" and if in writing must be conspicuous *– or –* Uses "as is" or "with all faults" type language
Implied Warranty of Fitness for Particular Purpose (§2-315)	Warranty that goods will be capable of being used in a particular way the buyer expects	Seller who (1) knows or should know that Buyer intends to use the good for a particular purpose and (2) knows or should know that Buyer is relying upon Seller's skill or judgment	Must be in writing, conspicuous and use general disclaiming language such as "There are no warranties which extend beyond the description on the face hereof" *– or –* Uses "as is" or "with all faults" type language

81 There may be other ways to disclaim the implied warranties, such as by trade usage. Because the focus of this book is on drafting to *prevent* problems, I did not include other ways a seller might try to argue that an implied warranty was disclaimed since these arguments are used when preventive measures have failed. Please review the relevant UCC section for other ways to disclaim warranties which are not related to preventive drafting.

Table 5.1 (continued)

Type of warranty	What is it?	To whom does it apply?	How can you disclaim it?
Express Warranty (§2-313)	Warranty that any model or factual statement regarding the good which becomes the basis of the bargain is accurate	Any seller making an affirmative factual statement or promise about the good or who provides a sample or description of the good	Not enforceable in theory; however, integration clause may effectively exclude express warranties where the contract contains a "no express warranty" provision because of the parol evidence rule

6

Contract clauses and issues related to performance and breach

If a contract has been properly formed, each party should fulfill the covenants (promises) they made in the contract. These covenants may be subject to the occurrence of certain conditions. If all conditions have been met, a party fails to perform, and there is no available defense to performance, then that party will be in breach of contract.

Contracts can be very long and each party may have many obligations. Does the failure to fulfill *any* promise mean the party breached the contract? Some promises may be an essential part of the contract, such as payment of money due. But other obligations may be less material, such as meeting certain deadlines. What happens if a party fails to fulfill an ancillary or minor obligation?

A party breaches if that party fails to perform precisely as required under the contract. There are two kinds of breaches – material and minor. A material breach means the non-breaching party did not get the benefit of her bargain. A minor breach means that although the other party's performance wasn't *perfect*, the non-breaching party received essentially what she wanted under the contract. The non-breaching party can sue for either a material or minor breach; however, there is a significant difference between the two. If the breach was material, the non-breaching party can immediately terminate the contract and sue the other party for breach of contract. If the breach was minor, however, the non-breaching party cannot terminate the contract although it can sue for damages caused by the minor breach. Whether a party has committed a breach of either kind may depend upon timing and/or the order of performance.

One party might be expected to do something *but only after a condition has been met*. A condition is the occurrence of some event that triggers performance or some other event. A condition can either be something that is within one party's control or it can be an external event.

The determination of breach often hinges upon interpretation. Courts will interpret an agreement according to its language and in context of the entire agreement, with some courts adhering primarily to the plain language of the agreement and others focusing on the context in which the agreement was made. The primary objective of the courts in interpreting a contract is to accomplish the intent and purpose of the parties.[1]

The parties may specify what constitutes a material breach:

Example clause

The disclosure of the information in Section 2.3 by Client to any other person or entity constitutes a material breach of this Agreement.

6.1 Doctrinal concept: covenants

Principle: A covenant is a promise. In some cases, the covenant must be performed only under certain conditions. Unless otherwise stated or indicated by the contract, the performances of the parties are due simultaneously.

A covenant can be dependent, concurrent, or independent. A dependent covenant depends upon the occurrence of some act or condition, such as the performance of the other party. The party is not required to perform the undertaken dependent covenant until the act or condition happens. A concurrent covenant requires that both parties perform their covenants at the same time. A party who is ready, willing, and able to perform may sue for breach if the other party fails to perform or anticipatorily repudiates, meaning that before the time for performance she indicates unequivocally that she will not perform what she promised. An anticipatory repudiation is treated like a breach. Independent covenants are promises which are not mutually dependent and they can be enforced by a party regardless of whether that party has also performed.

The determination of whether a covenant is enforceable may depend upon whether it is dependent or independent. Whether a clause is dependent or independent hinges upon the interpretation of the contract. Because of the mutual dependency of performances (meaning that each party's performance obligation depends upon the performance of the other), covenants

1 Hand v. Grow Construction, Inc., 983 So. 2d 684, 686–687 (Fla. 1st DCA 2008) (quoting James v. Gulf Life Ins. Co., 66 So. 2d 62, 62 (Fla. 1953)).

are generally considered concurrent or dependent.[2] Generally, if a covenant is an essential part of the consideration for the contract, it will be a dependent covenant. The parties, however, can expressly state that covenants be construed as independent.

Example clause:

SEPARABILITY. Each and every covenant and agreement contained in this Agreement shall for all purposes be construed to be a separate and independent covenant and agreement, and a breach of any covenant or agreement contained in this Agreement by either party shall in no way or manner discharge or relieve the other party from its obligation to perform each and every covenant and agreement in this Agreement.

CASE HIGHLIGHT

RICHLAND TOWERS, INC. v. DENTON, 139 So. 3d 318 (Fla. App. 2 Dist. 2014)

Richland Towers, Inc. and Richland Towers, LLC, the former employer and an affiliated company, sued former employees David Denton and Dale West for breach of contract and tried to enforce restrictive covenants in their employment agreements. The restrictive covenants precluded Denton and West from engaging in a competing business for a certain period of time and prohibited them from hiring or attempting to hire employees or independent contractors of the employer. They also imposed confidentiality and nondisclosure obligations. Denton and West argued that the agreements were unenforceable because they had not been fully paid. The lower court held that Richland Towers' failure to pay certain bonuses as required constituted a prior breach that rendered the agreements unenforceable. In doing so, the lower court determined that the parties' obligations under the contract were dependent covenants and relied upon the recitals clause which stated that "in consideration of the covenants and agreements herein contained and the moneys to be paid hereunder, the Employer hereby employs the Employee and the Employee hereby agrees to perform services as an employee of the Employer, upon the following terms and conditions[.]"

The District Court of Appeal disagreed and reversed the lower court's decision. In reaching its conclusion, it cited the following provision in the employment agreement:

2 Hand v. Grow Construction, Inc., 983 So. 2d 684, 687 (2008) (noting that covenants in a contract are considered dependent unless the contract evidences a contrary intention).

CASE HIGHLIGHT *(continued)*

"*Covenants Independent.* Each restrictive covenant on the part of the Employee set forth in this Agreement shall be construed as a covenant independent of any other covenant or provision of this Agreement or any other agreement which the Corporation and the Employee may have, fully performed and not executory, and the existence of any claim or cause of action by the Employee against the Corporation, whether predicated upon another covenant or provision of the Agreement or otherwise, shall not constitute a defense to the enforcement by the Corporation of any other covenant."

The District Court of Appeal stated that "the plain language" of the clause "compels our conclusion that the parties unambiguously intended that the covenants were independent."

The parties can clearly establish an obligation as dependent upon the occurrence of another action or event by drafting it as a condition. Conditions are discussed in the next section.

6.2 Doctrinal concept: conditions

Principle: The performance of a contractual obligation may depend upon the occurrence of another event.

A condition precedent means that something (an act or event) must occur before there is a right to performance. A condition can be either express or constructive (implied-in-law).[3] An express condition is created by the parties whereas a constructive condition is created by a court where it makes sense to do so. We've already discussed one type of express condition, satisfaction clauses, in the section on consideration. A satisfaction clause is an example of an express condition because the contract states that payment is conditioned upon one party being satisfied by the work product. Words such as "on the condition that," "provided that," "subject to," "only if" and the "if . . . then" duo are typically used to signal an express condition.

3 There are also implied-in-fact conditions, which are treated as express conditions for the purposes of this book. In addition, there are two subcategories of express conditions, conditions subsequent and conditions precedent. A condition precedent triggers performance while a condition subsequent discharges a duty to perform. *See* CALAMARI & PERILLO ON CONTRACTS, §11.7, at p.416 (5th ed., 2003); *see also* DBT GmbH v. J.L. Mining Co., 544 F. Supp. 2d 364, 380 (S.D.N.Y., April 8, 2008) ("A condition precedent is 'an act or event, other than a lapse of time, which, unless the condition is excused, must occur before a duty to perform a promise in the agreement arises' (citing Oppenheimer & Co., Inc. v. Oppenheim, Appel, Dixon & Co., 86 N.Y.2d 685, 660 N.E.2d 415, 418, 636 N.Y.S.2d 734 (N.Y. 1995)).

Example clause

The Offer is subject to Buyer obtaining Financing for construction loans.

Example clause

The transaction is contingent upon the Buyer obtaining engineer's reports and permits for construction.

The parties may expressly state certain conditions to the closing of a transaction. Here are some other examples of express conditions:

Example clause

The respective obligations of Buyer and Seller to effect the Closing of the transactions contemplated in this Agreement are subject to the fulfillment, prior to or at the Closing, of each of the following conditions:

(a) *Legal Proceedings.* No Governmental Body shall have enacted, issued, promulgated, enforced or entered any statute, rule, regulation, non-appealable judgment, decree, injunction or other order which is in effect on the Closing Date and which prohibits, restricts or delays consummation of the transactions contemplated by this Agreement or the Collateral Agreements and there shall be no pending lawsuit, claim or legal action relating to the transactions contemplated by this Agreement or any of the Collateral Agreements which seeks to prohibit or restrict the transactions contemplated by this Agreement.

(b) *Antitrust Laws.* Any applicable waiting period or approvals of a Governmental Body under the HSR Act or applicable foreign antitrust Laws, respectively, relating to the transactions contemplated by this Agreement or the Collateral Agreements shall have expired or been terminated."

Example clause

Conditions Precedent to Seller's Obligations

The obligations of Seller to effect the Closing of the transactions contemplated hereby are subject to the fulfillment, prior to or at the Closing, of each of the following conditions, any of which may be waived in writing by Seller: . . .

Express conditions must be strictly complied with or completely performed.[4] For example, in the following provision, the Licensee's obligation to provide notice is a condition to the Licensor's obligation to defend and indemnify. ("Indemnify" means to protect against loss or damage).

Example clause

Licensor shall defend Licensee, and indemnify same against third-party claims that use of the Software violates such third party's valid intellectual property rights, *provided that* Licensee gives Licensor prompt written notice of such claim.

In the Example Clause above, the Licensee must provide prompt written notice before the Licensor's duty to indemnify is triggered. In other words, the Licensor would not be in breach for failing to defend the Licensee until it receives notice of the claim. What if the Licensee fails to provide "prompt" written notice and instead provides written notice that is somewhat delayed? The Licensor may waive the right to receive timely notice. (Waiver is discussed in Chapter 6.3).

What if the Licensor does not waive the right to receive notice – is the Licensor's obligation to indemnify dismissed? The harsh results of strict compliance to express conditions may be alleviated through judicial construction. Courts prefer to construe clauses in a way that avoids a forfeiture.[5] Courts may relieve a party from even an express provision if equity requires it.[6] In the above example, the indemnification provision could have two different meanings. First, it could mean that the Licensee's failure to provide prompt notice results in a dismissal of the Licensor's obligation to defend and indemnify the Licensee from third-party intellectual property claims and

4 DBT GmbH v. J.L. Mining Co., 544 F. Supp. 2d 364, 380 (S.D.N.Y., April 8, 2008) (noting that "Express conditions must be literally performed, whereas constructive conditions, which ordinarily arise from language of promise, are subject to the precept that substantial compliance is sufficient" (citation omitted); *see also* Aetna Cas. and Sur. Co. v. Aniero Concrete Co., Inc., 404 F.3d 566, 597–601 (2d Cir. 2005) (holding that contractual requirement of third-party consent was a condition precedent to creation of the contract at issue)).

5 Johnson v. City of Hackensack, 200 N.J. Super. 185, at 190, 491 A.2d 14, 17 (1985) ("[L]anguage which may defeat an estate must be strictly construed and always against rather than in favor of forfeiture."); Ballard v. MacCallum, 15 Cal. 2d 439, 444 (1940) ("We have two possible constructions, one of which leads to a forfeiture and the other avoids it. In such a case, the policy and rule are settled both in the interpretation of ordinary contracts and instruments transferring property, that the construction which avoids forfeiture must be made if it is at all possible."); 34 Cal. Jur. 3d, Forfeiture and Penalties §14 ("As is true of statutory forfeitures and penalties, contractual forfeitures are not favored by the courts, and contracts that provide for the forfeiture of vested property rights are construed strictly to prevent forfeitures. Accordingly, whenever there are two possible constructions of a forfeiture provision in a contract, the construction that avoids the forfeiture must be adopted if it is possible to do so.").

6 Ballard v. MacCallum, 15 Cal. 2d 439, 444 (1940).

a forfeiture of Licensee's contractual right. In the alternative, the clause could mean that Licensee's failure to provide prompt notice results in a deferral or a delay of Licensor's obligation to defend and indemnify until it receives notice of the claim from the Licensee. As the latter construction would avoid forfeiture, it is likely that a court would adopt that one.

Troubleshooting: Because courts tend to construe clauses to avoid forfeitures, parties should draft clearly and specifically to indicate that a provision is a condition and that certain consequences will follow for failure to meet the condition. Even then, a court may find that a party has impliedly waived the condition.[7]

Caveat: A court's determination of whether a forfeiture would result takes into account equitable factors.

CASE HIGHLIGHT

DBT GMBH v. J.L. MINING CO., 544 F. Supp. 2d 364 (S.D.N.Y. April 8, 2008)

The plaintiffs, DBT GmbH and DBT America, entered into a Global Purchase Agreement ("GPA") with defendants, J.L. Mining, The Marmon Group, Ltd., and Marmon Wire & Cable. Under the GPA, the plaintiffs purchased certain assets from defendants and defendants agreed to indemnify plaintiffs subject to the following in paragraph 3.10 of the GPA:

> "Purchasers shall not undertake the fulfillment of any Warranty Obligation without the Sellers' prior approval if the estimated reimbursable cost thereof would be in excess of $5,000."

The plaintiffs sued defendants for, among other things, failing to indemnify plaintiffs. The plaintiffs argued that the failure to comply with the "prior approval" requirement was not a condition precedent to indemnification for warranty claims exceeding $5,000. The court disagreed:

"Here, paragraph 3.10 unambiguously requires Marmon's prior approval for reimbursement of warranty claims in excess of $5,000: 'Purchasers shall not undertake the fulfillment of any Warranty Obligation without the Sellers' prior approval if the estimated reimbursable cost thereof would be in excess of $5,000.' . . . There is no evidence that DBT believed otherwise: all of its internal guidance reflected the prior approval requirement, and DBT does not dispute that it sought such approval for some warranty

. . .

7 *See* Chapter 6.3.

CASE HIGHLIGHT *(continued)*

Finally, DBT argues that its failure to comply with the prior approval provision should be excused to avoid 'a disproportionate forfeiture.' Where contractual language is clear, the Court may excuse the nonoccurrence of a condition by waiver, breach or forfeiture . . . In this context, 'forfeiture' is defined as 'the denial of compensation that results when the obligee loses [its] right to the agreed exchange after [it] has relied substantially, as by preparation or performance on the expectation of that exchange' [citations omitted]. . . As described above, DBT has failed to allege facts indicating that it reasonably relied on the inapplicability of the prior approval provision. There is thus no basis for a determination of forfeiture here.

Defendants are therefore entitled to summary judgment on Plaintiffs' claims related to the Shenhua Settlement."

In short, the plaintiffs could not prove that they relied on the inapplicability of the prior approval clause. On the contrary, they had complied with the prior approval requirement for other claims and therefore, the court found, there was no forfeiture.

In some situations, the parties might have included a condition if they had thought about it. This is known as an omitted term. For example, assume an indemnification provision did not contain an express notice provision so that it stated as follows:

"Licensor shall defend Licensee, and indemnify same against third-party claims that use of the Patent violates such third party's valid patent rights."

The result could be harsh for the Licensor if its obligation to defend and indemnify were unqualified. It would not be fair for the Licensee to be able to sue the Licensor for breach of its indemnification obligation if the Licensor did not even know that the Licensee was being sued. This is where constructive conditions come in handy. A court is likely to find that a constructive condition to the Licensor's indemnification obligation is that the Licensee must provide the Licensor with notice within a reasonable time of finding out about the third-party claim, even though the provision does not expressly state it.

Constructive conditions typically arise where one party needs to do something or is expected to do something before the other party performs. For example, if I hire someone to mow the lawn in front of my house, unless we expressly agree otherwise, I won't have to pay until the mowing is finished (or substantially finished). The mowing of the lawn is a constructive condition to my obligation to pay. But, unlike an express condition, the mowing of the lawn does not have to be perfectly performed; it need only be substantially performed before it triggers my obligation to pay. If the lawn is pretty much mowed except for a patch near the driveway, I can't refuse to pay for the work that was done. Theoretically, I would be able to offset the damages caused by the imperfect performance although in this example, those damages would be negligible.

CASE HIGHLIGHT

HAND v. GROW CONSTRUCTION, INC., 983 So. 2d 684 (Fla. App. 1 Dist. 2008)

A real estate contract between the buyers/appellants, William and Jane Hand, and the seller/appellee, Grow Construction, Inc. contained the following provisions:

> "5. IMPROVEMENTS. Seller agrees to provide the labor, services and materials necessary to complete the improvements to the Property in a workmanlike manner free from defects. The improvements are specifically described, and will be made in accordance with the plans and specifications attached hereto as Exhibit B and by reference made a part hereof, hereinafter collectively referred to as the Plans and Specifications."

. . .

> "11. CLOSING DATE. This transaction shall be closed and Seller shall deliver title to the Property within ten (10) days after the issuance of a certificate of occupancy for the improvements to be made by [Seller]."

On the closing date, the transaction was not finalized. The buyers alleged that the seller breached the contract by failing to tender a building free from defects and refusing to bring itself into compliance with the contract. The seller counterclaimed, alleging that the buyers breached the contract by refusing to pay the entire purchase price on the closing date. The seller acknowledged that the building contained at least one defect but argued that the buyers had a unilateral obligation to close the transaction by paying the full purchase price once a certificate of occupancy was obtained, regardless of any defects in construction. The buyers argued that paragraphs five and eleven contained dependent covenants so that their duty to deliver the purchase price depended upon the seller's duty to deliver a building free from material defects and in compliance with the contract specifications. They also argued that the certificate of occupancy merely established a timeline for scheduling a closing date and was not a trigger for their payment obligation.

The trial court agreed with the sellers, finding that the buyers' "contractual obligation to close arose upon issuance of the certificate of occupancy" which "was not dependent upon the building being free from defects." Accordingly, the trial court ruled that the buyers breached the contract.

The appellate court reversed the trial court's ruling, stating that contract provisions must be construed in accordance with the plain language of the contract and in the context of the entire contract. It stated:

CASE HIGHLIGHT *(continued)*

"[T]he meaning of paragraph eleven clearly and unambiguously sets a date for closing and requires [Seller] to deliver title to the real property on that date, but it does not clearly and unambiguously state that Appellants duty to deliver the purchase price was independent of any other duties in the contract."

The appellate court further found that if the parties had wanted to use the certificate of occupancy to trigger an unconditional duty to purchase the building on the part of the Buyers, the parties could have more clearly articulated that intention. The Seller's promise to construct the improvements was the "essential consideration" for the Buyers' promise to pay the purchase price. According to the court, the Buyers' obligation to pay the purchase price and the Seller's obligation to build the improvements in accordance with the plans were concurrent duties even though the certificate of occupancy had been issued. The court concluded that "at some point, the improvements could be considered so defective as to relieve Appellants of their obligation to pay the purchase price."

APPLYING WHAT YOU LEARNED

Contract clauses and issues related to performance and breach

1. If you were representing a client in the Seller's position in *Hand v. Grow Construction, Inc.* what would you do so that the Buyer's obligation to complete the purchase would be triggered upon issuance of the certificate of occupancy (regardless of Seller's performance)?
2. If you were representing a client in the Buyer's position, what would you do so that your client Buyer would not have an obligation to complete the purchase until the building conforms to contract specifications and is defect free?

6.3 Doctrinal concept: waivers

Principle: A party may waive a breach or a condition. Unlike a modification, a waiver does not require consideration.

A waiver is commonly defined as a voluntary and intentional relinquishment of a known right.[8] What this means is that a party who receives the benefit of a provision may waive the right to enforce that provision. Unlike a

8 JOSEPH M. PERILLO, CONTRACTS §11.29(c)(7th ed., 2014); Geis v. Colina Del Rio, LP, 362 S.W.3d 100, 111 (2011).

modification, which requires additional consideration in most jurisdictions, a waiver of a condition or right does not require consideration. A waiver can also be retracted and the condition or requirement reinstated as long as there is reasonable notice and time for the other party to meet the condition or requirement. A waiver can be express or implied.

CLASSIC CASE

CLARK v. WEST, 86 N.E. 1 (1908)

The parties entered into an agreement where plaintiff was to write a series of law books. The contract contained a clause which provided:

> "the first party [the plaintiff] agrees to totally abstain from the use of intoxicating liquors during the continuance of this contract, and the payment to him in accordance with the terms of this contract of any money in excess of $2 per page is dependent on the faithful performance of this as well as the other conditions of this contract . . ."

The contract also stated:

> "in consideration of the above promises of the first party [the plaintiff], the second party [the defendant] agrees to pay to the first party $2 per page . . . on each book prepared by the first party under this contract and accepted by the second party, and if said first party abstains from the use of intoxicating liquor and otherwise fulfills his agreements as hereinbefore set forth, he shall be paid an additional $4 per page in manner hereinbefore stated."

The plaintiff completed the work and the defendant paid him $2 per page but refused to pay the additional $4 per page because he did not totally abstain from drinking intoxicating liquors. The plaintiff alleged that the defendant, long before the completion of the manuscript, knew that the plaintiff used intoxicating liquors and did not object to the breach but continued to accept the pages of the manuscript, continued to pay the plaintiff, and that the defendant, knowing that the defendant used intoxicating liquors, repeatedly represented that it would pay the plaintiff the royalty. The defendant argued that total abstinence was the consideration for the additional $4 per page and therefore could not be waived. The plaintiff argued that the stipulation for total abstinence was a condition precedent which was intended to work a forfeiture of the additional compensation in the event of breach, and that it could be waived without new consideration.

The court concluded:

"The compensation for the work specified in the contract was to be $6 per page, unless the plaintiff failed to totally abstain from the use of intoxicating liquors during the continuance of the contract, in which event he was to receive only $2 per page. That is the obvious import of the contract construed in the light of the purpose for which it was made, and in

CLASSIC CASE *(continued)*

accordance with the ordinary meaning of the plain language. It is not a contract to write books in order that the plaintiff shall keep sober, but a contract containing a stipulation that he shall keep sober so that he may write satisfactory books. When we view the contract from this standpoint, it will readily be perceived that the particular stipulation is not the consideration for the contract, but simply one of its conditions . . . .

If that conclusion is well founded, there can be no escape . . . that this condition could be waived; and, if it was waived, the defendant is clearly not in a position to insist upon the forfeiture which his waiver was intended to annihilate. The forfeiture must stand or fall with the condition. If the latter was waived, the former is no longer a part of the contract. Defendant still has the right to counterclaim for any damages which he may have sustained in consequence of the plaintiff's breach, but he cannot insist upon strict performance."

Assume that Buyer enters into a contract with Seller, where Seller will deliver a shipment of apples to Buyer every month and Buyer pays Seller on the 25th of each month. One month, Buyer makes payment on the 30th. If Seller accepts the payment without objection, Seller has impliedly waived the right to payment on the 25th. Seller can tell Buyer that it will accept the late payment this time, but will require payment by the 25th for the next month. In other words, Seller can reinstate the requirement that future payments be made by the 25th. If Seller wants to be sure that accepting the late payment doesn't affect its right to receive future payments by the 25th it can include a "non-waiver" clause in the agreement.[9]

Example clause

The waiver or failure of Licensor to exercise in any respect any right provided for herein shall not be deemed a waiver of any further right hereunder.

The parties can modify the common law rule of waiver by contract and require that waivers be in writing.[10]

9 Awards.com, LLC v. Kinko's Inc., 42 A.D.3d 178, 187–188 (2007) (noting that non-waiver clauses are "uniformly enforced" and that acceptance of late payments did not constitute a waiver of timely future payments).

10 Gergora v. Flynn, 486 So. 2d 5, 7 (1986) (finding that Lessors did not waive their right to rescind lease by accepting rent payments after tenants materially breached agreement where lease expressly provided that waivers must be in writing); Rybovich Boat Works, Inc. v. Atkins, 587 So. 2d 519, 522 (2009) (finding that time is of the essence provision could not be waived due to anti-waiver provision requiring that waivers be in writing).

Example clause

No modification, release, discharge or waiver of any provisions of this Agreement shall be of any force or effect unless in writing and signed by the Lessor.

Example clause

This Agreement may not be modified, supplemented or amended except by a written instrument signed by authorized representatives of each Party and referring specifically to this Agreement. No waiver of any of the provisions of this Agreement will be effective unless it is in writing and signed by the party against whom it is asserted and any such waiver shall only be applicable to the specific instance to which it relates and shall not be deemed to be a continuing or future waiver of any breach. The failure of either Party to enforce any provision of this Agreement shall in no way be construed to be a waiver of such provision, nor in any way to affect the rights of either Party to enforce each and every provision of this Agreement thereafter.

Reflection Prompt: Compare the two Example Clauses above. How different are they? Under what circumstances might the differences in language matter?

Some rights and duties are not waivable.[11] For example, a beneficiary cannot waive the obligation of a fiduciary to act in good faith.

6.4 Doctrinal concept: substantial performance

Principle: A party who substantially – even if not perfectly – performs under the contract, obligates the other party's counter-performance.

As previously noted, express conditions need to be strictly complied with before they trigger the related performance. Constructive conditions, on the other hand, do not need to be strictly complied with before triggering the related performance. This creates an important difference between constructive and express conditions when a breach occurs. If an express condition is not met, and is not waived or excused, the related performance is not triggered. Therefore, the party responsible for the related performance cannot

11 *See* In re Washington Builders Ben. Trust, 173 Wash. App. 34, 73 (2013) (noting that a trustee to a trust may not be relieved of the duty to act in good faith); Solfanelli v. Corestates Bank, N.A., 203 F.3d 197, 201 (3d. Cir. 2000) (bank's duty to conduct a commercially reasonable sale is not waivable by contract).

be sued for breach. This is not the case with constructive conditions. If a party has substantially performed (meaning it pretty much did what it was supposed to do, even if it did not do it perfectly), then the related performance is triggered. In determining whether a party has substantially performed, the courts consider whether the essential purpose of the contract was met and whether the breach was wrongful or in bad faith.

The concepts of substantial performance and material breach are related – a party who has substantially performed has not materially breached. A party who has materially breached, has not substantially performed. Furthermore, and perhaps more importantly, a material breach excuses the non-breaching party's performance.[12]

Under the doctrine of substantial performance, if the breaching party (Substantial Performer) performs substantially, even if not perfectly, then the other party (Other Party) must perform. The minor breach committed by Substantial Performer does not excuse Other Party's performance. Consequently, if Other Party fails to perform, Substantial Performer may sue for expectation damages offset by damages caused by her minor breach.

CLASSIC CASE

JACOB & YOUNGS v. KENT, 129 N.E. 889 (1921)

The plaintiff built a country home for the defendant at a cost of more than $77,000 and sued to recover the balance of $3,483.46. The defendant lived in the house for nine months before complaining of defective performance. One of the specifications for the plumbing work was that "all wrought-iron pipe must be well galvanized, lap welded pipe of the grade known as 'standard pipe' of Reading manufacture." The defendant learned that some of the pipe was the product of other factories. The plaintiff was ordered to redo the work but the plumbing was encased in the walls of the residence and would have required demolition at substantial expense. Defendant refused to make the final payment and plaintiff sued.

The court found that the use of other wrought-iron pipe was not fraudulent or willful and was the result of the oversight and inattention of the plaintiff's subcontractor. Plaintiff tried to introduce evidence that the brands that were installed were the same in quality, appearance, market value, and cost as the Reading pipe. The court stated that if admitted, the evidence would indicate that the defect was insignificant in relation to the project:

12 Mustang Pipeline Company, Inc. v. Driver Pipeline Company, Inc., 134 S.W.3d 195, 196 (2004) ("It is a fundamental principle of contract law that when one party to a contract commits a material breach of that contract, the other party is discharged or excused from further performance").

CLASSIC CASE *(continued)*

"[A]n omission, both trivial and innocent, will sometimes be atoned for by allowance of the resulting damage, and will not always be the breach of a condition to be followed by a forfeiture . . .

In the circumstances of this case, we think the measure of the allowance is not the cost of replacement, which would be great, but the difference in value, which would be either nominal or nothing . . . It is true that in most cases the cost of replacement is the measure. The owner is entitled to the money which will permit him to complete, unless the cost of completion is grossly and unfairly out of proportion to the good to be attained. When that is true, the measure is the difference in value."

Reflection Prompt: Why did the court determine that plaintiff had substantially performed? What are plaintiff's damages? What are defendant's damages?

Troubleshooting: A court's determination of a minor breach may not coincide with what a party thinks is "minor" or "material." If one party (Party A) believes that the other party's breach is material and ceases performance, but the court disagrees, then Party A may itself be liable for breach. One of the primary purposes of contracts is to reduce the likelihood of a dispute. If a party views a particular obligation as material, then that party should insist upon a contract clause that expressly states that the failure to perform that obligation is a material breach, such as in the following:

Example clause

Failure on the part of RESELLER to obtain the signature of its End-Users on such Sublicense Agreement and/or failure of RESELLER to return such Sublicense Agreement to LICENSOR within ten (10) days of execution of such Sublicense Agreement shall constitute a material breach by RESELLER of this Agreement which entitles LICENSOR to terminate this Agreement immediately.

Example clause

Licensee acknowledges and agrees that its failure to pay the license fees required herein or failure to comply with the License restrictions or U.S. export controls shall constitute a material breach.

The contract may also specify that engaging in a particular action constitutes a material breach:

Example clause

Any assignment by Licensor shall be void, deemed a material breach of this Agreement and result in the immediate termination of this Agreement.

Troubleshooting: Be sure to indicate what should happen in the event that one party breaches. Will the agreement automatically terminate? Will there be a notice and cure period? If there is a notice period, what constitutes notice?

Caveat: The doctrine of substantial performance does not apply to the sale of goods. Instead, the "perfect tender" rule permits the buyer to reject goods which "fail in any respect to conform to the contract."[13] The buyer's rejection of goods, however, does not necessarily result in the cancellation of the contract because the seller has the right to cure if the time for performance has not expired or the seller had "reasonable grounds" to believe the non-conforming tender would be acceptable and the seller "seasonably notifies" the buyer that the seller intends to substitute a conforming tender.[14] A party seeking to terminate a contract for the sale of goods must still act in accordance with the standard of good faith and fair dealing.[15] The parties should indicate the duration of the cure period.

13 UCC §2-601.

14 UCC §2-508. The Restatement arguably requires an opportunity to cure in some cases. RESTATEMENT (SECOND) CONTRACTS, §242 (noting that a "material failure of performance" suspends performance of the other party and "discharges those duties if it has not been cured during the time in which performance can occur"); JOSEPH M. PERILLO, CONTRACTS, §11.13(a) (7th ed., 2014) (noting that despite Restatement provision, "many common law cases hold that the breaching party has no right to cure unless the contract expressly provides for such a right").

15 UCC §1-304; good faith is defined as "honesty in fact and the observance of reasonable commercial standards of fair dealing." *See also* UCC §1-201(20); RESTATEMENT (SECOND) CONTRACTS, §205.

Example clause

Company must cure a default within ninety (90) days of receipt of written notice of such default.

Example clause

Either Party (the "Terminating Party") may terminate this Agreement at any time in the event of a breach by the other Party ("Breaching Party") that remains uncured thirty (30) days after the Breaching Party receives written notice of such breach. Termination is effective immediately and automatically upon the expiration of the applicable notice period, without further notice or action by either Party. Termination is in addition to any other remedies that may be available to the Terminating Party.

Reflection Prompt: What is the difference between a "default" and a "breach"? What happens upon expiration of the notice period under each scenario?

Most courts permit immediate termination if the breach goes to the essence of the contract or if the breaching party's conduct (such as dishonesty or disloyalty) warrants immediate termination *even if* the agreement contains an express cure provision.[16]

If the parties have bargained for completion of work under a services contract according to a timetable, the contract should indicate whether failure to meet that timetable constitutes a material breach. In the absence of an express provision, a court is unlikely to find that failure to meet a target date is a material breach. This result may be unsatisfactory for someone who has hired a particular contractor, or agreed to pay a certain price, because of assurances that services would be rendered according to the negotiated timetable.

Assume that Genex hires Brand Builders to construct a building according to a certain timeline (the frame is constructed by April 1, the windows installed by April 15th, etc). Genex has interviewed several contractors but has agreed to hire Brand Builders, even though its quoted prices are higher than its competitors, because it has promised to deliver the services in accordance

16 Southland Corp. v. Froelich, 41 F. Supp. 2d 227, 246 (E.D.N.Y. 1999) (material breach that goes to essence of the contract constitutes grounds for rescission without opportunity to cure); LJL Transportation, Inc. v. Pilot Air Freight Corporation, 599 Pa. 546, 567–568 (2009) (franchisee's self-dealing justified franchisor's immediate termination of agreement even though agreement contained a 90-day cure provision).

with the timeline. Brand Builders misses the first deadline. In the absence of a contract provision stating otherwise, that missed deadline will probably not be considered a material breach of Brand Builders' obligations under the contract. Recall that only material breaches allow the non-breaching party to terminate the contract. If the delay in performing services does not constitute a material breach, then Genex cannot terminate the contract – if it does, Genex itself will have breached. To prevent this, Genex might include a "time is of the essence" clause:

Example clause

Time is of the essence for the completion of the work described in this contract. Any delay in the completion of the work described herein shall constitute a material breach of this contract.

The clause indicates that the timeliness of performance is important to the parties.[17] Without some kind of a "time is of the essence" clause, a court will probably not find a small delay to be a material breach.[18]

On the other hand, the parties may agree that the timetable is merely an estimate of projected target dates. The contractor, for example, may have expressly stated that he can't guarantee the deliverables by a certain date. In such a case, the parties should include this provision in the contract:

Example clause

The parties agree that time is not of the essence in the completion of the work described in this contract. All parties shall act to complete the work described within a reasonable time.

Caveat: As with other provisions, a "time is of the essence" clause does not guarantee a court will find that a small delay does in fact constitute a material breach. The parties must have intended it, and not just included it in a

---

17 The Colorado Supreme Court explained the meaning of the "time is of the essence" clause as follows: "As we understand and construe that clause it means that the performance by one party at the time specified in the contract is prerequisite and essential in order to enable him to require performance of its terms by the other party thereto. It means that time is such a material matter as to require exact compliance with the terms of the contract in this respect before there is any right to require a counter-performance." Dunton v. Stemme, 117 Colo. 327, 332 (1947).

18 Tulisano v. Schonberger, 74 Conn. App. 101, 106 (2002) ("When the parties to a real estate contract want to fix a specific date for performance, we generally have required them to express specifically in the contract that time is of the essence; otherwise, performance within a reasonable time will satisfy the contract").

boilerplate or "stock" provision.[19] Several courts have noted that no "talismanic" words are required.[20] The *absence* of language indicating that the parties intended that time is an essential element of the contract makes it unlikely that a court will find that a delay constitutes a material breach unless there are circumstances indicating otherwise.[21] On the other hand, specific language regarding the timing of performance and other evidence regarding the intent of the parties to make time an essential element of the agreement may be better than the standard "time is of the essence" clause alone. Ultimately, the enforceability of "time is of the essence" provisions will depend on whether a court finds the parties intended the clause. A court may also consider extrinsic evidence to prove time was of the essence despite the absence of such a clause provided it does not contradict or vary the express terms of the contract.[22] Where time is of the essence, no notice of default may be required.[23]

CASE HIGHLIGHT

ARNHOLD v. OCEAN ATLANTIC WOODLAND CORP., 284 F.3d 693 (7th Cir. 2002)

The Buyers entered into a final settlement agreement with the Seller concerning the drawn-out and contentious prospective sale of farmland in Will County, Illinois. The settlement agreement contained the following clause in paragraph 15:

19 Ordinarily, time is not of the essence in contract performance but the intention of the parties may make it so. MHI P'ship, Ltd. v. DH Real Estate Inv. Co., 2008 Tex. App. LEXIS 6462, at *10–11; Davis v. Dawson, Inc., 15 F. Supp. 2d 64, 120 (D. Mass. 1998) ("time is of the essence" clause was not "boilerplate" nor was it waived or modified); *see also* RESTATEMENT (SECOND) CONTRACTS, §242, comment (d) (1981).

20 Arnhold v. Ocean Atl. Woodland Corp., 284 F.3d 693, 699 (7th Cir. 2002); Sunshine Cloak & Suit Co. v. Roquette Bros., 30 N.D. 143, 149 (1915) ("[I]t is not necessary to declare in so many words 'that time is of the essence of the contract,' but it is sufficient if it appears that it was the intention of the parties thereto that time should be of the essence thereof").

21 Chariot Holdings, Ltd. v. Eastmet Corp., 153 Ill. App. 3d 50, 58 ("[T]he contract contains no clause that expressly provides that 'time is of the essence,' and the circumstances and facts before us do not suggest that the parties intended that time was an essential element of the contract at the time the contract was entered into.").

22 Katemis v. Westerlind, 142 Cal. App. 2d 799, 804–805 (1956) ("Where the time for performance is stated and if time is not expressly made of the essence by a written contract, it is held that extrinsic evidence is admissible to show time was considered by the parties as of the essence; and that such evidence does not contradict or vary the writing, but confirms it by showing that it means just what its terms provide"). The court further noted, however, that extrinsic evidence is admissible to show that time was considered by the parties as of the essence of a written contract "only when it does not tend to contradict or vary the terms of the contract." *Id.* at 806.

23 Rybovich Boat Works, Inc. v. Atkins, 587 So. 2d 519, 521 (2009) (finding that where "time is of the essence no notice of a default is required"). In *Rybovich*, the court found that "the 'time of the essence' provision in the contract clearly required the buyer to set a date and time for closing and when buyer failed to do so by the latest date permitted in contract, buyer was in default". *Id.*

CASE HIGHLIGHT *(continued)*

> "It is intended by Sellers and Purchasers that January 25, 2001 shall be the absolute final date for closing . . . If closing has not occurred on or before January 25, 2001, for any reason other than Sellers' default . . . Purchaser shall have no right to purchase or otherwise encumber the Property or Homestead parcel, the Contract shall be terminated, and Purchaser shall have no rights with respect to the Property or Homestead Parcel."

The Buyers failed to meet the closing deadline but sought to enforce the agreement. The magistrate judge denied the motion and the Buyers appealed.

The U.S. Court of Appeals for the Seventh Circuit noted that the only issue before it was whether the Buyers materially breached the settlement agreement by failing to close the property by January 25, 2001.

The court first noted that contracting parties may make "time is of the essence" a provision of the contract, meaning that performance by one party within the time frame specified is "essential to enable him to require counter-performance by the other party." It further stated:

"Timely performance often is an absolute requirement even if the contract does not contain the talismanic phrase 'time is of the essence'; it is well-settled that 'the intention of the parties as expressed by the agreement controls,' [citations omitted], and courts 'will give effect to this provision when no peculiar circumstances have intervened to prevent or excuse strict compliance' [citations omitted]. . . .

When analyzing the materiality of a time-essence clause, the factfinder initially must ask whether performance by a particular date was truly of such significance that the contract would not have been made if the provision had not been included. A negative answer to this initial question means that the clause did not meet the materiality test and that the breach was minor, provided that the party has completed performance within a reasonable period of time [citations omitted]. On the other hand, an affirmative answer to the first question does not end the materiality inquiry . . . '[E]ven where the parties clearly intended to regard a specific payment date as crucial, equity will refuse to enforce such a provision when to do so would be unconscionable or would give one party an unfair advantage over the other' [citation omitted]. As a result, even if the factfinder concludes that timely performance is an essential element of the contract, he or she must also decide whether to award damages and require counterperformance in spite of the breach."

The court found that the provision in paragraph 15 was an essential term of the settlement agreement:

"The extent to which a time-essence clause should be strictly enforced 'depends upon the parties' intentions, which are to be determined both by the language used in the agreement and the circumstances surrounding the agreement' [citations omitted]. When considering extrinsic evidence, the factfinder should focus, in descending order of importance, on: (1) the parties' negotiations over the contract at issue; (2) their course of performance; (3) their prior course of dealing; and (4) trade usage in the relevant industry [citations omitted].

CASE HIGHLIGHT *(continued)*

In the case before us, the district court considered the language of the settlement agreement, along with the substance of the parties' negotiations and their course of performance prior to January 26, 2001. All three categories of evidence support a finding of materiality. The explicit and unequivocal language of the contract is an unambiguous expression of intent, referring to January 25, 2001 as an 'absolute, final date for closing' that 'shall' be enforced without exception. These contract terms were chosen with precision after extensive negotiations during which Ocean Atlantic conceded, in its own words, 'that failure to close . . . shall result in Plaintiffs' unequivocal right to terminate the contract.' Extrinsic evidence establishing the bitterness of the parties' protracted relationship also supports the magistrate's finding that the parties intended strict adherence to the January 25, 2001 closing date."

Troubleshooting: Parties should use specific terms that clearly express the intent of the parties to make adherence to time frames an essential element of the contract. In addition, the contract language should indicate what happens in the event that time frames are not met.

Most courts agree that a party cannot use a "time is of the essence" clause to escape a contract if the failure to perform within a timely manner is his fault or he has taken advantage of the delay in performance.[24] A "time is of the essence" clause may also be waived by the party who benefits from the provision (the party whose timely performance is not at issue).[25]

Caveat: With an option contract, time is ordinarily of the essence. Option contracts are to be strictly construed because the period of time in which an option is to be exercised is essential to the agreement.[26]

---

24 Kalinowski v. An-Chi Yeh, 9 Haw. App. 473, 479 (1993) (ordering specific performance of a contract to purchase a condominium unit when delay was caused by party seeking to cancel agreement); Kimm v. Andrews, 270 Md. 601, 612 (1974) (noting that "contract may nevertheless be specifically enforced if the failure to perform within the designated time results from the act or fault of the party against whom specific performance is demanded"); Alk v. Lanini, 61 Ore. App. 158, 162 (1982), *review denied* 294 Ore. 613 (1983) ("party to a contract cannot take advantage of his own failure to perform, and defendants were responsible, at least in part, for the fact that the transaction did not close on schedule").

25 Phoenix Ltd. P'ship of Raleigh v. Simpson, 201 N.C. App. 493, 501, 688 S.E.2d 717, 723 (2009) (defendants waived the "time is of the essence" clause).

26 Ex Parte Keelboat Concepts, Inc., 938 So. 2d. 922 (2005); Franzier v. Northeast Mississippi Shopping Ctr., Inc., 458 So. 2d 1051, 1055 (Miss, 1094); Poole v. McCarty, 229 Miss. 170, 90 So. 2d 190 (1956). There are two exceptions to the general rule that time is of the essence in the exercise of option contract: (1) the optionor had waived the right to timely performance; or (2) the optionee's failure to exercise the option within the required time is the optionor's fault. Ex Parte Keelboat Concepts, Inc., 938 So. 2d 922, 925–926.

Remember, a material breach means that the breaching party has not substantially performed – and so can't sue to recover under the contract (although it may seek restitution, which is covered in Chapter 8.1). A material breach also excuses the non-breaching party's performance and allows that party to sue.

Some contractual obligations will be unqualified, which means that each party has to do what it agreed to do or else it will be in breach of the contract (unless it can successfully avoid the contract under an available defense). In the following clause, the Licensee must pay the $500,000 license fee and not just *try* to come up with the money:

Example clause

Licensee shall pay a $500,000, non-refundable, upfront pre-paid royalty fee for its license to use and its right to distribute and sublicense Localized Licensed Software Products.

In some cases, however, one or both parties are supposed to do something but the requirement that they succeed in doing it is not absolute – what is required is that the party *try*. In that case, a party's obligation to perform is subject to "reasonable efforts."

CLASSIC CASE

WOOD v. LUCY, LADY DUFF-GORDON, 118 N.E. 214 (1917)

The defendant was a style leader and "creator of fashion." Clothing manufacturers sought her certificate of approval to help sell their products. She entered into an agreement with the plaintiff where he was to have the exclusive right, subject to her approval, to place her endorsements on clothing designed by others and to try to sell or license her own creations. In return for this exclusive right, she would receive half of all profits and revenues from any contracts he made. The agreement was to last at least one year and was then renewable year to year unless terminated upon 90 days' notice. The plaintiff sued the defendant, claiming that she placed her endorsement on clothing without his knowledge and withheld profits. The defendant claimed that the contract was unenforceable as the plaintiff did not bind himself to anything. The court disagreed:

"It is true that he does not promise in so many words that he will use reasonable efforts to place the defendant's indorsements and market her designs. We think, however, that such a promise is fairly to be implied . . .

CLASSIC CASE *(continued)*

His promise to pay the defendant one-half of the profits and revenues resulting from the exclusive agency and to render accounts monthly was a promise to use reasonable efforts to bring profits and revenues into existence."

The parties may expressly include a "reasonable efforts"-type requirement in their contract:

Example clause

Licensee must use commercially reasonable efforts, but not less than those comparable to what it uses for its own products, to monitor, ensure enforceability, and enforce agreements with End Users of Customer Services and will promptly notify Licensor of any substantial noncompliance.

Example clause

ChronX shall use reasonable commercial efforts to promote, distribute and sell Products in the United States.

Example clause

PharmCo. must use diligent, good faith efforts to enforce all PharmCo Patent Rights.

In the following Example Clause, as long as the sales representative uses his or her "best efforts" to sell the company's products – even if those efforts are unsuccessful – he or she will not be in breach.

Example clause

Representative shall solicit orders for Company Products at the prices and on the terms established by Company and in accordance with the general policies set forth by Company. Representative agrees to use Representative's best efforts to represent and solicit orders for Products, and that Representative's efforts will be of the highest quality, in good taste, and will enhance the professional image and reputation of Company and Company Products.

The parties may include their own definition of standards such as "good faith" or "reasonable commercial efforts" in the agreement.

Example clause

"Reasonable Commercial Efforts" means diligent and good faith efforts to accomplish the applicable performance but does not require any expenditure of funds.

The definition in the above Example Clause is different from what one might expect at common law where reasonable commercial efforts may mean *some* expenditure of funds, even if not a substantial amount.[27] A court may not be able to enforce a "best efforts" clause without clear guidelines or articulated criteria.[28]

A standard such as "best efforts" or "reasonable efforts," would likely make it easier for a party to be relieved of a performance obligation than an impracticability defense. The precise meaning of these standards differs and is based upon jurisdiction and industry norms.[29] If both are used in the contract, however, "best efforts" is generally perceived as a tougher standard than "reasonable efforts."[30] Some courts have held that a party subject to a "best efforts" standard must exercise diligent, good faith, and reasonable efforts even if not "all" of their efforts.[31] Reasonable efforts, on the other hand, refers to efforts that would be made by a reasonable person or entity

27 *See*, for example, Citri-Lite Co. v. Cott Bevs., Inc., 721 F. Supp. 2d 912, 927–928 (E.D. Cal. 2011) ("Viewing the evidence in a light most favorable to Citri-Lite, Cott's non-allocation of funding for marketing efforts at Food Lion, its focus on other retailers besides Food Lion, its lack of any particular marketing plan for Food Lion, and its lack of promotions after being prompted to do so by the food broker, suggest that Cott did not use commercially reasonable efforts to promote and sell Slim-Lite at Food Lion").

28 Ashokan Water Services, Inc. v. New Start, LLC, 807 N.Y.S.2d 550, 553 (2006) (noting that there is authority that a best efforts clause should contain clear guidelines against which to measure efforts, but that numerous courts have applied an express "best efforts" clause without articulated objective criteria).

29 Citri-Lite Co. v. Cott Bevs., Inc., 2011 U.S. Dist. LEXIS 112901, at *9 (E.D. Cal. Sept. 30, 2011)("Within the beverage industry, it is understood that a 'best efforts' clause imposes a higher standard of performance than a 'commercially reasonable efforts' clause"); *but see* California Pines Property Owners Ass'n v. Pedotti, 141 Cal. Rptr. 3d 793, 801 (2012) (stating "when a contract does not define the phrase 'best efforts,' the promisor must use the diligence of a reasonable person under comparable circumstances. Diligence is certainly required, but the obligation is framed within the bounds of reasonableness").

30 In re Chateaugay Corp., 198 B.R. 848, 854 (1996) ("The standard imposed by a 'reasonable efforts' clause such as that contained in §7.01 of the Agreement is indisputably less stringent than that imposed by the 'best efforts' clauses contained elsewhere in the Agreement").

31 Great W. Producers Coop. v. Great W. United Corp., 200 Colo. 180, 613 P.2d 873, 878 (1980) ("The 'best efforts' obligation required that [defendant] and its board of directors make a reasonable, diligent, and good faith effort to accomplish a given objective . . ."); First Union National Bank v. Steele Software Systems Corp., 838 A.2d 404, 429 (2003) ("A promise to use 'best efforts' does not necessarily mean that the promisor is

in similar circumstances. Commercially reasonable efforts mean efforts that would be made by a reasonable business person. "All reasonable efforts" or "all commercially reasonable efforts" may indicate a greater level of effort than "reasonable" or "commercially reasonable" efforts.[32] The determination of whether a party has met the standard depends upon the factual circumstances and any definition contained in the agreement.[33] Beware that a party that enters into a contract to use "best efforts" without intending to do so may be liable for fraud.

At least in theory, a requirement to exercise best efforts or reasonable efforts is distinguishable from the covenant of good faith and fair dealing.[34] Most states,[35] the Restatement[36] and the UCC[37] recognize that a covenant of good faith and fair dealing exists in the performance of every contract.

Troubleshooting: If there is a duty to perform in good faith, some drafters might wonder whether it is necessary to include a requirement of "best efforts" or "reasonable efforts" in the contract. The requirement of good faith and fair dealing generally deals with a party's honesty and whether that party acted ethically. "Reasonable efforts"-type standards address the level of skill and effort required for performance. A party may act in good

---

required to give all of its efforts toward assisting or promoting the promisee's interests or product, or that the promisor is prohibited from promoting competing products").

32 Castle Props. v. Lowe's Home Ctrs., 2000 Ohio App. LEXIS 1229, 2000 WL 309395, at *7 (C.A. Ohio, March 20, 2000) (finding that phrase "all commercially reasonable efforts" was not ambiguous and "is capable of only one reasonable construction, that Lowe's was required to make every effort to obtain the required zoning that a reasonable business entity would have made under similar circumstances"). The court added, however, that the "word 'all' is limited by the words 'commercially reasonable'". *Id.*

33 Chen v. Cayman Arts., Inc., 2011 U.S. Dist. LEXIS 99678, 2011 WL 3903158, at *10 (S.D. Fla. Sept. 6, 2011) ("Florida law recognizes that "[t]he definition of 'best efforts' may vary depending upon the factual circumstances surrounding the transaction and the intent of the parties in entering into the transaction" (citing First Nat'l Bank of Lake Park v. Gay, 694 So. 2d 784, 788 (Fla. Dist. Ct. App. 1997)); First Union National Bank v. Steele Software Systems Corp., 838 A.2d 404, 428 (2003) ("Best efforts" is "a term 'which necessarily takes its meaning from the circumstances'") (citing Bloor v. Falstaff Brewing Corp., 454 F.Supp. 258, 266 (S.D.N.Y. 1978), aff'd, 601 F.2d 609 (2d Cir. 1979)); Triple-A Baseball Club Assocs. v. Northeastern Baseball, Inc., 832 F.2d 214, 225 (1st Cir. 1987), cert. denied, 485 U.S. 935, 108 S.Ct. 1111, 99 L.Ed. 2d 272 (1988) (best efforts "cannot be defined in terms of a fixed formula . . . [but] varies with the facts and the field of law involved"); Mark Technologies v. Utah Resources Intern., 147 P.3d 509, 511–512 (Utah. App. 2006) (best efforts clause must be "measured subjectively in the context of the particular facts and circumstances involved").

34 Mark Technologies v. Utah Resources Intern., 147 P.3d 509, 511–513 (Utah. App. 2006) (finding that the word "diligence" was not required and that "best efforts" clause imposes obligations that are different than those implied under the covenant of good faith and fair dealing).

35 Dick Broadcasting Co., Inc. of Tennessee v. Oak Ridge FM, Inc., 395 S.W.3d 653, 660 (2013) ("It is well-established that '[i]n Tennessee, the common law imposes a duty of good faith in the performance of contracts.'" Wallace v. Nat'l Bank of Commerce, 938 S.W.2d 684, 686 (Tenn. 1996))

36 RESTATEMENT (SECOND) CONTRACTS, §205.

37 UCC §1-304.

faith yet lack the skill and resources to perform at a commercially reasonable level. Negotiating the inclusion of a standard provides an opportunity for the parties to clarify and shape their expectations. Providing a definition of what a standard means may be especially useful if the parties' expectations differ from what might be considered commercially reasonable to a third party. Finally, the duty to perform in good faith – while standard in U.S. law and in many countries – is not universal. Notably, English contract law does not recognize a general duty of good faith, although there are some exceptions.[38] Furthermore, the meaning of the standard of good faith or reasonable/best efforts may vary depending upon the country.

Caveat: An agreement to use reasonable efforts to *enter* into a contract may be construed as an "agreement to agree" and unenforceable. By contrast, an agreement to use reasonable efforts in the *performance* of contractual duties is enforceable.[39]

Troubleshooting: Instead of simply referring to a standard such as "reasonable efforts" or "best efforts," the parties should specify what actions a party must take in certain circumstances and/or what actions constitute a breach. The parties may also want to include the consequences of a breach by allocating costs, or outlining each party's responsibilities. Note, for example, the different obligations created by the following two clauses:

Example clause

Licensee shall make reasonable efforts to ensure that End User signs the Sublicense Agreement and that End User adheres to the obligations in the Sublicense Agreement.

Example clause

Licensee shall ensure that End User signs and returns a signed copy of the Sublicense Agreement to Licensee prior to delivery of any Software. Licensee shall retain a copy of each signed Sublicense Agreement and shall produce

38 Even English law recognizes such a duty may be an implied term of a contract, especially in contracts involving long-term, fiduciary, or employment relationships. *See* Yam Seng Pte Ltd v. International Trade Corporation Ltd., [2013] EWHC 111 (QB) (noting that there is no legal principle of good faith of general application in English contract law but recognizing a duty of good faith where it is the presumed intention of the parties).

39 Cyberlock Consulting, Inc. v. Information Experts, Inc., 939 F. Supp. 2d 572, 581 (E.D. Va. 2013) (finding agreement to use "reasonable efforts" to negotiate later agreement was "agreement to agree" and unenforceable). *But see* SIGA Technologies, Inc. v. PharmAthene, Inc., 67 A.3d 330 (Del. 2013) (finding agreement to negotiate in good faith was binding).

such copy to Licensor upon Licensor's request. Licensee shall ensure that End User adheres to the obligations in the Sublicense Agreement by providing quarterly audits. Upon failure of End User to fulfill any material obligation relating to Product under those agreements, Licensor may, in addition to any other remedies available, require Licensee to terminate such End User's rights to Customer Service. If Licensee fails to satisfy the foregoing obligations, Licensee will be responsible for all reasonable costs incurred by Licensor, including without limitation, attorneys' fees, in connection with enforcement actions undertaken by Licensor.

Reflection Prompt: What happens if the Licensee fails to obtain an End User's signature on a Sublicense Agreement according to each Example Clause?

Clauses which purport to terminate an agreement upon bankruptcy, referred to as *ipso facto* clauses, are generally unenforceable,[40] but are still commonplace in many agreements.[41]

Example clause

Either party may terminate this Agreement upon 30 days' prior written notice if: (a) the other party materially breaches the Agreement and fails to cure the breach within such 30-day period; (b) the other party files a petition seeking

---

40 11 U.S.C. §365(e)(1)

> Notwithstanding a provision in an executory contract or unexpired lease, or in applicable law, an executory contract or unexpired lease of the debtor may not be terminated or modified, and any right or obligation under such contract or lease may not be terminated or modified, at any time after the commencement of the case solely because of a provision in such contract or lease that is conditioned on—
>
> (A) the insolvency or financial condition of the debtor at any time before the closing of the case;
> (B) the commencement of a case under this title; or
> (C) the appointment of or taking possession by a trustee in a case under this title or a custodian before such commencement.

See also 11 U.S.C. §541(1):

> (1) Except as provided in paragraph (2) of this subsection, an interest of the debtor in property becomes property of the estate under subsection (a)(1), (a)(2), or (a)(5) of this section notwithstanding any provision in an agreement, transfer instrument, or applicable nonbankruptcy law—
>
> (A) that restricts or conditions transfer of such interest by the debtor; or
> (B) that is conditioned on the insolvency or financial condition of the debtor, on the commencement of a case under this title, or on the appointment of or taking possession by a trustee in a case under this title or a custodian before such commencement, and that effects or gives an option to effect a forfeiture, modification, or termination of the debtor's interest in property.

41 If the party does not actually file a bankruptcy case, the other party may terminate if the other party declares itself insolvent. In addition, there may be other applicable law (i.e. intellectual property law) which allows a party to reject performance by a third party. The last scenario is further discussed in Part III. D (2).

bankruptcy protection, has an involuntary bankruptcy petition filed against it, has a receiver appointed, or otherwise declares its inability to maintain its business or pay its debts as they become due; (c) the other party makes an assignment for the benefit of creditors; or (d) the other party ceases to do business.

Caveat: A material breach does not necessarily result in termination if the agreement requires the parties to take certain actions (such as providing notice) in order to terminate. On the other hand, the parties may want the ability to terminate the agreement for reasons other than a material breach of the contract or because they do not want to have to prove a material breach:

Example clause

Licensee may terminate the License at any time upon 90 days' prior written notice to Licensor.

Caveat: Drafting a termination clause that expressly states that a party can terminate at any time and *without notice* is an example of greedy drafting. As explained in Chapter 4.1, a court may find termination-at-will clauses render a contract illusory. A party that terminates without notice may be found to violate its obligation to perform in good faith and in accordance with standards of fair dealing. Thus, parties should include a notice provision even if they want to be able to terminate without cause.

Troubleshooting: Remember to specify what should happen upon termination in order to avoid misunderstandings and conflict. It is especially important to address who will bear what costs:

Example clause

If either Company or Contractor is unable to fulfill the terms of this Agreement after reasonable effort, then either party has the right to terminate this Agreement. In the event of termination, neither party will be liable to the other for any unfulfilled obligation with the exception that Company shall reimburse Contractor for travel expenses incurred prior to termination in accordance with Section 1.2 of this Agreement and Contractor will refund fees paid in accordance with Section 1.6 of this Agreement.

7

Contract clauses and parties other than the original parties to the contract

A person who was not an original party to the contract may seek to enforce its terms against one of the original parties or one of the original parties may seek to enforce the contract against a third party. This chapter explores what happens when a third party becomes involved in a contract after formation.

7.1 Doctrinal concept: third-party beneficiaries

Principle: Persons who are not parties to the contract may have rights to enforce performance if the parties so intended.

Traditionally, only the parties to a contract have rights and obligations under it, even if non-parties are affected by it.[1] For example, a coffee shop may benefit from the contract between an adjacent bookstore and the shopping center owner because the bookstore's customers often purchase a coffee after visiting the bookstore. Yet, the coffee shop would not be permitted to sue the shopping center if the shopping center breached its contract with the bookstore. Third parties do, however, have enforceable rights under the contract in cases where the parties so intended.

If the purpose of the contract was to benefit the third party, that third party is an intended beneficiary. Typically, an intended beneficiary is someone who is a creditor of one of the parties or someone to whom one of the party's intends to make a gift.[2] A third party who benefits from the contract but is

---

1 "Privity of contract" refers to the "connection or relationship which exists between two or more contracting parties." BLACK'S LAW DICTIONARY, 5th ed. (1979) 1079. While contractual privity was traditionally essential to enforcement of a contract, this is no longer true due to the law governing product liability, warranties and third party beneficiaries. *Id.*

2 The Restatement First classified third parties who could enforce a contract as "creditor" or "donee" beneficiaries. RESTATEMENT (FIRST) CONTRACTS, §133(1) (a), (b) and (c). If the purpose of the contract

not an intended beneficiary is an incidental beneficiary and does not have any rights under the contract.

If the parties to a contract intended a third party to benefit from it, there should be no problem when that third party seeks to enforce the contract. The reality is more complicated. Typically only one of the parties actually wants the third party to benefit from the contract. The other party understands and agrees, but it is not necessarily the *desire* of the other party to benefit the intended beneficiary. For example, assume Sally and Mark enter into a contract where Sally agrees to sell her car to Mark for $5,000. Rather than paying her, Sally wants Mark to pay Ray the money because she has previously borrowed money from Ray. Both Sally and Mark intend Ray to benefit from the contract even though Sally is the only one who *wants* Ray to get paid. Mark doesn't care whether he has to pay Sally or Ray. (He doesn't actually want to pay anyone – what he wants is the car.) But he agrees to pay Ray as part of the deal with Sally.

Assume that Mark doesn't pay Ray. What happens? Sally can sue to enforce her right to have Mark pay Ray. But what if Sally is out of the country – or worse, dead? Ray can seek to enforce his rights under the contract against Mark.

What if we changed the facts so that Sally, Mark, and Ray are not individuals but corporations? Assume that Sally Corp. is a large banking institution and Mark Corp. is a software company. Under their contract, Sally Corp. licenses software from Mark Corp. and Mark Corp. agrees to indemnify Sally Corp. against any infringement claims arising from using the software. Under the agreement, Sally Corp's affiliated companies may also use the software. What happens if a third party sues an affiliate for software infringement? Can that affiliate require Mark Corp. to indemnify it from the infringement claim? The answer is yes if the affiliate is an intended third-party beneficiary. Sally Corp. can greatly increase the likelihood that a court will find the affiliate to be an intended beneficiary by including a provision that expressly states that affiliated companies are intended third-party beneficiaries, such as the one that follows:

---

was to make a gift or confer a right upon a third party, that party was a donee beneficiary. *Id.* §133(1)(a). If the purpose of the contract was not to make a gift but to satisfy a duty of one of the parties to the third party, that third party was a donee beneficiary. *Id.* at §133(1)(b). The Restatement (Second) Contracts replaces the donee and creditor categories with the intended beneficiary category. RESTATEMENT (SECOND) CONTRACTS, §302. *See also* E. ALLAN FARNSWORTH, CONTRACTS (4th ed., 2004) §10.3 at 658 (noting the "surprising similarity" between the donee and creditor categories and the intended beneficiary category but stating that there are "some significant differences"); LON L. FULLER, MELVIN ARON EISENBERG & MARK GERGEN, BASIC CONTRACT LAW, 9th ed. (2013) 953–954.

Example clause

The Corporation's Affiliates shall be deemed to be third party beneficiaries under this Agreement with the right to seek enforcement and make claims under this Agreement.

A third party identified in the contract as an intended third-party beneficiary may enforce the contract.[3]

Conversely, the parties may wish to include a clause such as the following to make clear that no third party may enforce the agreement.

Example clause

This Agreement does not and is not intended to confer any rights or remedies upon any person or entity other than the Parties.

7.2 Doctrinal concept: assignment and delegation

Principle: Generally a party to a contract can assign its rights or delegate its duties under a contract provided it would not materially change the bargain for the other party.

Third-party issues arise where assignment or delegation is involved. While the rights of third-party beneficiaries are created at the time the contract between the parties is formed, with assignment and delegation, the rights (and/or obligations) of third parties do not arise until *after* the contract is created *and* the assignment and/or delegation has occurred. Assignment is the transfer of a *right*, including rights under a contract. Delegation refers to one party tasking its *obligations* under the contract to another.

Unless the contract states otherwise, a party may assign his contractual rights unless the assignment would materially change the duty of the other party (the obligor), materially increase the burden on the obligor, materially impair the obligor's chance of obtaining return performance or materially reduce its value to the obligor.[4] For example, a software developer may not want a customer/licensee to assign the right to use customized software to a third

3 Richland Towers, Inc. v. Denton, No. 2D12-5493, March 12, 2014, District Court of Appeals of Florida, Second District, 39 Fla. L. Weekly D535 (The cessation of business by employer Richland Towers, Inc. did not affect the ability of affiliates to enforce restrictive covenants against former employees). *Id.* at 2.

4 RESTATEMENT (SECOND) CONTRACTS, §317(2)(a).

party because the licensor wants to be sure that any use of the software will be with compatible operating systems or there might be something about the combination of certain technologies that would make the licensor vulnerable to a claim of infringement.

A party may delegate duties unless the party who is supposed to receive the performance has a substantial interest in having the original party perform.[5] A party may have a substantial interest where the contract is one for services that involves the other party's particular expertise or abilities. For example, an interior decorator or a portrait painter would probably not be able to delegate her performance under a contract.

A delegation of duties does not mean the original party is no longer liable for performance. *The party who is delegating his duties is still responsible for the performance.*[6] Assume Dave enters into a contract with José where Dave is supposed to maintain José's yard. José does not have a substantial interest in having Dave do the job – Dave isn't doing any landscaping or design, he's merely trimming hedges and mowing the grass. Dave decides he is too busy to take care of José's lawn and so he enters into an agreement with Frances where he delegates his duty to maintain José's lawn to her. If Frances fails to maintain José's lawn, José has a claim against Dave. José also has a claim against Frances *as he is a third-party beneficiary* of the contract between Dave and Frances.[7] Dave, too, has a claim against Frances, for breaching her obligation under their agreement.

The above outlines the general law governing assignments and delegations. As with many other areas of contract law, the parties may modify the default rules of contract law by including a provision in their agreement:

Example clause

Neither party may assign any of its rights or delegate any of its duties under this Agreement. Any purported assignment or delegation is void.

Caveat: Some courts resist enforcing an anti-assignment clause. They may refuse to invalidate it on the grounds of public policy, or they may construe the clause to prohibit only the delegation of duties and not the assignment of rights. If the clause requires the consent of a party to an assignment but does not

5 RESTATEMENT (SECOND) CONTRACTS, §318(2).

6 In order to release the delegating party, all three parties need to sign a novation.

7 José would only be allowed to recover once for his damages.

indicate the standard of conduct required of the party to refuse consent (referred to as a "silent consent clause"),[8] many courts read into the clause an obligation to act reasonably.[9] Furthermore, Article 9 of the UCC renders ineffective a clause prohibiting assignment of accounts, promissory notes, chattel paper, and payment intangibles.[10] A further caveat is that federal law may complicate the issues associated with assignment clauses, especially where the assignment involves intellectual property rights.[11] The Bankruptcy Code may also limit the effect of an anti-assignment clause in an executory contract or an unexpired lease where one of the parties is undergoing bankruptcy proceedings.[12]

Some contracts reference an assignment of the agreement or an assignment of rights under the Agreement, without distinguishing an assignment of rights from a delegation of duties. The following clause is an example:

Example clause

Neither Party may, or has the power to, assign this Agreement without the prior written consent of the other Party.

Both the UCC and the Restatement state that a provision that prohibits assignment of "the contract" prohibits only the delegation of duties and not

8 Dick Broadcasting Co., Inc. of Tennessee v. Oak Ridge FM, Inc., 395 S.W.3d 653, 659 (defining a "silent consent" clause as one that "requires consent of the non-assigning party" but "is silent regarding the standard of conduct required of a party desiring to refuse consent to a requested assignment").

9 Kendall v. Ernest Pestana, 40 Cal. 3d 488, 496 (1985) (noting that where a lease contains a clause permitting assignment only with the consent of the lessor, a "growing minority" view requires that such consent may be withheld "only where the lessor has a commercially reasonable objection to the assignment"); Campbell v. Westdahl, 148 Ariz. 432, 715 P.2d 288, 292 (Ariz. Ct. App. 1985) (noting the "modern trend is to impose a standard of reasonableness on the landlord in withholding consent to a sublease [6] unless the lease expressly states otherwise"). Similarly, in Julian v. Christopher, 320 Md. 1 (1990), the Court of Appeals of Maryland modified the common law rule expressed in Jacobs v. Klawans 225 Md. 147, 169 A.2d 677 (1961), which allowed a landlord to withhold consent arbitrarily and unreasonably where the lease contained an anti-assignment clause. The Court of Appeals of Maryland offered two policy justifications for modifying *Klanwans*: "The first is the public policy against restraints on alienation. The second is the public policy which implies a covenant of good faith and fair dealing in every contract." *Id.* at 8. *See also* Dick Broadcasting Co., Inc. of Tennessee v. Oak Ridge FM, Inc., 395 S.W.3d 653, 660 (2013) (holding that the implied covenant of good faith and fair dealing is applicable to an assignment clause requiring the consent of the non-assigning party); *But see* B & R Oil Co., Inc. v. Ray's Mobile Homes, Inc. 139 Vt. 122, 123, 422 A.2d 1267 (1980) (upholding view that lessor has the right to "arbitrarily withhold his consent to an assignment"); Dress Shirt Sales, Inc. v. Hotel Martinique Associates) 12 N.Y.2d 339, 343, 236 N.Y.S.2d 613, 190 N.E.2d 10 (1963) (noting that defendants had "an unqualified contractual privilege to refuse to accept" assignment).

10 UCC §9-406.

11 Food Consulting Group, Inc. v. Azzalino, 270 F.3d 821, 824 (9th Cir. 2001) (noting that federal law answers the threshold question of whether an implied, nonexclusive copyright license can be granted but that state law determines the contract question whether a copyright holder has, in fact, granted such a license).

12 11 USC §365(f); 11 USC §365(c).

the assignment of rights.[13] They also state that a term prohibiting assignment of rights does not forbid assignment of a right to damages for breach of contract.[14] A court's decision whether to enforce anti-assignment clauses may depend upon whether the assignment involves an executory contract (in which case the anti-assignment clause is likely to be upheld), or whether it involves assignment of rights based upon a contract, such as the right to collect money or damages for breach of contract (in which case the anti-assignment clause will not invalidate the assignment but will give rise to a cause of action for breach of the covenant not to assign).

It is a good idea to distinguish between an assignment of the *contract* and an assignment of rights arising from the contract.[15] The following provision expressly references both rights and obligations:

Example clause

Neither Party may, or has the power to, assign, transfer or delegate this Agreement or any of the rights or obligations under this Agreement without the express prior written consent of the other Party, which consent shall not be unreasonably withheld.

Putting it in context – negotiating an assignment clause:

The parties may want to limit the ability to assign to only one party, or to permit assignment only under some circumstances. This is especially true if the contract involves an ongoing relationship and where a party was selected due to its unique attributes or qualifications. Assume, for example, Manufacturer X selects Distributor Y to be the exclusive distributor of its products in North America. Manufacturer X most likely made its selection

13 RESTATEMENT (SECOND) CONTRACTS, §322; UCC §2-210. *See also* Traicoff v. Digital Media, Inc., 439 F.Supp. 2d 872 (S.D. Ind. 2006) (finding that a failure of anti-assignment provision to "clearly state" intent to prohibit assignment of rights under contract required application of "generally accepted rule" interpreting prohibition against assignment of "the contract" to "refer only to the delegation of contractual duties, not assignment of rights.") *Id.* at 880.

14 RESTATEMENT (SECOND) CONTRACTS, §322(2)(a); UCC §2-210(2); Pagosa Oil and Gas, L.L.C. v. Marrs and Smith Partnership, 323 S.W.3d 203 (Tex. App. El Paso, 2010) (rev. denied, June 11, 2010) (stating that Texas law recognizes a distinction between a contracting party's ability to assign rights under a contract containing an anti-assignment provision, and that same party's ability to assign a cause of action arising from breach of that contract).

15 Public Service Com'n of Maryland v. Panda-Brandywine, L.P., 375 Md. 185, 825 A.2d 462, 469 (Md. 2003) ("In a bilateral contract, each party ordinarily has both rights and duties – the right to expect performance from the other party to the contract and the duty to perform what the party has agreed to perform. Although both are often the subject of transfer, the law does distinguish between them, using the term "assignment" to refer to the transfer of contractual rights and the term "delegation" to refer to the transfer of contractual duties").

of Distributor Y after careful consideration of Distributor's Y's reputation, resources, and ability to sell products, knowledge of the relevant marketplace, and knowledge of Manufacturer X's product. There may have been other factors involved, such as how comfortable the relevant team at Manufacturer X was in dealing with the team that would handle the account at Distributor Y. Given the careful and subjective selection criteria and process, the benefit of the bargain to Manufacturer X could be undermined if Distributor Y were to assign its contract to another distributor.

While Manufacturer X's reasons for prohibiting assignment may be understandable, Distributor Y may want to carve out an exception to the "no-assignment" clause to allow assignment of the contract to a successor entity in the event of a merger or acquisition of substantially all of its assets. The distribution agreement between Manufacturer X and Distributor Y may make Distributor Y more attractive as an acquisition, increase its valuation and/or enhance its bargaining power during negotiations with a potential acquiring company. Distributor Y may ask for a clause like the following in the contract:

Example clause

Except as provided in this Section, no Party may, or has the power to, assign any of its rights or delegate any of its obligations under this Agreement without the prior written consent of the other Party; provided, however, that each Party may assign its rights and delegate its obligations under this Agreement without the approval of the other Party (i) to an entity which acquires all or substantially all of its assets or (ii) to any wholly-owned subsidiary or Affiliate or successor entity in a merger, acquisition, restructuring or reorganization of Distributor. Any permitted assignee shall assume all obligations of its assignor under this Agreement. Any purported assignment in violation of this section shall be void and of no effect.

While the ability to assign the rights and delegate the obligations under a contract in the event of a merger or acquisition may benefit Distributor Y, Manufacturer X might be unhappy if the surviving or acquiring entity is one of its main competitors. It would be wise for Manufacturer to include language which prohibits assignment by Distributor Y in the event that it is acquired by a competitor of Manufacturer X:

Example clause

Except as provided in this Section, neither Party may, or has the power to, assign this Agreement or any of its rights under this Agreement, or delegate any of its obligations under this Agreement without the prior written consent of the other Party; provided, however, that either Party may assign its rights and delegate its obligations under this Agreement without the approval of the other Party (i) to an entity which acquires all or substantially all of its assets or (ii) to any wholly-owned subsidiary or Affiliate or successor entity in a merger, acquisition, restructuring or reorganization of Distributor. Any permitted assignee shall assume all obligations of its assignor under this Agreement. Notwithstanding the foregoing, in no event may Distributor assign this Agreement to a competitor of Manufacturer as determined by Manufacturer in its sole discretion. Any purported assignment in violation of this section shall be void and of no effect.

Distributor Y may be concerned that granting Manufacturer X the right to determine who is a "competitor" may grant it discretion that could be abused. Although Manufacturer X's discretion would be subject to the covenant of good faith, to avoid future problems over who is a competitor, Distributor Y may want Manufacturer X to identify its competitors in the contract, either by name or by industry.

Troubleshooting: If the list of names will be updated – which is likely – it should be attached to the document as a schedule rather than incorporated within the assignment provision itself. A schedule may be updated more easily than a revision to the body of the agreement.

Example clause

Except as provided in this Section, neither Party may, or shall have the power to, assign any of its rights or delegate any of its obligations under this Agreement without the prior written consent of the other Party; provided, however, that either Party may assign its rights and delegate its obligations under this Agreement without the approval of the other Party (i) to an entity which acquires all or substantially all of its assets or (ii) to any wholly-owned subsidiary or Affiliate or successor entity in a merger, acquisition, restructuring or reorganization of Distributor. Any permitted assignee shall assume all obligations of its assignor under this Agreement. Notwithstanding the foregoing, in no event may Distributor assign this Agreement to a competitor of Manufacturer listed on Schedule 1, which may be updated from time to time by agreement of the parties. Any purported assignment in violation of this section shall be void and of no effect.

CLASSIC CASE

SALLY BEAUTY CO. v. NEXXUS PRODUCTS CO., INC., 801 F.2d 1001 (7th Cir., 1986)

Nexxus Products Company ("Nexxus") and Best Barber & Beauty Supply Company, Inc. ("Best") entered into a contract which made Best the exclusive distributor of Nexxus hair care products in the state of Texas. Nexus cancelled the agreement when Best was acquired by and merged into Sally Beauty Company, Inc. ("Sally Beauty"). Sally Beauty was a wholly-owned subsidiary of Alberto-Culver Company ("Alberto-Culver"), a major manufacturer of hair care products and a competitor of Nexxus. Sally Beauty claimed that Nexxus breached by cancelling the contract. Nexxus claimed that the contract was not assignable or, in the alternative, that it was not assignable to Sally Beauty. The district court ruled for Nexxus, finding that the contract was one for personal services and therefore not assignable. The U.S. Court of Appeals for the Seventh Circuit affirmed, but on the theory that under §2-210 of the Uniform Commercial Code, the contract could not be assigned to the wholly-owned subsidiary of a direct competitor.

The distributorship agreement was treated as a sale of goods contract and subject to the provisions of the UCC, which is the rule in the majority of jurisdictions.[16] The Seventh Circuit stated that the fact that the contract was considered one for the sale of goods, instead of a personal services contract, did not mean that it was freely assignable.

> "The Code . . . sanctions delegation except where the delegated performance would be unsatisfactory to the obligee . . . Consideration is given to balancing the policies of free alienability of commercial contracts and protecting the obligee from having to accept a bargain he did not contract for."

The court noted that in the exclusive distribution agreement, Nexxus had contracted for Best's "best efforts" in promoting Nexxus products in Texas and that "Sally Beauty's position as a wholly-owned subsidiary of Alberto-Culver is sufficient to bar the delegation of Best's duties under the agreement" as Sally Beauty's efforts were subject to the control of Alberto-Culver, a competitor of Nexxus. The court limited its holding, however, to the particular facts of the case:

> "We hold merely that the duty of performance under an exclusive distributorship may not be delegated to a competitor in the marketplace – or the wholly-owned subsidiary of a competitor – without the obligee's consent."

16 Sally Beauty Co. v. Nexxus Products Co., Inc., 801 F.2d 1001, 1005 (7th Cir. 1986) (citing to Kirby v. Chrysler Corp., 554 F. Supp., 743 (D.Md. 1982)); Quality Performance Lines v. Yoho Automotive, Inc., 609 P.2d 1340 (Utah 1980); Meuse-Rhine-Ijssel Cattle Breeders of Canada, Ltd. v. Y-Tex Corp., 590 P.2d 1306 (Wyo. 1979).

Caveat: Parties who have an ongoing or long-term relationship without contract terms that allow for termination for convenience may want to prevent or restrict contract assignment. The parties should carefully consider whether prohibiting or restricting assignment is enough, however, to preserve their expectations. A change of control does not constitute an assignment. The parties should carefully consider the impact of a change of control on their agreement. As the following Case Highlight illustrates, a party might get around the intended effect of an anti-assignment provision through other maneuvers.

CASE HIGHLIGHT

VDF FUTURECEUTICALS, INC. v. STIEFEL LABORATORIES, INC., 792 F.3d 842 (7th Cir. 2015)

The plaintiff, VDF Futureceuticals ("VDF"), entered into an agreement where it licensed rights to commercialize CoffeeBerry-based skincare products to J&J Technologies, LC ("J&J"). J&J was allowed to sublicense its rights. As part of the agreement, J&J agreed to pay to VDF royalties of 15 percent of any revenues that J&J obtained from selling the licensed product and any royalties that J&J received from sublicensees. (The royalties to be received by VDF were "running royalties," which means they were based on the number of sales by J&J or its sublicensees). The agreement also provided for a minimum, alternative royalty in the event that the running royalties fell below a specified level. The license agreement stated that it could not be assigned without VDF's written permission but it did not forbid a change of control of J&J.

J&J entered into a sublicense agreement with Stiefel. Several years later, Stiefel purchased J&J stock from its three owners and J&J became a Stiefel subsidiary. Two months after purchasing J&J, Stiefel and J&J amended the sublicense agreement to reduce the royalties that Stiefel owed J&J, thus diverting some of the license-revenue stream from VDF and J&J to Stiefel.

Stiefel's internal documents indicated that it purchased J&J stock rather than seeking an assignment of J&J's license both to avoid having to seek VDF's permission for the assignment and to reduce the royalties that Stiefel would have to pay J&J under the sublicense agreement. VDF sued claiming, among other things, that Stiefel and J&J had engaged in a de facto unauthorized assignment of the agreement. The district court granted summary judgment in favor of defendants on this claim. The Second Circuit Court of Appeals agreed, noting a "fatal problem" with the plaintiffs' claim of unauthorized assignment:

"[B]y failing to place any restrictions on who could own its licensee J&J, VDF exposed itself to being taken advantage of by a change of ownership at J&J that would result in operating changes and alter its relationship to VDF. Had Stiefel bought J&J's license, or instead bought J&J and dissolved the company so that when the dust settled all that Stiefel would

CASE HIGHLIGHT *(continued)*

have obtained from the purchase was the license, Stiefel would have violated the terms of the license by obtaining it without VDF's consent . . . That didn't happen. J&J remained in existence after its acquisition by Stiefel, as VDF's licensee and Stiefel's sublicensor . . .

That the change in how J&J was operated was adverse to the licensor's interests is why with clearer foresight VDF would have included restrictions in the license on changes in the ownership of its licensee, J&J. Its failure to do so was fatal, because 'the courts have held that the sale of all the stock in a closely held corporation whose principal asset is a contract does not violate a nonassignment clause even when the stock is sold to a person to whom, previously, the counterparty had explicitly refused that the contract be assigned. If the counterparty to a contract with a corporation wishes to limit the persons to whom ownership or control of the corporation can be sold, it must do this through specific language to that effect in the contract (a "change of control" clause); a nonassignment clause will not suffice' [citations omitted] . . . Were this not the rule, routine anti-assignment clauses would impede liquidity in the market for corporate control."

As the above Case Highlight illustrates, depending upon the nature of the transaction, the parties may want to include a provision that permits termination upon a change in control.

Example clause

Manufacturer has the right to terminate this Agreement in the event of a Change in Control upon thirty (30) days' written notice to Distributor. "Change in Control" is defined as the sale of all or substantially all of the property or assets of Distributor.

Example clause

If the majority of the Distributor's voting stock is transferred or its ownership or control is in any way substantially changed, the Company has the right to terminate this Agreement upon thirty (30) days' written notice.

Reflection Prompt: Under what circumstances might the differences in the two Example Clauses be relevant?

The parties may also define "assignment" in a way that encompasses a change in control:

Example clause

The Distributor may not assign any rights or delegate any obligations under this Agreement except with the prior written consent of Company. Any sale, transfer, or other assignment of more than ten percent (10%) of the corporate stock of Distributor shall be considered an assignment of this Distributorship for purposes of this Agreement. Any attempted assignment of rights or delegation of obligations by Distributor in violation of this Section shall be void and unenforceable.

Caveat: As noted in the Introduction, background laws affect the enforceability and interpretation of contracts. Federal laws may determine the validity of an attempted assignment of intellectual property rights. Bankruptcy law may also affect whether an assignment of intellectual property rights is valid.[17]

Although the UCC generally permits a party to delegate his or her duty, delegation may be prohibited by contract or if the other party has a substantial interest in having the original promisor perform. Delegation does not, however, relieve the original promisor of any duty to perform or any liability for breach.[18]

Based upon the case law, it's a good idea to make sure that any anti-assignment clause is clearly drafted to reflect the parties' intent. If the parties want all assignments to be ineffective (and not just provide the other party with the right to sue for breach of covenant not to assign), the provision should use words that specifically state that any attempted assignment is void and without legal effect.

Example clause

Any attempt by either party to assign any right or delegate any duty under this Agreement shall be void, deemed a material breach of this Agreement and result in the immediate termination of this Agreement.

17 *See* In Re Supernatural Foods, LLC, 268 B.R. 749 (2001) (finding clause in license agreement permitting assignments in connection with sale of substantially all of company's assets constituted consent to assignment in liquidation proceedings). *But see* In Re Sunterra Corporation, 361 F.3d 257 (2004) (finding that agreement to assignment to successor in interest was not consent to debtor's assumption of contract).

18 UCC §2-210.

Example clause

Contractor shall not assign or transfer this agreement or assign any rights or delegate any obligations hereunder except with the prior written consent of Principal. Any attempt at assignment without such written consent shall be deemed null and void and of no effect.

Reflection Prompt: Why would a party want the Agreement to immediately terminate upon an attempted assignment? When would a party want the Agreement to continue to be effective?

The Restatement[19] and the UCC[20] both state that an assignment of "the contract" includes a delegation of duties, but some courts have held otherwise where the transaction was not one for the sale of goods.[21] If the parties intend the assignment of a contract to include a delegation of duties, it is a good idea for the parties to expressly state that the assignee will assume those duties.

Example clause

Assignee hereby assumes all of Assignor's right, title, interest and obligations under the Assumed Agreement and agrees to perform all obligations and satisfy all conditions to be performed or satisfied by Assignor under the provisions of the Assumed Agreement.

CASE HIGHLIGHT

ALLHUSEN v. CARISTO CONST. CORP., 303 N.Y. 446 (1952)

The defendant, a general contractor, subcontracted with Kroo Painting Company ("Kroo") for certain painting work in New York City public schools. The contracts between the defendant and Kroo contained the following provision:

19 RESTATEMENT (SECOND) CONTRACTS, §328.

20 UCC §2-210(5).

21 *See*, for example, In re Mortgages, Ltd., 405 B.R. 669, 671–672 (2009) (noting that Arizona contract law is contrary to the Restatement's rule of implied delegation and that "an assignment alone does not imply a delegation or assumption of duties" and that "assignment of a contract" does not operate to "cast on the assignee the assignor's liabilities"); 6A C.J.S. Assignments §94, 485–486 (2004) ("An assignment of contractual rights does not necessarily carry with it a delegation of contractual duties, even if the assignment contract specified that it was binding on the assigns of the parties to the contract").

CASE HIGHLIGHT *(continued)*

> "The assignment by the second party [Kroo] of this contract or any interest therein, or of any money due or to become due by reason of the terms hereof without the written consent of the first party [defendant] shall be void."

Kroo subsequently assigned certain rights under its contracts with the defendant to Marine Midland Trust Company, which then assigned those rights to the plaintiff. These rights included "moneys due or to become due." The court noted that the *contracts* were not assigned and there was no improper delegation of contractual duties. The defendant did not provide written consent to either of the assignments.

The plaintiff sought to recover $11,650 allegedly due for work done by Kroo. The defendant demanded dismissal of the plaintiff's claim on the basis that the contract provision cited above prohibited the assignment to the plaintiff. Special Term held that the prohibition against assignments "must be given effect" and dismissed the complaint. The Appellate Division affirmed. The plaintiff appealed the judgment of the Appellate Division to the Court of Appeals.

The Court of Appeals observed that the specific language in the clause had not yet been construed by state courts but that similar clauses which have been subject to interpretation were usually held to be either (1) personal covenants limiting the covenantee to a claim for damages in the event of a breach or (2) ineffectual because of the use of uncertain language. That did not, however, mean that there could be no contractual prohibition against the assignment of a claim. Rather, "in the absence of language clearly indicating that a contractual right thereunder shall be nonassignable, a prohibitory clause will be interpreted as a personal covenant not to assign."

Importantly, the court noted that the language in the contract "expressly provided that the 'assignment . . . shall be void."

The court concluded:

> "In the light of the foregoing, we think it is reasonably clear that, while the courts have striven to uphold freedom of assignability, they have not failed to recognize the concept of freedom to contract. In large measure they agree that, where appropriate language is used, assignments of money due under contracts may be prohibited. When 'clear language is used', and the 'plainest words . . . have been chosen', parties may 'limit the freedom of alienation of rights and prohibit the assignment' [citation omitted]. We have now before us a clause embodying clear, definite and appropriate language, which may be construed in no other way but that any attempted assignment of either the contract or any rights created thereunder shall be 'void' as against the obligor. One would have to do violence to the language here employed to hold that it is merely an agreement by the subcontractor not to assign. The objectivity of the language precludes such a construction. We are therefore compelled to conclude that this prohibitory clause is a valid and effective restriction of the right to assign."

Judgment affirmed.

Caveat: A delegation of duties does not mean that the delegating party is no longer liable for performance. In order to relieve one of the original parties from the contract and substitute a new party, the parties must enter into a novation. A novation is an agreement among the three parties – the original parties and the new party – that extinguishes the original contract and forms a new contract. Thus, a novation constitutes both a release of one of the original parties and a new contract between the remaining original contracting party and the new substituted party. In order to be effective, the novation must contain language expressly releasing the original party.

CASE HIGHLIGHT

BOSWELL v. LYON, 401 N.E.2d 735 (Ind. Ct. App. 1980)

Boswell and Snyder entered into a contract with Hadley for the conditional sale of an apartment building for the purchase price of $30,000, to be paid by a $3,000 down payment and monthly payments of $135. The balance was to bear interest at five percent per annum, with a final balloon payment of the remaining balance due no later than March 9, 1974. The contract contained the following provision:

> "6. Assignment of contract. Neither this contract, Purchaser's interest therein, nor Purchaser's interest in the Real Estate, shall be sold, assigned, pledged, mortgaged, or transferred by Purchaser without the written consent of vendor."

. . . .

Boswell and Snyder assigned their rights under the contract to Batties. Hadley consented to the assignment by an instrument which stated:

Assignment

September 25, 1964

This is to certify that for value received and subject to the consent of the owner of the property described in the within Conditional Sales Contract, the undersigned do hereby sell, assign, transfer and set over unto MARK D. BATTIES all of his right, title and interest in and to the said conditional Sales Contract.

/s/ CHARLES E. BOSWELL
Charles E. Boswell
/s/ STEPHEN J. SNYDER
Stephen J. Snyder

CASE HIGHLIGHT *(continued)*

ACCEPTANCE

September 25, 1964

The undersigned hereby accept the above assignment of the within Conditional Sales Contract and hereby expressly agree to be bound by all of the terms and conditions of said Conditional Sales Contract.

/s/ MARK D. BATTIES

Mark D. Batties

CONSENT

September 25, 1964

The undersigned, owner of the property described in the within Conditional Sales Contract, hereby consents to the above assignments and acceptance thereof.

/s/ MARTHA S. HADLEY

Martha S. Hadley

By Elmer E. Lyon

Attorney in Fact

. . . .

Hadley later assigned her rights under the contract to Lyon on July 10, 1968. There was no issue concerning this assignment from Hadley to Lyon. On February 1, 1969, Batties assigned his rights under the contract to Roberts. Lyon consented to that assignment using the same form as used in the 1964 assignment with Batties as the assignor, Roberts as the assignee and Lyon as the vendor.

In 1973, Lyon's attorney notified Snyder by letter that the final payment on the 1960 contract was due on March 9, 1974 and that both Snyder and Boswell would face potential liability in the event of a default. The letter also indicated that Roberts, the current assignee under the contract, did not appear to be in a financial position to meet the large balloon payment. Roberts defaulted on two monthly payments in 1973 and Boswell, Snyder, and Batties were all notified of the default by letter. On March 9, 1974, the contract balance of $21,896 came due but remained unpaid. Lyon then filed suit against Boswell, Snyder, Batties, and Roberts.

Boswell and Snyder asserted that the term "assignment" in the 1960 contract was ambiguous as it did not state whether the purchasers would remain secondarily liable once the contract was assigned. The court ruled that the assignment clause was not ambiguous and no genuine issue of material fact existed as to the parties' intent in using that clause.

Boswell and Snyder also claimed that the conduct of the parties surrounding the assignment created a question of fact as to whether the parties intended to create a novation. The court stated:

> "A novation simply means the substitution of one debtor for another by mutual agreement of the parties . . . Only if a party has agreed to a substitution in the place of the other party is that other party relieved of liability . . . While there is a paucity of case law on the subject of novation in Indiana, it is reasonable to conclude that novation consists of four elements: an existing valid

CASE HIGHLIGHT *(continued)*

> contract; all parties must agree to a new contract; the old contract must be extinguished by the new contract; and the new contract must be valid . . . Whether a novation has occurred is a matter of the intent of the parties."

The court, reviewing the 1964 assignment, found that the assignment involved both the assignment of rights and the delegation of duties but that there was no language indicating a release of liability. It concluded:

"The document before us assigned the rights and interests of Boswell and Snyder, and delegated contractual obligations to Batties and no more. The agreement did not mention novation, relieving of contractual liabilities, substitution of parties to the contract, or extinguishing the old contract. Without some such indicator, we cannot conclude that his assignment was equivocal or uncertain or that a novation could have been in any way intended . . .

[N]othing in the language used by the parties in any way infers an intent to relieve Boswell and Snyder of their contractual obligations and to substitute Batties in their stead. As a matter of law there was no novation."

Finally, Boswell and Snyder argued that, even if they remained liable on the 1960 contract after the 1964 assignment, the assignment from Batties to Roberts in 1969, done with the consent of Lyon, discharged them because they never received notice of it. The court rejected this argument:

"The general rule is that absent a provision to the contrary a party may delegate his duties under a contract . . . An exception is made if the duty is of a personal nature and performance by an assignee would vary materially from performance by the obligor . . . The duty of payment of the purchase price is not so personal in nature as to be a non-delegable duty, and the parties here did not contract to make it such . . . it is fundamental that, absent a novation, such a delegation does *not* relieve the assignor of his contractual liabilities . . .

Just as Boswell and Snyder had the right to delegate their duty of paying the contract price to Batties, he in turn had the same right to delegate that duty to a second assignee, Roberts. Batties' assignment to Roberts did not relieve him of his contractual liability to Boswell and Snyder to perform the duty of paying the purchase price.

This round robin of contractual liability theoretically could go on indefinitely, but does not alter the underlying contractual obligation of Boswell and Snyder."

Finally, the court noted that Boswell and Snyder could have made Battie's duty of payment non-delegable or they could have required him to receive their consent to any delegation by including "appropriate language in the assignment. They did not do so. The obligation of Boswell and Snyder not having been altered by the assignment and consent thereto, they remained liable as a matter of law."

As *Boswell v. Lyon* illustrates, an assignment of a contract (i.e. the delegation of duties) does not release the assigning/delegating party from liability. To release the assigning/delegating party, all parties (the original parties and the assignee) must enter into a novation. A novation typically requires: (1) a valid existing contract; (2) the agreement of all (original and new) parties to a new contract; (3) a valid new contract; and (4) an extinguishment of the old contract in favor of the new one.[22] The novation should contain a provision expressly releasing the assigning party.

Example clause

The Parties hereby intend and agree that [Substituted Party] be substituted for [Original Party] and hereby completely release [Original Party] from the obligation to Obligor.

Example clause

In consideration of this novation, the parties to this novation agreement release [Original Party] from any and all further obligations to perform under the above referenced Agreement and acknowledge and agree that [Original Party] is fully relieved of liability to any party to this novation agreement arising out of the above referenced Agreement.

Troubleshooting: A party (Obligee) to a contract (Original Contract) may consent to an assignment of the Original Contract by the other party (Assignor) to a third party (Assignee) but may refuse to sign a novation which releases the Assignor. The Assignor could, in this case, request that an indemnification clause be included in the agreement which effectuates the assignment. The Assignor would still be liable to the Obligee under the Original Contract, but the Assignee would have to cover Assignor's costs and liabilities to the Obligee.

Example clause

Partnership will indemnify and hold harmless Departing Partner and his heirs, successors and assigns from and against any and all claims, demands, losses, damages, costs, expenses and liabilities, including but not limited to reasonable attorney fees and costs, arising out of or in any way connected to (i) the operation or ownership of the Partnership, (ii) any inaccuracy in or breach of any representation or warranty of Partnership, or (iii) any breach or default by Partnership under any of the Partnership's covenants or agreements contained in this Agreement. The Partnership agrees to assume all rights and responsibilities of the Partnership Interest from and after the Closing Date.

22 Ashbaugh v. Horvath, 859 N.E.2d 1260, 1265 (2007).

In some cases, a later party may acquire rights obtained under the original contract through a legal change that doesn't involve assignment of a contract. A party may, for example, merge with another legal entity, thus creating a successor entity.[23] A party may also succeed an original party through the acquisition of property.[24] The original parties may express their intent to bind such future parties (including those who have not expressly agreed to the obligations through a contract assignment) by including a provision commonly referred to as a "successors and assigns" clause:

Example clause

This Agreement binds and inures to the benefit of the Parties and their respective heirs, successors and assigns.

Example clause

All representations, warranties and covenants of Seller contained herein survive the Closing and inure to the benefit of Buyer and its legal representatives, heirs, successors or assigns.

Reflection Prompt: In what type of transaction would it be better to use the first Example Clause? What about the second?

Note that the two Example Clauses above are in the present tense so that they become immediately effective and do not require further action.

The legal effect of the "successors and assigns" language is to benefit and bind later parties. As previously noted, an assignment of a contract does not

23 A merger statute may govern rather than contract principles. *See* HD Supply Facilities Maintenance, Ltd. v. Bymoen, 210 P.3d 183, 188 (2009) (finding that when a successor corporation acquires restrictive employment covenants as the result of a merger, contract principles regarding non-assignability do not apply).

24 As Stoebuck & Weaver explain, a later purchaser of real property may succeed to interests in a prior contract affecting the land if the covenants run with the land: "Enforcement between the original parties is a matter of the law [34] of contract . . . But the doctrine with which we are concerned here is the doctrine, generally regarded as part of the law of real property, under which the covenant by the original parties may be enforced by or against persons who succeed to interests they held in the burdened or benefited land. The doctrine of 'running' is analogous to the contract doctrines of assignment of rights and delegation of duties; it is a doctrine whereby remote parties are bound or benefited by contractual covenants made by the original parties. *However, while a party must consensually undertake assignment or delegation, the law of running covenants imposes a duty or confers a benefit upon remote parties, not because they consensually agree, but because the covenant bore a certain relationship to parcels of land and because they stepped into a certain relationship with the same parcels.* The essence of the law of running covenants has to do with what these relationships must be for the remote parties to be bound or benefited." 17 WILLIAM B. STOEBUCK & JOHN W. WEAVER, WASHINGTON PRACTICE: REAL ESTATE: PROPERTY LAW §3.2, at 126 (2nd ed. 2004) (cited in Deep Water Brewing, LLC v. Fairway Res. Ltd., 152 Wash. App. 229, 258 (2009)).

necessarily include a delegation of duties. Some courts have held that a successors and assigns clause eliminates the need for an express assumption of duties by the assignee.[25] (Others have not, however, making an express assumption of those duties advisable.)

A successors and assigns clause may affect subsequent parties who are not assignees but who have succeeded to an original party's interest, such as the heirs to the original party. A right of first refusal to purchase property is typically found to be personal to the grantee absent the intent of the parties to bind their successors.[26] In order to be effective, a copyright transfer must be in writing and signed by the owner or owners of the copyright interest being transferred.[27] A "successors and assigns" clause allows the transferee of that copyright interest to later transfer that interest. In addition, a successors and assigns clause may keep out parol evidence that the parties agreed to restrict the assignability of a property interest. Finally, the omission of the clause may lead a court to find that the parties expressly intended to exclude it.[28]

CASE HIGHLIGHT

DEEP WATER BREWING, LLC v. FAIRWAY RES. LTD., 215 P.3d 990 (Wash. App. Div. 3 2009)

Developers and Ahlquists, who were restaurant owners, entered into an agreement granting an easement and right of way to developers and restricting the developers from building in a manner that would affect the sight or views from the restaurant building to the lake. The

25 *See* Citizens Suburban Company v. Rosemont Development Co., Inc., 244 Cal. App. 2d 666, 675 (1966) ("At common law an assignment transfers the benefits of an executory contract but not its burdens, unless the assignee expressly assumes the latter . . . A clause binding 'successors and assigns' is designed to eliminate the necessity for an express assumption of burdens."); Roe v. Ladymom, 318 S.W.3d 502, 519 (2010) (Successors and assigns clauses "make a contract expressly assignable and have the effect of making a successor or assignee obligated to perform the assignor's obligations without an express agreement of assumption").

26 *See* Malone v. Flattery, 797 N.W.2d 624 (2011) (finding that rights of first refusal are presumed personal unless express language evidences intent to the contrary); Winn v. Stevenson, 1992 WL 12034051 (Va, Feb. 3 1992) (finding that because there was no successors and assigns clause, "the parties to the present contract did not intend to bind their successors, but instead included the preemptive right clause to create a personal obligation limited to the Seller"). *Id.* at *3.

27 17 U.S.C. §204(a) ("A transfer of copyright ownership, other than by operation of law, is not valid unless an instrument of conveyance, or a note or memorandum of the transfer, is in writing and signed by the owner of the rights conveyed or such owner's duly authorized agent").

28 Winn v. Stevenson, 26 Va. Cir. 271, 1992 WL 12034051 at *3 (Va. Feb. 3, 1992) ("By the Buyer's own admission, no words or references to heirs or assigns may be found anywhere in the closing statement. Virginia courts have held that the omission of a particular term from a contract reduced to writing shows a specific intent to exclude it").

CASE HIGHLIGHT *(continued)*

right of way was deeded to Key Development, which purchased the property. The right of way agreement was never recorded. The preamble to the right of way agreement provided that the Key Bay Homeowner's Association would protect the Ahlquists' rights. The Ahlquists sold the restaurant to Robert and Roberta Kenagy who were aware of the right of way agreement. Kenagy leased the building to his business, Deep Water Brewing, LLC. Sometime later, Robert Kenagy learned that some of the homeowners in the Key Bay development were allowed to build multi-story homes. The Kenagys sued the developers and the homeowners' association for declaratory judgment and injunctive relief to enforce the provisions in the right of way agreements that protected their view.

The trial court found that there was a valid and enforceable contractual relationship between the Kenagys, as Ahlquist's successors in interest and third-party beneficiaries of the easement and right of way agreements. The defendants appealed.

The Court of Appeals noted that although the recorded deed said nothing about protecting the views of the lake, the real estate purchase and sale agreement provided:

> "All representations, warranties and covenants of Seller contained herein shall survive the Closing and shall inure to the benefit of Buyer and its legal representatives, heirs, successors or assigns."

Therefore, the covenants assuring preservation of the view of the lake survived the deed conveying the property.

The court then addressed whether the Kenagys were third-party beneficiaries who were entitled to the benefit of the covenants as successors to the Ahlquists' interest. The court found that they were not third-party beneficiaries to either the easement or the right of way agreements as the original parties to the easement or the right of way agreement did not intend, at the time they entered into the agreement, to confer a benefit upon them.

The court next asked whether the agreements were to run with the land (i.e. whether they were "running real covenants"). The court set forth the following elements of running real covenants:

> "(1) the covenants must have been enforceable between the original parties, such enforceability being a question of contract law except insofar as the covenant must satisfy the statute of frauds; (2) the covenant must "touch and concern" both the land to be benefitted and the land to be burdened; (3) the covenanting parties must have intended to bind their successors in interest; (4) there must be vertical privity of estate, *i.e.*, privity between the original parties to the covenant and the present disputants; and (5) there must be horizontal privity of estate, or privity between the original parties."

The court concluded that the covenants were running real covenants as all the elements had been met, that the parties intended the covenant to restrict the height of development on the property to benefit successor estate-in-land holders like the Kenagys, and that the Kenagys could enforce them.

A "successors and assigns" clause might be viewed by some courts as consent to assignments. If the parties want to clarify that assignments are only allowed in certain situations, they should include a provision to that effect:

Example clause

This Agreement binds and inures to the benefit of and is binding upon the parties, their respective successors in interest and permitted assigns. Nothing in this section permits assignment other than as expressly permitted in section XXX.

APPLYING WHAT YOU LEARNED

Contract clauses and parties other than the original parties to the contract

Inventor, LLC. sued FirstCo, Inc., alleging infringement of two patents held by Inventor. The parties settled and entered into a Settlement Agreement which contained the following clause:

"The license and covenant not to sue granted in this Agreement is personal to FirstCo and shall not be assigned or transferred, in whole or in part, by FirstCo or by operation of law without the prior written consent of Inventor provided, however, that FirstCo may transfer or assign its rights under this Agreement in connection with the merger, sale or transfer of all or substantially all of (i) its stock or (ii) its assets related to its design or production of defined Products."

The Settlement Agreement also contained the following clause:

"Unless otherwise restricted herein, this Agreement shall be binding upon and inure to the benefit of and be enforceable by the parties hereto and their respective successors and assigns."

As part of the settlement, FirstCo agreed not to challenge the validity of the patents and to pay royalties on the sale of any FirstCo products using Inventor's patents.

Later, FirstCo took out a loan with Guaranty Biz and pledged, as collateral, its products, including those incorporating Inventor's patents. FirstCo defaulted on its loan and surrendered its collateral. Guaranty Biz then sold the collateral to SecondCo. Inventor sued SecondCo, alleging that it violated the Settlement Agreement by not paying royalties on products using Inventor's patents. SecondCo claims that it was not bound by the Settlement Agreement.

Is SecondCo bound by the Settlement Agreement?

8

Contract clauses addressing remedies

The remedy for breach of contract is typically in the form of damages, which refers to monetary compensation for injury caused by the breach. In the alternative, a party may seek the equitable remedies of specific performance or an injunction. The standard remedy for breach of contract, however, is to award damages. The courts are reluctant to award equitable remedies absent special circumstances.

8.1 Doctrinal concept: damages

Principle: In the event of a breach, the standard measure of recovery for breach of contract is expectation damages.

The objective of contract law is to protect the reasonable expectations of the parties. In the event that one party breaches its contractual obligation to the other party, the standard measure of recovery for the non-breaching party is generally the expectancy measure, which is compensation equal to what the party would have received if the contract had been performed. The expectancy measure includes foreseeable consequential damages, meaning those damages that could reasonably be expected to result from a breach of the contract.

CLASSIC CASE

HAWKINS v. MCGEE, 84 N.H. 114, 146 A. 641 (1929)

The defendant was a surgeon who repeatedly solicited plaintiff for permission in order to perform a skin graft surgery on plaintiff's hand which he promised would result in "a hundred percent good hand." The operation was unsuccessful and resulted in the deformity of plaintiff's hand. The court explained the expectation measure as follows:

CLASSIC CASE *(continued)*

"[T]he true measure of the plaintiff's damage in the present case is the difference between the value to him of a perfect hand or a good hand, such as the jury found the defendant promised him, and the value of his hand in its present condition, including any incidental consequences fairly within the contemplation of the parties when they made their contract . . .

The extent of the plaintiff's suffering does not measure this difference in value. The pain necessarily incident to a serious surgical operation was a part of the contribution which the plaintiff was willing to make to his joint undertaking with the defendant to produce a good hand. It was a legal detriment suffered by him which constituted a part of the consideration given by him for the contract. It represented a part of the price which he was willing to pay for a good hand, but it furnished no test of the value of a good hand or the difference between the value of the hand which the defendant promised and the one which resulted from the operation."

The calculation for expectation damages depends upon the type of transaction and the situation of the injured party. In a breach of a construction contract where the breach is by the contractor, the building owner's expectation damages would be measured by the cost of completion or how much more it would cost the building owner to have the building completed than if the contractor had completed the job at the contract price. For example, a contractor enters into a contract with building owner to construct a building for $100,000. Then the contractor informs the building owner that he has decided to accept another job elsewhere. At this point, the building owner has not yet paid the contractor any money. Assume that the building owner finds another contractor to complete the project for $150,000. The building owner's expectation damages would be the difference between what he expected to pay for the work ($100,000) and what he ended up having to pay ($150,000). In order to give him the benefit of his bargain, the building owner should get $50,000 in expectation damages (the amount he paid in excess of what he expected to pay under his contract with the contractor). But what if, at the time of the breach, the building owner had paid the contractor $10,000 (and all other facts remained the same)? The building owner's expectation damages would be $60,000 (the $50,000 plus the $10,000 advance payment).

If the cost of completing the job would be grossly disproportionate to the economic benefit of doing so or if it would result in economic waste, the breaching party might argue for diminution in value as the proper measure for damages. Diminution in value applies where the provision breached was incidental to the contract, and not its main purpose.

If we assume that the breaching party was the building owner and the injured party was the contractor, the calculation of expectation damages would differ. The benefit of the bargain for the contractor is not a completed building at the contract price but profit from the job. The contractor's expectation damages are his lost profits and must also include any costs incurred and deduct any payments already made. For example, assume the contract price is $100,000. The contractor estimates it will cost him $60,000 to complete the building. His anticipated profit is $40,000, which would be his expectation damages. Imagine, however, that at the time the building owner breached, the contractor had purchased materials in the amount of $20,000. In order to give the contractor his anticipated profit of $40,000, he should also be reimbursed the $20,000 that he already spent ($40,000 + $20,000 = $60,000). If some of those materials could be resold, that amount should be deducted from his damages calculation. If, for example, the materials could be resold for $15,000, the contractor's damages calculation could be $40,000 (his anticipated profit) + $20,000 (his costs incurred) – $15,000 (the amount he could receive for reselling those materials) = $45,000 (expectation damages).

CLASSIC CASE

PEEVYHOUSE v. GARLAND COAL & MINING CO., 382 P.2d 109 (1962)

The Peevyhouses owned a farm and leased the premises to Garland Coal & Mining Co., ("Garland") so it could strip mine for coal. Garland agreed to perform restorative and remedial work at the end of the five-year lease period. The coal mining company failed to restore the land and the Peevyhouses sued for $25,000 (slightly less than the estimated cost of restoration). Garland introduced expert testimony that the "diminution in value" of plaintiff's farm due to the failure to restore the land as required under the contract was $300. The Peevyhouses argued that the measure of damages is what it would cost them to obtain performance of the work that was not done due to Garland's default. Garland argued that the measure of damages was the cost of performance limited to the total difference in the market value before and after the work was performed.

The court found that the "relative economic benefit" was the proper consideration:

> "We therefore hold that where, in a coal mining lease, lessee agrees to perform certain remedial work on the premises concerned at the end of the lease period, and thereafter the contract is fully performed by both parties except that the remedial work is not done, the measure of damages in an action by the lessor against the lessee for damages for breach of contract is ordinarily the reasonable cost of performance of the work; however where the contract provision breached was merely incidental to the main purpose in view, and where the economic benefit which would

CLASSIC CASE *(continued)*

> result to lessor by full performance is grossly disproportionate to the cost of performance, the damages which lessor may recover are limited to the diminution in value resulting to the premises because of the non-performance."

The court reduced the sum to $300 for the Peevyhouses.

APPLYING WHAT YOU LEARNED

Contract clauses addressing remedies

The Smiths own a ranch in Wyoming. They want to lease their property to Big Wind Co. so it can install energy-generating windmills for a period of 15 years. The ranch is in a beautiful part of the state and has been in the Smith family for generations. It is very important to the Smiths that Big Wind Co. restore the land to its original condition at the end of the lease term. What steps should they take to reduce the likelihood that they will end up like the Peevyhouses?

There are certain limitations on a party's ability to recover expectation damages. The mitigation principle means that an injured party is not permitted to recover damages that could have been avoided by reasonable efforts (note that the party does not have to undertake any undue burden in order to minimize damages). For example, a construction company hired to build a bridge for a town cannot continue building the bridge after the town anticipatorily repudiates.[1] While the construction company can recover lost profits, it cannot recover the costs incurred after it learned of the town's breach.

Another limitation is that the damages must have been reasonably foreseeable. General or direct damages are foreseeable by the nature of the breach. Special or indirect damages (which refer to consequential and incidental damages) are recoverable only if the breaching party knew or should have known about special circumstances which would give rise to these damages. For example, if Mechanic promises to fix Driver's car by Monday and fails to fix it for two weeks, Mechanic should expect that Driver will have to rent a car during that time (which is why most car repair facilities offer a loaner car). Assume, however, that a convention was in town during those two weeks,

1 Rockingham County v. Luten Bridge Co., 35 F.2d 301 (4th Cir. 1929).

taxi drivers were on strike and Driver operates her vehicle as an independent car service (assume regulations prevent her from using a rental car for this purpose). Unless Mechanic knew that Driver used her car to operate a car service business, he would not be liable for her lost profits. If he knew about her car service business, the profits that she would typically make during a two-week period (but could not because of Mechanic's breach) would be reasonably foreseeable. However, even if he did know that she owned a car service business, unless he knew about the convention and the taxi drivers' strike, he would not be liable for Driver's lost profits other than what she would typically make during an ordinary two-week period. Even if he knew about the convention and the taxi drivers' strike, expectation damages must not be speculative, meaning that they must be calculable to a reasonable certainty, and there must be causation, meaning the breach was a substantial factor in causing the damages. Driver will have a hard time proving her lost profits with reasonable certainty. There is too much speculation involved in determining how much money she *would have made* during those two weeks when the convention was in town and the taxi drivers were on strike. These events are one-time events and there is no basis for estimating how much money she would have earned. There must be some basis for arguing for the lost profits, such as a past history of performance.

In some cases, expectation damages may not be appropriate. It may be too difficult or speculative to ascertain damages to a reasonable certainty or the purpose of the contract may not be to make a profit. For example, assume that New Co. is a fledgling software company that has developed software for the banking industry. Because it is a new company without a reputation, New Co. has had trouble landing bank clients. New Co. enters into a contract with Big Bank where New Co. agrees to develop software for Big Bank's operations at a low price. New Co. will have to expend resources greater than what it plans to make on the contract with Big Bank. New Co.'s purpose in entering into the contract with Big Bank is not to make money from the contract, but to make money *in the future* by using its contract with Big Bank to attract other bank customers. If Big Bank breaches, New Co.'s expectation damages would likely be limited to the contract price and would not include the speculative lost profits that New Co. would have (hopefully) made in the future. Expectation damages would not be sufficient to compensate it for the substantial development costs it incurred in reliance upon the contract. An injured party like New Co. may choose to seek reliance damages instead of expectation damages. Reliance damages are the costs incurred in reliance upon the contract. In the New Co. example, the reliance damages include New Co.'s costs in developing the software.

Importantly, reliance damages include even those costs which were incurred *prior* to contract formation with the breaching party. The rationale is that the injured party had incurred costs in contemplation of eventually entering into a contract with someone who could perform and that the breaching party was aware of these previously incurred costs at the time of contract formation.

CLASSIC CASE

SECURITY STOVE & MFG. CO. v. AMERICAN RYS. EXPRESS CO., 227 Mo.App. 176 (1932)

The plaintiff planned to display a furnace at a convention of the American Gas Association in Atlantic City. The furnace was equipped with a special oil and gas burner. Although the plaintiff intended only to show, and not to sell, the furnace, he thought displaying the furnace at the convention would put him in a good position to meet with an executive of a company that was interested in selling oil and gas burners. The plaintiff engaged the defendant to have the furnace shipped express from Kansas City to Atlantic City, explaining to the defendant and emphasizing the need to have it arrive in Atlantic City in time for the convention. The shipment containing the furnace was contained in 21 packages. The plaintiff made arrangements to go to Atlantic City, including renting a booth at the convention. When the plaintiff arrived at the convention, he found the shipment had arrived with only 20 packages. The missing package contained the gas manifold, which was the part of the oil and gas burner that controlled the flow of gas in the burner. This was the most important part of the exhibit and a replacement could not be found. The package eventually arrived after the convention ended and the plaintiff had returned to Kansas.

The plaintiff sued, alleging that he relied upon the defendant's promise to deliver the packages on time, and seeking damages which included the express and freight charges, the railroad fare to Atlantic City from Kansas City, the hotel room, employee wages, and the rental charges for the booth at the convention. The defendant objected that the plaintiff was seeking to recover costs that he would have had to incur anyway, even if the contract had been performed. The court stated:

"There were no profits contemplated. The furnace was to be shown and shipped back to Kansas City. There was no money loss, except the expenses, that was of such a nature as any court would allow as being sufficiently definite or lacking in pure speculation. Therefore, unless plaintiff is permitted to recover the expenses that it went to, which were a total loss to it by reason of its inability to exhibit the furnace and equipment, it will be deprived of any substantial compensation for its loss. The law does not contemplate any such injustice. It ought to allow plaintiff, as damages, the loss in the way of expenses that it sustained, and which it would not have been put to if it had not been for its reliance upon the defendant to perform its contract. There is no contention that the exhibit would have been entirely

CLASSIC CASE *(continued)*

valueless and whatever it might have accomplished defendant knew of the circumstances and ought to respond for whatever damages plaintiff suffered. In cases of this kind the method of estimating the damages should be adopted which is the most definite and certain and which best achieves the fundamental purpose of compensation . . .

While it is true that plaintiff had already incurred some of these expenses . . . before entering into the contract . . . plaintiff arranged for the exhibit knowing that it could call upon defendant to perform its common law duty to accept and transport the shipment . . . The whole damage, therefore, was suffered in contemplation of defendant performing its contract, which it failed to do, and would not have been sustained except for the reliance by plaintiff upon defendant to perform it. It can, therefore, be fairly said that the damages or loss suffered by plaintiff grew out of the breach of the contract, for had the shipment arrived on time, plaintiff would have had the benefit of the contract, which was contemplated by all parties, defendant being advised of the purpose of the shipment."

Reflection Prompt: Do you think the plaintiff would have eventually tried to make money from his furnace?

Another alternative to the expectation measure is restitution. Restitution is the recapture of a benefit conferred which would leave one party unjustly enriched. Restitution is granted where the breach by a party is substantial and essentially means that the other party is seeking to rescind or undo the contract. In other words, restitution is not based upon the contract and for the non-breaching party the recovery amount may even exceed the contract price. Restitution is not available if the party seeking restitution has fully performed and no performance by the other party remains due except for the payment of a definite sum of money.[2] Restitution is mutual in nature, meaning that the breaching party must return the value of the performance received by the other party but the non-breaching party must also return any benefit received. Even the breaching party can seek restitution as long as the breach was not willful. Recovery for the breaching party (unlike for the non-breaching party) cannot exceed the contract price.

2 RESTATEMENT (SECOND) CONTRACTS, §373.

CLASSIC CASE

OSTEEN v. JOHNSON, 473 P.2d 184 (1970)

Osteen hired Johnson to help her record and promote her new album. They agreed that Johnson would advertise Osteen through mailings for one year, arrange and furnish recording facilities for her to use, prepare two records, press and mail copies of one of the records and, if the first was successful, press and mail copies of the second record. Osteen sued Johnson and sought return of the amounts she had paid to him, alleging that he did not promote her and failed to press and mail copies of her second record even though the first was successful. The court found that although Johnson did promote her, he failed to press and mail the second record and that this failure was a substantial breach that justified the remedy of restitution. Because the defendant did partially perform, the court stated that he, too, should be compensated for the reasonable value of his services:

> "It shall, therefore, be the ultimate order of this court that prior to restoring to the plaintiffs the $2,500 paid by them to the defendant, further proceedings be held during which the trial court shall determine the reasonable value of the services which the defendant rendered on plaintiffs behalf."

Reflection Prompt: Why were expectation damages inappropriate in this case?

The UCC contains damages measures which apply where the contract involves a sale of goods. The UCC damages provisions allow the injured party a certain amount of flexibility to protect its commercial interests in the event of breach. If the buyer breaches, the seller has the option to resell the goods and sue for the difference between the resale price and the contract price, and/or withhold delivery or stop delivery of the goods.[3] The injured buyer also has options if the seller breaches. She may cover, which means that she may in good faith and without unreasonable delay buy substitute goods. If she covers, the UCC allows her the difference between the cover price and the contract price. She does not, however, have to cover. If she doesn't cover, she gets the difference between the market price and the contract price. If the buyer accepts the goods, but they are nonconforming, the seller has still breached the contract (i.e. a breach of warranty) and the buyer is entitled to damages. In that case, the buyer would receive the difference between the value of the goods accepted and the value they would have been if they had

3 UCC §2-703.

been as warranted.[4] In a breach of warranty scenario, courts have determined that the cost of repair provides the adequate measure *even if the cost of repairing the goods exceeds the contract price for the goods.* The seller may want to include a provision that limits the buyer's recovery and the seller's liability and/or allows the seller discretion to select the best remedial measure.

Example clause

Seller warrants that the Products are free of defects in materials and workmanship under normal use and service. Seller's *sole* obligation under this warranty shall be to repair or replace, at seller's option, without charge, any parts which shall prove defective within 24 months from date of delivery. This warranty is in lieu of any representation or warranty, express or implied, including, but not limited to, the warranty of merchantability and the warranty of fitness for a particular purpose.

Example clause

LIMITATION OF LIABILITY. Except as otherwise agreed herein, the Seller shall not be liable for special or consequential damages, such as, but not limited to, damage or loss of other property or equipment, loss of profits or revenue, loss of use of power system, cost of capital, cost of purchased or replacement power, or claims of customers of purchaser for service interruptions. The remedies of the purchaser set forth herein are exclusive, and the liability of Seller with respect to any contract, or anything done in connection therewith such as the performance or breach thereof, or from the manufacture, sale, delivery, resale, installation or technical direction of installation, repair or use of any equipment covered by or furnished under this contract whether in contract, in tort, under any warranty, or otherwise, shall not, except as expressly provided herein, exceed the price of the equipment or part on which such liability is based.

Reflection Prompt: Examine the differences between the two Example Clauses above. Could you draft a better clause by using language from each clause?

The UCC permits exclusive remedies and limitations of liability, including exclusion of consequential damages, as long as the limitation or exclusion is not unconscionable and as long as circumstances do not cause the limited or

4 UCC §2-714.

exclusive remedy to "fail of its essential purpose."[5] A remedy fails of its essential purpose if it deprives a party of a substantial benefit of the bargain even if it seems reasonable on its face.[6] For example, a seller's warranty to "repair or replace" defective goods may deprive the buyer of the benefit of the bargain if the seller is unwilling to repair or replace the good within a reasonable time.[7]

The UCC permits limitation of consequential damages unless the exclusion or limitation is unconscionable and expressly states that excluding consequential damages for personal injury in the case of consumer goods is "prima facie unconscionable."[8] There are also consumer protection statutes that limit the effectiveness of such clauses in the context of consumer goods and services. By contrast, courts typically uphold such clauses in commercial transactions between two businesses where the loss is economic.[9]

A question arises regarding whether, under the UCC, a consequential damages disclaimer is effective even where a remedy fails of its essential purpose. There are three different approaches.[10] The dependent approach finds that a limited remedy which fails of its essential purpose destroys any limitation or exclusion of consequential damages in the contract.[11] Under this approach, the enforceability of the consequential damages exclusion *depends* upon the validity of the limitation of remedy. The independent approach adopts the view that a limitation of consequential damages must be judged on its own merits and enforced unless unconscionable, regardless of whether a limited remedy failed of its essential purpose.[12] A third, and less common approach, is the case-by-case approach, which examines the individual facts of the case, including the type of goods, the parties, and the precise nature

5 UCC §2-719.

6 City of New York v. Bell Helicopter Textron, Inc., 2015 WL 3767241 (E.D. N.Y. June 16, 2015) at *6.

7 *Id.* at 7 (citing to JAMES J. WHITE, ROBERT S. SUMMERS & ROBERT A. HILLMAN, UNIFORM COMMERCIAL CODE §13:20 (6th ed. 2014).

8 UCC §2-719(3).

9 Cayuga Harvester, Inc. v. Allis-Chalmers Corp., 95 A.D.2d 5, 20 (N.Y. App.1983) ("In cases involving transactions of a commercial nature, courts have rarely found unconscionability and it has been held that 'when businessmen contract in a commercial setting, a presumption of conscionability arises'") (citations omitted). *But see* Tokyo Ohka Kogyo America, Inc. v. Huntsman Propylene Oxide LLC, 35 F. Supp. 3d 1316 (D. Ore. 2014) (finding limitation of liability clause between two businesses unconscionable and unenforceable).

10 Razor v. Hyundai Motor America, 854 N.E.2d 607, 615–622 (2006) (discussing dependent, independent and case-by-case approach and concluding that the independent approach accords best with the UCC and is the better reasoned one).

11 Adams v. J.I. Case Co., 125 Ill. App. 2d 388, 402–403, 261 N.E.2d 1 (1970) (finding that "limitations of remedy and of liability are not separable from the obligations of the warranty").

12 Chatlos Systems v. National Cash Register Corp., 635 F.2d 1081, 1086 (3d Cir. 1980) (finding the "better reasoned approach" is to "treat consequential damage disclaimer as an independent provision, valid unless unconscionable").

and purpose of the contract.[13] Although the dependent approach used to be the majority view, the majority of jurisdictions now follow the independent approach.[14]

Generally, consequential and incidental damages are available under the UCC. These can be limited or excluded by the parties in their contract through limitation of liability provisions.

Table 8.1 summarizes the limitation of liability provisions under the UCC.

Table 8.1 Summary of limitation of liability provisions under UCC §2-719

Type of limitation of liability (§2-719)	Requirements	Split views
Exclusion of consequential damages	Must not be unconscionable (§2-719(3)) – exclusion for bodily injury in case of consumer goods considered unconscionable – does limitation *operate* in an unconscionable manner? (§2-719(3) cmt. 3) – *Cf*: §2-302(1) – looks at facts at time of contract formation	Should unconscionability be determined at time of contract formation or should it consider parties' conduct and facts arising after formation?
Exclusive remedies (e.g. repair, replace, or refund)	Must not "fail of essential purpose" (§2-719(2))	If remedy fails of essential purpose, does consequential damages exclusion also fail? Two main views: *Independent approach* (majority) – No; consequential damages provision should be enforced unless unconscionable. *Dependent approach* – Yes; enforceability of consequential damages exclusion depends upon the validity of limitation of remedy.

13 AES Technology Systems, Inc. v. Coherent Radiation, 583 F.2d 933, 941 (7th Cir. 1978).

14 Razor v. Hyundai Motor America, 854 N.E.2d 607, 616–617 (noting that while the dependent approach may have been the majority view 15–20 years ago, "the majority of jurisdictions" now follow the independent approach.).

The UCC's various provisions often cause much confusion as they interrelate and may sometimes seem to conflict with one another. The creation of a warranty – and the effectiveness of a warranty disclaimer – should be distinguished from the liability which attaches to a warranty.[15] The UCC permits parties to limit their liability or the available remedy for breach of warranty. They may also disclaim warranties *altogether*, in which case there would be no breach of warranty – and thus no recovery for its breach.[16] Finally, some states prohibit certain types of limitations or exclusions which is why the parties may want to include the following provision in their limitation of liability clause:

Example clause

Some states do not allow limitations on how long an implied warranty lasts, or the exclusion or limitation of incidental and consequential damages, so the limitations or exclusions set forth regarding this limited warranty may not apply to you. You may also have other rights which vary from state to state.

Caveat: Some consumer protection statutes do not permit a general statement that a limitation of liability clause is invalid in "some states"; rather, the clause must specify the states which do not permit the clause.[17]

The availability of limitation of liability provisions is not limited to transactions governed by the UCC.[18] There are different ways that parties can limit their liability. They can limit the amount of damages, exclude certain types of damages, or limit the type of damages for which they may be found liable:

---

15 *See* City of New York v. Bell Helicopter Textron, Inc., 2015 WL 3767241 (E.D.N.Y. June 16, 2015) (noting that "whether a remedy fails of its essential purpose under UCC §2-719 is entirely separate from whether the seller has properly disclaimed warranties under UCC §2-316(2)"). *Id.* at 8.

16 UCC §2-316 cmt. 2 (noting that the UCC treats limitations of remedy separately from the creation of liability under a warranty and that "[i]f no warranty exists, there is of course no problem of limiting remedies for breach of warranty.").

17 *See* N.J. Stat. Ann. § 56:12-16 ("No consumer contract, warranty, notice or sign as provided for in this act, shall contain any provision by which the consumer waives his rights under this act. Any such provision shall be null and void. No consumer contract, notice or sign shall state that any of its provisions is or may be void, unenforceable or inapplicable in some jurisdictions without specifying which provisions are or are not void, unenforceable or inapplicable within the State of New Jersey; provided, however, that this shall not apply to warranties.").

18 CompuSpa, Inc., v. IBM, 228 F.Supp. 2d 613, 626 (D. Md. 2002) ("New York courts generally enforce limitation of liability clauses in breach of contract and tort actions 'unless a special relationship between the parties, a statute, or public policy imposes liability.' Metropolitan Life Ins. Co. v. Noble Lowndes Int'l, Inc., 192 A.D.2d 83, 89, 600 N.Y.S.2d 212, 215 (N.Y. App. Div. 1993); Mom's Bagels of New York, Inc. v. Greenebaum, 164 A.D.2d 820, 559 N.Y.S.2d 883 (N.Y. App. Div. 1990); Rivkin v. Brackman, 167 A.D.2d 239, 561 N.Y.S.2d 738 (N.Y. App. Div. 1990).").

Example clause

IN NO EVENT WILL EITHER PARTY BE LIABLE TO THE OTHER IN CONTRACT OR TORT OR OTHERWISE FOR ANY LOST REVENUES, LOST PROFITS, INCIDENTAL, INDIRECT, CONSEQUENTIAL, SPECIAL OR PUNITIVE DAMAGES.

Example clause

TO THE FULLEST EXTENT PERMITTED BY LAW, AND NOTWITHSTANDING ANY OTHER PROVISION OF THIS AGREEMENT, THE TOTAL LIABILITY, IN THE AGGREGATE, OF THE COMPANY AND THE COMPANY'S OFFICERS, DIRECTORS, PARTNERS, EMPLOYEES AND CONTRACTORS, AND ANY OF THEM, TO THE CUSTOMER AND ANYONE CLAIMING BY OR THROUGH THE CUSTOMER FOR ANY AND ALL CLAIMS, LOSSES, COSTS OF DAMAGES, INCLUDING ATTORNEYS' FEES, AND COSTS AND/ OR FEES OF ANY NATURE WHATSOEVER OR CLAIMS EXPENSES RESULTING FROM OR IN ANY WAY RELATED TO THE AGREEMENT FROM ANY CAUSE OR CAUSES SHALL NOT EXCEED THE TOTAL MONEY AMOUNTS RECEIVED BY THE COMPANY UNDER THIS AGREEMENT, OR THE TOTAL AMOUNT OF $10,000, WHICHEVER IS GREATER. IT IS INTENDED THAT THIS LIMITATION APPLY TO ANY AND ALL LIABILITY OR CAUSE OF ACTION HOWEVER ALLEGED OR ARISING, UNLESS OTHERWISE PROHIBITED BY LAW.

Example clause

NEITHER PARTY SHALL BE LIABLE TO THE OTHER FOR LOSS OF PROFITS OR REVENUE; LOSS OF USE OR OPPORTUNITY; LOSS OF GOODWILL; COST OF SUBSTITUTE FACILITIES, GOODS OR SERVICES; COST OF CAPITAL; OR FOR ANY SPECIAL CONSEQUENTIAL, INDIRECT, PUNITIVE, OR EXEMPLARY DAMAGES.

CUSTOMER AGREES TO LIMIT THE COMPANY'S LIABILITY TO THE CUSTOMER TO THE TOTAL FEES PAID BY CUSTOMER TO COMPANY. THIS LIMITATION APPLIES REGARDLESS OF THE CAUSE OF ACTION OR LEGAL THEORY PLED OR ASSERTED.

Reflection Prompt: There is a potential problem with all three clauses if they appear in a contract for the sale of consumer goods. Can you guess what it is?

It may be helpful to distinguish three different types of clauses: limitation of liability, exculpatory, and indemnity.[19] All three clauses raise policy concerns although generally, courts are more likely to enforce provisions that seek to limit liability than provisions that seek to preclude liability altogether.[20]

A limitation of liability clause limits the amount and/or type of damages a party would have to pay under the contract. The enforceability of limitation of liability clauses varies from state to state because they raise public policy concerns. Some drafters include a provision expressly stating that the limitation is subject to applicable law:

Example clause

TO THE FULLEST EXTENT PERMITTED BY LAW, IN NO EVENT SHALL SELLER OR ITS SUPPLIERS HAVE ANY LIABILITY FOR ANY SPECIAL, INDIRECT OR CONSEQUENTIAL DAMAGES INCLUDING, WITHOUT LIMITATION, DAMAGES FOR LOST PROFITS, OR COSTS OF PROCUREMENT OF SUBSTITUTE GOODS, TECHNOLOGY OR SERVICES, ARISING IN ANY WAY OUT OF THIS AGREEMENT UNDER ANY CAUSE OF ACTION, WHETHER OR NOT SELLER HAS BEEN ADVISED OF THE POSSIBILITY OF SUCH DAMAGES. THIS SECTION DOES NOT LIMIT LIABILITY FOR BODILY INJURY OF A PERSON.

---

19 Valhal Corp. v. Sullivan Associates, Inc., 44 F.3d 195, 202 (3d Cir. 1995) (noting that "there are (real) differences between a contract which insulates a party from liability," such as exculpatory clauses and indemnity and hold harmless clauses, "and one which merely places a limit upon that liability"); Fort Knox Self Storage, Inc. v. Western Technologies, Inc., 140 N.M. 233, 142 P.3d 1, 5 (N.M. Ct. App. 2006) ([t]he limitation of liability clause in this case does not seek to contract away all liability for Western's negligence but seeks to limit the amount of damages Western must pay for its own negligence"); Blaisdell v. Dentrix Dental Sys., 284 P.3d 616, 622 (Utah 2012) (finding a limitation of liability clause enforceable) *But cf*: Lanier at McEver, L.P., 284 Ga. 204, 663 S.E.2d 240 (2008), (finding the limitation of liability clause violated Georgia public policy as set forth in the relevant statute which stated that an agreement in connection with a construction contract "purporting to indemnify or hold harmless the promisee against liability for damages arising out of bodily injury or damage to property caused by or resulting from the sole negligence of the promisee . . . is against public policy and is void and unenforceable.") *Id.* at 242 (quoting Official Code of Georgia Annotated §13-8-2(b)).

20 Saia Food Distribs. & Club, Inc. v. SecurityLink from Ameritech, Inc., 902 So. 2d 46, 54 (Ala. 2004) ("We do not interpret this language as allowing SecurityLink to escape all liability for any breach of its contract with Saia Food or for SecurityLink's negligence, if any. SecurityLink and Saia Food merely agreed to limit the amount of damages for which SecurityLink could be held responsible. The parties' agreement to limit SecurityLink's exposure is enforceable"); Prescription Counter v. AmerisourceBergen Corp., 2007 U.S. Dist. LEXIS 84102, at *34 (D.N.J. Nov. 14, 2007) (Georgia state law allows parties to limit liability and limit or exclude consequential damages unless unconscionable).

A limitation of liability clause must be prominent, clear and unambiguous[21] and intended by the parties.[22] The clause must include the types of risks that are covered or a court may decide that the clause does not apply to a particular action. For example, a clause that is intended to limit liability for a party's negligent acts should specifically mention that it covers a party's negligent acts.[23] Other factors considered by the courts are whether the parties were free to bargain during contract negotiations,[24] the amount of the limitation, especially compared to the potential liability of the party seeking enforcement, and whether there are conflicting provisions.[25] As a general rule, if the clause seeks to free a party from any and all liability for breach, or if the limitation amount is too low, it is less likely to be enforceable.

Here are some examples of disputed limitation of liability provisions with a brief discussion of whether they were found enforceable.

Example #1

"7. LIMITATION OF LIABILITIES. In no event will Dentrix be liable to you for any indirect, incidental, consequential, special, or exemplary damages arising out of or in connection with your use or inability to use the Product, the breach of any express or implied warranty, or otherwise in connection with the Product, its Software, the Documentation and/or the license even if Dentrix has been advised of the possibility of such damages. In no event shall Dentrix be held liable to you whenever registry files are examined and/or

21 Monitronics Int'l, Inc. v. Veasley, 323 Ga. App. 126, 135–136 (2013) (limitation of liability clause on back of one-page, two-sided contract which is not set off in its own paragraph and which appears toward the end of long sentence and is not capitalized, lacked requisite indicia of prominence, and was unenforceable.).

22 Turnbough v. Ladner, 754 So. 2d 467, 469 (Miss. 1999) (limitation of liability clauses must be "fairly and honestly negotiated and understandingly entered into" and "are not upheld unless the intention of the parties is expressed in clear and unmistakable language").

23 Gross v. Sweet, 49 N.Y.2d 102, 109; 400 N.E.2d 306, 311 (1979) (stating that although "the law grudgingly accepts the proposition that men may contract away their liability for negligently caused injuries, they may do so only on the condition that their intention be expressed clearly and in 'unequivocal terms'").

24 Thrash Commer. Consts., Inc. v. Terracon Consultants, Inc., 889 F. Supp. 2d 868, 873 (S.D. Miss. 2012) ("[A] party's ability to negotiate with respect to a clause that limits liability [which here would include the limitation of liability clause as well as the waiver of consequential damages provision], bears directly on the enforceability of such provision . . . under Mississippi law, "[c]lauses that limit liability are given strict scrutiny . . . and are not to be enforced unless the limitation is fairly and honestly negotiated and understood by both parties") (citations omitted).

25 TSI Seismic Tenant Space, Inc. v. Superior Court, 149 Cal. App. 4th 159, 167 (finding "it was an abuse of discretion for the court to only consider what Geocon would *pay* to Sunbow by virtue of the limitation of liability clause, without also considering its proportionate share of *culpability*, and its potential for liability to TSI, Swanson, and the other defendants for indemnity").

edited. Because some states do not allow the exclusion or limitation of liability for consequential or incidental damages, the above limitation may not apply to you.

In no event shall Dentrix's total liability for any damages, direct or indirect, in connection with the Product, its Software, the Documentation and/or this License exceed the license fees paid for your right to use this Product whether such liability arises from any claim based upon contract, warrants, tort or otherwise."[26]

[Court held that provision properly limits liability of Dentrix for tort claims, was not unconscionable, was entered into between two sophisticated parties, and the remedy provisions did not fail of their essential purpose. The court also held that provision did not violate Utah Products Liability Act, which renders unenforceable sales contracts that require a purchase or end user to indemnify manufacturer for harms caused by defective product. The clause was a limitation of liability and not an indemnification clause.]

Example #2

> "Lessor shall not be liable for damages to person or property sustained by the Lessee, his family, servants, agents or visitors, due to the building or any of the appurtenances being out of repair or arising from leakage or stoppage of gas, plumbing, steam, water, sewer pipes or from defective wiring or from defective construction of any of the aforesaid. It is agreed that the common areas and grounds, on which the demise premises are located, recreational facilities, laundry rooms and equipment, hallways, walkways, stairways, parking lots, lawns and all other areas and equipment to be used in common by all occupants of the apartment building and grounds, are provided and maintained gratuitously by Lessor, and that their use is not appurtenant to the premises hereby leased; and the Lessee hereby expressly agrees that the same shall be made use of Lessee, his family, servants, agents or visitors, such use shall be at his, or their own risk, and that the lessor shall, in no event, be, or become liable thereby for any loss, or damage, to persons or property, whether such property be contained in the storerooms, in the common areas, in the leased premises or in any other portion of said building and grounds, even though such loss or damage shall be caused by the negligence of Lessor, or its agents, servants, or employees."[27]

[Court found clause was against public policy because of the vast number of people affected by residential leases, the inequality of bargaining power caused by the need for housing, the fact that people who are not parties to the contract could suffer as a result of the clause, and desire to promote responsible maintenance by landlords to avoid personal injuries by tenants and third parties.][28]

---

26 Blaisdell v. Dentrix Dental Sys., 284 P.3d 616, 617 (Utah 2012).

27 Ransburg v. Richards, 770 N.E.2d 393, 394 (Ind. Ct. App., 2002).

28 *Id.* at 402–403.

EXAMPLE #3

"agrees to and shall indemnify and save harmless the Contractor * * * for and against any claims, suits, losses, demands and expenses arising from any death of or injury to any person or any loss or damage to property occasioned or alleged to be occasioned by Contractor's * * * performance or failure to perform its obligations under this agreement whether due to Contractor's negligence or otherwise."[29]

[Court found that clause was an invalid limitation of liability under New York statute prohibiting limitation of liability for contractor's negligence.]

EXAMPLE #4

"[t]his receipt is a storage contract, articles listed are accepted for storage until December 31, of dated year, subject to the terms and conditions hereof, in accepting this receipt, the depositor agrees to be bound by all its terms and conditions and acknowledges that this receipt is the entire agreement with the furrier, which cannot be changed except by endorsement herein signed by the furrier. If no value is specified, or if no separate insurance covering the garment is declared at the time of issuance of this receipt, insurance in the amount of $1.00 will be placed on the garment . . . I understand and agree that Cedar Lane Furs' liability for loss or damage from any cause whatsoever, including their own negligence or that of employees and others, is limited to the declared valuation."[30]

[Court found clause was unenforceable because contract was pre-printed form, plaintiff had no opportunity to negotiate terms and was in inferior bargaining position, defendant did not bring the limitation to plaintiff's attention or inquire as to value of each fur piece nor did form provide a space to include valuation figure, and fire was caused by defendant's negligence.][31]

EXAMPLE #5

"16. Liability. Neither BANKDIRECT nor its assignee shall be liable for any loss or damage to the Insured by reason of failure of any insurance company to issue or maintain in force any of the Policies or by reason of the exercise by BANKDIRECT or its assignee of the rights conferred herein, including, but not limited to BANKDIRECT's exercise of the right of cancellation, except in the event of willful or intentional misconduct by BANKDIRECT."

[Court found that BankDirect did not meet its burden of establishing as a matter of that limitation of liability met fair notice requirement of conspicuousness. Clause was located in paragraph 16, in the second column of page that appeared to be the third page of the agreement, and clause was in the same small print and font as the rest of the agreement. No symbols or other marks called attention to it, language was not bolded or in caps, apart from the name "BANKDIRECT" and the heading was "Liability" instead of "Limitation of Liability."][32]

---

29 Tate v. Clancy – Cullen Storage Co., 577 N.Y.S.2d 377, 378 (1991).

30 Jasphy v. Osinsky, 364 N.J. Super. 13, 16 (Superior Ct. New Jersey, November 5, 2003).

31 *Id.* at 17.

32 Plasma Fab. LLC v. BankDirect Capital Finance, LLC, 468 S.W. 3d 121, 128 (Tex. App. – Austin 2015).

CLASSIC CASE

HADLEY v. BAXENDALE, 9 Exch. 341, 156 Eng. Rep. 145 (1854)

Plaintiffs owned a flour mill whose engine crank shaft broke, which prevented the milling of corn. They sent an employee to the office of the defendants to have the crank shaft delivered for repair. The employee told the carrier that the mill was stopped and that the shaft must be sent immediately. The delivery of the shaft was delayed by neglect of the carriers and the consequence was that the plaintiffs did not receive the new shaft for several days and they lost profits due to the inability to operate the mill. The defendants argued that the lost profits sought by plaintiffs were too remote. The court stated:

"Where two parties have made a contract which one of them has broken, the damages which the other party ought to receive in respect of such breach of contract should be such as may fairly and reasonably be considered either arising naturally, i.e., according to the usual course of things, from such breach of contract itself, or such as may reasonably be supposed to have been in the contemplation of both parties, at the time they made the contract, as the probable result of the breach of it. Now, if the special circumstances under which the contract was actually made were communicated by the plaintiffs to the defendants, and thus known to both parties, the damages resulting from the breach of such a contract, which they would reasonably contemplate, would be the amount of injury which would ordinarily follow from a breach of contract under these special circwumstances so known and communicated. But, on the other hand, if these special circumstances were wholly unknown to the party breaking the contract, he, at the most, could only be supposed to have had in his contemplation the amount of injury which would arise generally, and in the great multitude of cases not affected by any special circumstances, from such a breach of contract. For had the special circumstances been known, the parties might have specially provided for the breach of contract by special terms as to the damages in that case, and of this advantage it would be very unjust to deprive them . . .

CLASSIC CASE *(continued)*

Now, in the present case . . . we find that the only circumstances here communicated by the plaintiffs to the defendants at the time the contract was made, were, that the article to be carried was the broken shaft of a mill, and that the plaintiffs were the millers of that mill.

But how do these circumstances shew reasonably that the profits of the mill must be stopped by an unreasonable delay in the delivery of the broken shaft by the carrier to the third person? Suppose the plaintiffs had another shaft in their possession put up or putting up at the time, and that they only wished to send back the broken shaft to the engineer who made it . . . Or, again, suppose that, at the time of the delivery to the carrier, the machinery of the mill had been in other respects defective, then, also, the same results would follow. Here it is true that the shaft was actually sent back to serve as a model for a new one, and that the want of a new one was the only cause of the stoppage of the mill, and that the loss of profits really arose from not sending down the new shaft in proper time, and that this arose from the delay in delivering the broken one to serve as a model. But it is obvious that, in the great multitude of cases of millers sending off broken shafts to third persons by a carrier under ordinary circumstances, such consequences would not, in all probability, have occurred; and these special circumstances were here never communicated by the plaintiffs to the defendants. It follows, therefore, that the loss of profits here cannot reasonably be considered such a consequence of the breach of contract as could have been fairly and reasonably contemplated by both the parties when they made this contract."

The court concluded that since the loss was not one that would have "flowed naturally" from breach of this kind of contract nor were the special circumstances communicated to or known by the defendants, loss of profits should not be taken into consideration in estimating plaintiffs' damages.

APPLYING WHAT YOU LEARNED

Contract clauses addressing remedies

1. What steps should the mill take the next time its crank shaft breaks and it needs to get it repaired as soon as possible? (Please assume that the defendant is the only shipping company in the county.)
2. What should (and do) shipping companies do to avoid having to pay for consequential damages in event of shipping delay?

Jurisdictions are split on the issue of whether exculpatory and indemnity clauses are enforceable.[33] An exculpatory clause frees one party from liability to the other party for a negligent or wrongful act:[34]

Example of exculpatory clause

In consideration for this service, I, individually and on behalf of my child, do hereby waive, release and forever discharge SuperMax Corp., its subsidiaries and affiliates and their respective agents, employees, officers, directors, shareholders, successors and assigns from any and all claims and causes of action of any kind or nature which are in any way related, directly or indirectly, to the use of SuperMax's facilities which I may have or that hereafter may accrue including any such claims or causes of action caused in whole or in part by the negligence of SuperMax Corp., its subsidiaries and affiliates, and their respective agents, employees, officers, directors, successors and assigns.

An indemnity clause makes one party responsible for the harms or losses that might be incurred by the other party:

Example of indemnification clause

I agree to indemnify, defend and hold harmless SuperMax, its subsidiaries and affiliates and their respective agents, employees, officers, directors, successors and assigns from any claims or causes of action of any kind arising from my or my child's use of the SuperMax facilities. By placing my signature below, I acknowledge and agree that I have read this agreement, understand all of the terms and conditions contained herein, and that this agreement will be in full force and effect during each of my visits to SuperMax.

Reflection Prompt: Should a contract contain both an exculpatory and indemnification provision in the same paragraph or should a drafter separate each into its own paragraph? Why or why not?

---

33 Ransburg v. Richards, 770 N.E.2d 393, 399 (C.A., Indiana, June 20, 2002) (Noting that there is "no majority rule" on the issue of exculpatory clauses).

34 BJ's Wholesale Club, Inc. v. Rosen, 435 Md. 714 at 724; 80 A.3d 345 (November 27, 2013).

Some states have statutes prohibiting indemnity or exculpatory provisions in certain contracts (such as construction contracts) if they seek to indemnify against one's own negligence[35] but others do not.[36] Many states have provisions invalidating waivers in residential leases and rental agreements.[37] Even in the absence of legislation expressly prohibiting such clauses, courts may still invalidate indemnity or exculpatory clauses if they determine they are against the public interest[38] or against public policy.[39] A clause is against public policy if it violates an expressed objective of the state constitution or the legislature or if it tends to injure the public or the public good.[40] Courts have tended to distin-

35 68 Pa. Stat. Ann. §491 (voiding agreements indemnifying architects, engineers, and surveyors from losses arising out of their work), NMSA 1978, §56-7-1 (a provision in construction contract indemnifying a party for its negligence, acts or omissions is void and against public policy); Cal. Civ. Code §2782 (barring indemnity for a party's "sole negligence" or "willful misconduct" of the promise in construction contracts); Cal. Civ. Code §1668 ("All contracts which have for their object, directly or indirectly, to exempt anyone from responsibility for his own fraud, or willful injury to the person or property of another, or violation of law, whether willful or negligent, are against the policy of the law"); Utah Code Ann. §13-8-1 (indemnification in construction contracts is void and unenforceable where covers damages "caused by or resulting from the fault of the promisee, indemnitee, others, or their agents or employees"); Utah Code Ann. §78B-6-707 (indemnification provision in sales contract that requires purchaser or end user to indemnify manufacturer is void if product defect caused injury or death).

36 Marshall v. Blue Springs Corp., 641 N.E.2d 92, 96 (C.A., Indiana, October 19, 1994) (stating that "in the absence of legislation to the contrary, it is not against public policy to enter into an agreement which exculpates one from the consequences of his own negligence" and noting that Indiana does not have such legislation); Sommer v. Federal Signal Corp., 79 N.Y.2d 540, 593 N.E.2d 1365 (Ct. of Appeal, NY, May 12, 1992) ("Absent a statute or public policy to the contrary, a contractual provision absolving a party from its own negligence will be enforced . . . however, a party may not insulate itself from damages caused by grossly negligent conduct . . . This applies equally to contract clauses purporting to exonerate a party from liability and clauses limiting damages to a nominal sum"). *Id.* at 553–554.

37 CA Civ. Code §1953 (voiding as contrary to public policy, "any provision of a lease or rental agreement of a dwelling by which the lessee agrees to modify or waive" certain rights or remedies, including right to notice or hearing required by law and right to have landlord exercise duty of care to prevent personal injury or personal property damage where that duty is imposed by law").

38 In determining whether a contract affects the public interest, many courts apply the factors set forth in Tunkl v. Regents of University of California, 60 Cal. 2d 92 (1963).

39 Monitronics Int'l, Inc. v. Veasley, 323 Ga. App. 126, 746 S.E.2d 793 (2013) (stating that it is "well settled that exculpatory clauses in which a business seeks to relieve itself from its own negligence are valid and binding in this State, 'and are not void as against public policy unless they purport to relieve liability for acts of gross negligence or wilful or wanton conduct' [citation omitted]. Nevertheless, because exculpatory clauses may amount to 'an accord and satisfaction of future claims and waive substantial rights, they require a meeting of the minds on the subject matter and must be explicit, prominent, clear and unambiguous' [citation omitted]. Moreover, any ambiguities in exculpatory clauses are 'construed against the drafters'" [citations omitted]. *Id.* at 134.

40 *See* Trotte v. Nelson, 684 N.E.2d, 1150, 1152–1153 (Ind. 1997) (noting that three situations where courts have refused to enforce private agreements on public policy grounds: "(i) agreements that contravene statute; (ii) agreements that clearly tend to injure the public in some way; and (iii) agreements that are otherwise contrary to the declared public policy of Indiana"); Tunkl v. Regents of University of California, 60 Cal. 2d 92, 96 (1963) (noting that while cases interpreting Cal. Civ. Code §1668 have been diverse, they have all "consistently held that the exculpatory provision may stand only if it does not involve 'the public interest'"); Lewis Operating Corp. v. Superior Court, 200 Cal. App. 4th 940, 941 (2011) (an exculpatory clause where the party seeking exculpation is engaged in performing a service "of great importance to the public, which is often a matter of practical necessity for some members of the public" affects the public interest and cannot stand).

guish those transactions involving an essential service, such as housing or child care, from those that involve recreational activities and have found that while the former involve the public interest, the latter do not.[41] Some states, however, have voided agreements for certain types of recreational activities and many states (but not all) have held that a parent may not release a minor's prospective claim for negligence.[42] Most jurisdictions recognize an exculpatory clause that relieves a party for negligence but will find that a provision seeking to exculpate a party for willful or gross negligence or recklessness is against public policy.[43]

CASE HIGHLIGHT

ROSENCRANS v. DOVER IMAGES, LTD., 192 Cal. App. 4th 1072 (2011)

As Plaintiff was driving into a motocross track facility with several cars behind him, he was handed a document and told to "Sign this." The document was titled "Release and Waiver of Liability Assumption of Risk and Indemnity Agreement" and contained nine paragraphs including the following language:

---

41 Lewis Operating Corp., *supra* note 39, at 947 (stating that "the law has . . . been consistent in enforcing exculpatory clauses, releases, and waivers in the recreational context" and enforcing a clause exculpating landlord from liability for an injury at onsite health club). *But cf:* N.Y. Gen. Obligations § 5-326 (Agreements which exempt operators of fee-paid "places of public amusement or recreation" from liability for negligence are "void as against public policy and wholly unenforceable").

42 Hawkins ex rel. Hawkins v. Peart, 2001 UT 94, 37 P.3d 1062–1066 (a "clear majority of courts treating the issue have held that a parent may not release a minor's prospective claim for negligence", citing Fedor v. Mauwehu Council, Boy Scouts of Am., 21 Conn. Supp. 38, 143 A.2d 466, 467–468 (Conn. Super. Ct. 1958); Meyer v. Naperville Manner, Inc., 262 Ill. App. 3d 141, 634 N.E.2d 411, 414–415, 199 Ill. Dec. 572 (Ill. App. Ct. 1994); Doyle v. Bowdoin Coll., 403 A.2d 1206, 1208 n.3 (Me. 1979); Fitzgerald v. Newark Morning Ledger Co., 111 N.J. Super. 104, 267 A.2d 557, 558–559 (N.J. Super. Ct. Law Div. 1970); Childress v. Madison County, 777 S.W.2d 1, 6–7 (Tenn. Ct. App. 1989); Munoz v. II Jaz Inc., 863 S.W.2d 207, 209–210 (Tex. App. 1993); Scott v. Pac. W. Mountain Resort, 119 Wn. 2d 484, 834 P.2d 6, 10–12 (Wash. 1992)) *But see contra* Aaris v. Las Virgenes Unified School Dist. (1998) 64 Cal. App. 4th 1112, 1120 [75 Cal. Rptr. 2d 801] (enforcing release signed by mother); *see also* Platzer v. Mammoth Mountain Ski Area 104 Cal. App. 4th 1253 (2002) (enforcing parents' release on behalf of child participating in ski school).

43 Core-Mark Midcontinent, Inc. v. Sonitrol Corp., 2012 COA 120, 300 P.3d 963, 971 (Colo. App. 2012) (stating that "numerous Colorado appellate decisions have held that a contract provision relieving a party from liability for its own willful and wanton conduct is against public policy.") *See also* Honeywell, Inc. v. Ruby Tuesday, Inc., 43 F.Supp. 2d 1074, 1079–1080 (D. Minn. 1999) (applying Alabama and Minnesota law); Lenny's, Inc. v. Allied Sign Erectors, Inc., 170 Ga. App. 706, 318 S.E.2d 140, 142 (1984); BJ's Wholesale Club, Inc. v. Rosen, 435 Md. 714, 80 A.3d 345 (November 27, 2013) (noting that although exculpatory clauses are generally valid, they are to be construed strictly and are invalid where they try to exclude liability for intentional harms or gross negligence, where the contract is the product of grossly unequal bargaining power, and where the transaction affects the public interest). *Id.* at 724–725. *See also* Cal. Civ. Code §1668 (stating that all contracts which "exempt anyone from responsibility for his own fraud, or willful injury to the person or property of another, or violation of law, whether willful or negligent, are against the policy of the state").

CASE HIGHLIGHT *(continued)*

> "Hereby releases, waives, discharges and covenants not to sue the owner of the Premises, any individual engaging in the Activities, rescue personnel, and the Premises inspectors, surveyors, underwriters, consultants and others who give recommendations, directions or instructions or engage in risk evaluation or loss control activities regarding the Premises, and each of them, their directors, officers, agents and employees[,] from all liability to the Undersigned for any and all loss or damage and any claim or demands therefore on account of injury to the person or property or resulting in death of the Undersigned arising out of or related to the use of the Premises for the Activities, whether caused by the negligence of the Releasees or otherwise."

At the bottom of the page, the signature lines were presented as follows:

Print Name Here	Sign Name Here	Witness	Date
______________	*I HAVE READ THIS RELEASE*	______________	________
______________	*I HAVE READ THIS RELEASE*	______________	________
______________	*I HAVE READ THIS RELEASE*	______________	________
______________	*I HAVE READ THIS RELEASE*	______________	________

Plaintiff printed his name and then signed it over the words, "I HAVE READ THE RELEASE."

He was subsequently injured and sued defendant for negligence. Defendant argued Plaintiff's claim was barred by the Release. Plaintiff argued that the Release was unenforceable based upon "fraud in the execution" because he did not know he was signing a Release but believed it was a "sign in sheet."

The court disagreed and found that Plaintiff had an opportunity to read the Release and therefore there was no fraud in the execution. Plaintiff's claims for ordinary negligence and negligent hiring and supervision were barred by the Release; however, due to public policy concerns, the Release did not bar Plaintiff's claim for gross negligence.

Reflection Prompt: Examine the Release critically. What are some problems with the Release? Given these problems, what arguments other than "fraud in the execution" could be raised to try to invalidate the Release?

Most courts will not construe a general indemnity clause to indemnify the indemnitee against losses resulting from its own negligent acts unless the intent to do so is clearly expressed.[44] Words stating that the indemnity

44 University Plaza Shopping Center v. Stewart, 272 So. 2d 507 (1973) (noting that a "contract of indem-

protects the indemnitee from "any and all claims" may not be sufficient to establish such an intent, as the following Case Highlight illustrates:

CASE HIGHLIGHT

UNIVERSITY PLAZA SHOPPING CENTER v. STEWART, 272 So. 2d 507 (Fla. 1973)

University Plaza Shopping Center ("Landlord") leased a building to Stewart ("Tenant"), who operated a barber shop in the premises. A gas line exploded underneath the barber shop, causing fatal injuries to a barber. The barber's widow sued Landlord for wrongful death, alleging that it negligently installed and/or maintained the gas line which caused the explosion. The Landlord filed a third-party complaint against the Tenant and its insurer, seeking to impose liability on them under the lease agreement which contained the following clause:

> "SECTION 11. INDEMNITY – LIABILITY INSURANCE. Tenant shall indemnify and save harmless the Landlord from and against any and all claims for damages to goods, wares, merchandise and property in and about the demised premises and from and against any and all claims for any personal injury or loss of life in and about the demised premises."

The trial court entered summary judgment for Tenant, stating that an indemnity agreement stated in general terms does not apply to liability resulting from the sole negligence of the indemnitee. The Supreme Court of Florida agreed, stating that "the general clause 'indemnify. . . against any and all claims' or equivalent language does not authorize indemnification for negligence committed by the indemnitee alone." It noted, however, that it was specifically limiting its decision to situations where the liability results "solely" from the negligence of the indemnitee.

Troubleshooting: In jurisdictions with anti-indemnification statutes for certain contracts, such as construction contracts, it may be a good idea for the indemnitee to ask to be added as an additional insured on an insurance policy. Many jurisdictions distinguish indemnification provisions which attempt to indemnify a party from its own negligence (and which are, therefore, unenforceable in those jurisdictions) from agreements to

nity will not be construed to indemnify the indemnitee against losses resulting from his own negligent act unless such *intention is expressed in clear and unequivocal terms*. . ." (emphasis in original) (citing 41 Am. Jur. 2d, Indemnity, §15 at 700).

procure insurance, which are viewed as agreements to allocate costs and are enforceable.[45] (The insured should review the insurance policy to understand the conditions of insurance, including the policy exclusions and exceptions).

Indemnification clauses often state that a party will indemnify the other for damages and claims "arising out of" an agreement. Generally, the courts have not interpreted "arising out of" to mean proximate causation under tort law. Instead, they have interpreted the words "arising out of" broadly, to mean originating, flowing from, or resulting from, the action and thus require only that there be some causal relationship between the injury and the action.[46]

Example clause

The Administration agrees to indemnify, save harmless, and defend CSXT from any and all casualty losses, claims, suits, damages or liability of every kind arising out of the Contract Service under this agreement . . .
(Court found that in order for indemnification provision to apply, it was sufficient that the action be "a cause" of the injury – there was no requirement that the indemnifying party acted negligently or "causally contributed" to the dangerous situation).[47]

The "arising out of" language may be used to limit the indemnifying party's obligation if it is part of an exclusion, such as in the following case:

45 *See* Cal. Civ. Code §2782 (stating that agreements to indemnify a party from damage arising from its "sole negligence or willful misconduct" are void and unenforceable but excepting "any insurance contract, workers' compensation, or other agreement issued by an admitted insured as defined by the Insurance Code"); Meadow Valley Contractors, Inc. v. Transcontinental Ins. Co., 2001 UT App. 190 (finding that Section 13-8-1 of the Utah Code, which prohibits indemnification provisions in construction contracts, does not invalidate agreement to obtain insurance and add party as additional insured); *but see* NM Stat. Ann. §56-7-1 (stating that "indemnify" includes "any requirement to name the indemnified party as an additional insured in the indemnitor's insurance coverage for the purpose of providing indemnification for any liability not otherwise allowed in this section.").

46 Meadow Valley Contractors, Inc. v. Transcontinental Ins. Co., 2001 UT App. 190, paragraph 14 ("Thus, while some nexus must exist between the flood damage and the BT Gallegos project, the phrase 'arising out of' does not require that BT Gallegos cause the damage.").

47 CSX Transp., Inc., Mass Transit Admin., 111 Md. App. 634, 640–642 (1996).

CASE HIGHLIGHT

FINN v. NATIONAL UNION FIRE INS. CO. OF PITTSBURGH, PENNSYLVANIA, 452 Mass. 690 (2008)

The defendant, National Union Fire Insurance Company of Pittsburgh, Pennsylvania ("National Union") issued a professional liability policy to plaintiff, Uniscribe Professional Services, Inc. ("Uniscribe"). An exclusion to the policy stated that coverage did not apply:

> "to any claim arising out of any misappropriation of trade secret or infringement of patent, copyright, trademark, trade dress or any other intellectual property right."

Uniscribe was hired by Jones Day, a law firm, to provide litigation support in connection with a case. Jones Day prohibited Uniscribe employees from removing documents from its offices and required Uniscribe employees to sign confidentiality agreements. Uniscribe authorized one of its employees to bring his nephew to assist with the litigation. The nephew subsequently sent confidential trade secret information about the litigation to a website.

Jones Day demanded that Uniscribe reimburse Jones Day $1,471,992.84 in losses it had sustained as a result of the disclosure. Uniscribe ultimately settled with Jones Day and sought coverage from National Union. National Union replied that the claim was excluded. Uniscribe sought declaratory judgment that National Union had a duty to defend and indemnify Uniscribe.

The court found the plain language of the intellectual property exclusion precluded coverage and that the phrase "arising out of" incorporated a greater range of causation than proximate cause under tort law. Furthermore, it stated that given the plain language of the exclusion, the court did not need to consider Uniscribe's reasonable expectations. Finally, the court found that Jones Day's claim arose out of the nephew's misappropriation of trade secrets.

APPLYING WHAT YOU LEARNED

Contract clauses addressing remedies

Question 1:

Parent wishes to enroll Child, who has a history of epileptic seizures, in a recreational swim program. Parent signs the following release.

CITY OF SANTA BARBARA RELEASE AGREEMENT

IN CONSIDERATION OF BEING PERMITTED TO PARTICIPATE IN THIS CITY ACTIVITY OR USE OF ANY CITY FACILITIES IN CONNECTION WITH THIS ACTIVITY, THE UNDERSIGNED AGREES TO THE FOLLOWING:

1. THE UNDERSIGNED HEREBY RELEASES, WAIVES, DISCHARGES AND COVENANTS NOT TO SUE THE CITY OF SANTA BARBARA, ITS EMPLOYEES, OFFICERS AND AGENTS (hereinafter referred to as 'releasees') from all liability to the undersigned, his or her personal representatives, assigns, heirs and next of kin for any loss, damage, or claim therefore on account of injury to the person or property of the undersigned, whether caused by any negligent act or omission of the releasees or otherwise while the undersigned is participating in the City activity or using any City facilities in connection with the activity.

2. THE UNDERSIGNED HEREBY AGREES TO INDEMNIFY AND HOLD HARMLESS the releasees from all liability, claims, demands, causes of action, charges, expenses, and attorney fees . . . resulting from involvement in this activity whether caused by any negligent act or omission of the releasees or otherwise.

3. THE UNDERSIGNED HEREBY ASSUMES FULL RESPONSIBILITY FOR AND RISK OF BODILY INJURY, DEATH OR PROPERTY DAMAGE while upon City property or participating in the activity or using any City facilities and equipment whether caused by any negligent act or omission of releasees or otherwise. The undersigned expressly agrees that the foregoing release and waiver, indemnity agreement and assumption of risk are intended to be as broad and inclusive as permitted by California law.

I acknowledge that I have read the foregoing and that I am aware of the legal consequences of this agreement, including that it prevents me from suing the City or its employees, agents or officers if I am injured or damaged for any reason as a result of participation in this activity. . . .

IF THE PARTICIPANT IS A MINOR, his or her custodial parent or legal guardian must read and execute this agreement. I hereby warrant that I am the legal guardian or custodial parent of who is a minor, and agree, on my own and said minor's behalf to the terms and conditions of the foregoing agreement.

Adult name (please print) ______________

Counselors permit Child to swim an hour after Child suffers a seizure. Child drowns. Is the release enforceable?

Question 2:

The parties sign an agreement that contains the following clause:

"Exclusion of Consequential Loss. In no circumstances shall either we or you be liable for indirect, consequential, reliance, or special loss or damages or for lost revenues, lost savings, lost business opportunity or lost profits of any kind."

The agreement is governed by New York law, which prohibits parties from limiting their liability for gross negligence or willful misconduct. Is the limitation of liability clause enforceable?

Troubleshooting: Be mindful of how the clauses relate and refer to each other. If one clause is deemed invalid, it may affect the operation of other clauses with unintended consequences.

CASE HIGHLIGHT

BUTLER MFG. CO. v. AMERICOLD CORP., 835 F. Supp. 1274 (D. Kan. 1993)

Plaintiffs were corporations who had stored goods in an underground warehouse facility owned by defendants. The goods were damaged by fire. The plaintiffs had signed contracts with the defendants which contained the following two provisions:

Condition of Rental 1:

> "It is expressly agreed that this contract is not intended to create the relationship of bailor and bailee but that of landlord and tenant, and Lessee expressly waives any right to claim that this contract is one for a bailment. Lessor undertakes only to provide Lessee with space of the character generally made available by Lessor for storage of goods and to act as the agent of Lessee in rendering the services outlined herein and on the other side hereof. Lessee assumes all risk of loss or damage to records stored or handled pursuant hereto and waives all rights of action against Lessor and releases it from all responsibility for loss of or injury to such records except for gross negligence or willful injury. Lessee expressly waives every presumption of law and fact that loss shall have occurred through negligence of Lessor, and Lessee agrees that Lessor shall not be liable for any loss sustained by Lessee unless such loss shall be occasioned by some specific, clearly proven, willful act or gross negligence of Lessor and then only to the extent elsewhere herein provided. Lessor shall not, in any event, be liable for any loss or damage caused by any act or neglect of any person or persons not in the employ of Lessor."

Condition of Rental 7:

> "(a) The rental storage rate is based upon the space occupied by the records. Lessee hereby declares the value of all records stored under the terms of this Record Storage Contract to be two dollars ($2.00) per cubic foot of space occupied. Such value shall be the agreed upon value for all purposes.
>
> (b) Lessor's liability shall be limited as set forth in paragraph 1, above, and its liability for any loss due to either damage or destruction of records or delay or inaccuracy in furnishing of information or due to any other cause whatsoever shall be limited to the declared value of the records and in no event shall Lessor be liable for any consequential or other damage in any amount whatsoever."

CASE HIGHLIGHT *(continued)*

The defendants, as "warehouseman," were subject to the Kansas state equivalent of Article 7 of the UCC, which states:
"Duty of care; contractual limitation of warehouseman's liability.

(1) A warehouseman is liable for damages for loss of or injury to the goods caused by his failure to exercise such care in regard to them as a reasonably careful man would exercise under like circumstances but unless otherwise agreed he is not liable for damages which could not have been avoided by the exercise of such care.

(2) Damages may be limited by a term in the warehouse receipt or storage agreement limiting the amount of liability in case of loss or damage, and setting forth a specific liability per article or item, or per unit of weight, beyond which the warehouseman shall not be liable."

The court found that condition 1 was an attempt by defendants to disclaim all liability for ordinary negligence and to allow recovery only for acts amounting to gross negligence or willful injury. The court noted that condition 1 was an impermissible attempt to impair the warehouseman's duty of care and forbidden under the UCC.

Then the court considered whether condition 7 effectively limited defendant's liability for ordinary negligence. First, it noted condition 7(b)'s cross-reference to condition 1 ("Lessor's liability shall be limited as set forth in paragraph 1, above . . ."). Then it noted that condition 7 limited defendant's liability "for any loss due to either damage or destruction of records . . . or due to any other cause whatsoever shall be limited to the declared value of the records" and that "in no event shall Lessor be liable for any consequential or other damage in any amount whatsoever."

The court found that the plain language of condition 1 was intended to eliminate all liability for defendants for their ordinary negligence and to allow recovery under the contract only if the actions of defendants amount to gross negligence or willful conduct. The court found that the cross-reference in condition 7(b) to condition 1 indicated that the parties intended the limitation on condition 1 to stand on its own. The remaining limitations on damages contained in condition 7 therefore were intended to apply to actions *other than those for ordinary negligence*:

> "Such intent can be seen from reading the cross reference in conjunction with the further language of condition 7(b) which refers to '*any* loss due to either damage or destruction of records' and the language referring to loss 'due to *any other cause whatsoever*' [emphasis added]. In short, the court finds that the only logical reading of the plain language of the conditions leads to the conclusion that the parties intended condition 1 to eliminate all liability on the part of defendants for negligent conduct, and that condition 7(b) is designed to limit the defendants' damages for other types of conduct."

Because the damages limitation provisions did not comply with the requirements of the Kansas statute, they were invalid. The court stated:

CASE HIGHLIGHT *(continued)*

> "The court finds that the damage limitation provisions do not comply with the requirements of K.S.A. §84-7-204, and therefore they cannot be given effect. K.S.A. §84-7-204 sets forth in straightforward terms the warehouseman's duty of care and specifically sets forth that a warehouseman may limit (not eliminate) his liability in damages for a breach of that duty by 'setting forth a specific liability per article or item, or per unit of weight.' Rather than follow the statutory requirements to properly limit liability for ordinary negligence, the Contracts purport to totally eliminate all liability for ordinary negligence (which is not allowed under the UCC) and to limit damages for all other conduct (which is not contemplated by the UCC and, as discussed later in this opinion, is not valid under Kansas common law)."

The court stated that because the legislature had provided a "specific method for warehousemen to limit their liability for ordinary negligence," and because the parties did not comply with it, the liability limitation provisions did not limit defendants' damages for ordinary negligence. In other words, the clause which attempted to exculpate the defendants from liability for ordinary negligence (condition 1) was invalid because it did not comply with the Kansas statute. The limitation of liability clause (condition 7) did not limit defendants' liability for ordinary negligence because it stated that it applied to damage caused by conduct *other than ordinary negligence as ordinary negligence was excluded under condition 1.* Kansas statute, however, prohibited the parties' exclusion of ordinary negligence, which left defendants liable for damages based upon ordinary negligence *and* without a limit on liability for ordinary negligence!

Next, the court considered whether the limitation of liability applied to acts of gross negligence and willful conduct. While condition 1 did not apply to gross negligence or willful injury, condition 7(b) did:

> "However, condition 7(b) provides that liability for '*any* loss due to either damage or destruction of records or delay or inaccuracy in furnishing information or *due to any other cause whatsoever* shall be limited to the declared value of the records and in no event shall Lessor be liable for any consequential or other damage in any amount whatsoever.' The plain meaning of that language includes limiting damages caused by defendants' gross negligence and willful or wanton conduct."

The court stated that Kansas law prohibits the enforcement of liability limitation provisions that limit damages for gross negligence and willful or wanton conduct. Therefore, the liability limitation language in condition 7(b) did not limit defendants' damages, essentially leaving the defendants without an effective limitation of liability:

> "The liability limitation provisions relating to defendants' liability for their ordinary negligence are not enforceable due to the failure of the contractual provisions to comply with Article 7 of the UCC. The contractual provisions purporting to limit defendants' liability for damages caused by defendants' gross negligence and willful or wanton conduct are unenforceable under Kansas common law."

Troubleshooting: It is a good idea to avoid greedy drafting and to include any legislative exclusion in the clause. While a court *could* imply the exclusion and uphold the clause, it may not, especially if the plain language of the clause makes clear that the parties intended the (invalid) exclusion. It is a good idea, then, to specifically state in an exculpatory and/or limitation of liability clause that it does not include legislative exclusions.

8.2 Doctrinal concept: liquidated damages

Principle: The parties to a contract may determine, in advance of a breach, a specific damages amount otherwise known as "liquidated damages" provided that it is reasonable under the circumstances.

Generally, a liquidated damages clause that operates as a penalty for non-performance, (rather than as a reasonable pre-estimate of damages) will not be enforceable.[48] The question of whether a liquidated damages clause is valid or whether it constitutes a penalty is a question of law for the courts to determine.[49] The language of the clause is not controlling; rather, the court looks at the reasonableness of the clause, the facts, and the intention of the parties.[50] A strong factor in favor of reasonableness is if damages would be impractical or difficult to prove.[51] The difficulty of proof of damages alone does not, however, demonstrate reasonableness.[52]

The following are examples of liquidated damages provisions that a court found unenforceable:

Example #1

Liquidated Damages Payment. If Contractor fails to commence commercial operation of the Gas-to-Electric Plant on or before the date specified in Paragraph 7(b)(15) . . . Seller may assess and collect from Contractor, at Seller's option, liquidated damages in an

48 RESTATEMENT (SECOND) CONTRACTS, §356; Med + Plus Neck & Back Pain Center v. Noffsinger, 311 Ill. App. 3d 853, 860, 726 N.E.2d 687 (2000) (liquidated damages amount "must be for a specific amount for a specific breach; they may not be a penalty to punish nonperformance or as a threat used to secure performance"); Checkers Eight Ltd. P'ship v. Hawkins, 241 F.3d 558, 561 (7th Cir. 2001) ("In interpreting contract provisions that specify damages, Illinois law draws a distinction between liquidated damages, which are enforceable, and penalties, which are not.").

49 Dean v. Kruse Foundation, Inc. v. Gates, 973 N.E.2d 583, 590 (Ind. App. 2012).

50 *Id.* at 591 ("To determine whether a stipulated sum payable upon breach of contract constitutes liquidated damages or a penalty, the facts, the intention of the parties, and the reasonableness of the stipulation under the circumstances of the case are all to be considered.").

51 *Id.* at 592; Arrowhead Sch. Dist. No. 75 v. Klyap, 2003 MT 294, 79 P.3d 250 (2003).

52 Arrowhead, *supra* note 52.

amount equal to Two Thousand Five Hundred and No/100 Dollars ($2,500.00) for each day after the Milestone Date that the Gas-to-Electric Plant fails to commence commercial operation. Such liquidated damages shall be paid by Contractor on a weekly basis in arrears each Monday after the Milestone Date until commercial operation has occurred. If Seller assesses and collects from Contractor such liquidated damages for any period of delay, such liquidated damages shall be in full and complete settlement of all claims, losses and damages of Seller resulting from such period of delay; provided, however, that if the delay exceeds ninety (90) days, Seller may also elect to terminate this Agreement in accordance with the provisions of Paragraph 11 of this Agreement [which includes default by the Contractor or default by Owner] and pursue any of the rights and remedies provided for therein. Seller and Contractor acknowledge and agree that the liquidated damages provided for therein constitute a reasonable forecast of the actual damages Seller would sustain as a result of such delay and are not intended as a penalty.[53]

[This clause was found to be an unenforceable penalty because it allowed Seller the option of collecting liquidated damages or terminating the Agreement with the option of also seeking actual damages. Providing the option of either liquidated damages or actual damages shows that the parties did not intend to establish a specific sum to constitute damages in the event of breach.]

Example #2

TERMS – If EMPLOYEE voluntarily terminate[s] his/her services during continuity of project, he/she shall owe Allied the sum of 5,000 dollars as liquidated damages for time and money spent by [A]llied to procure and start the project. If EMPLOYEE voluntarily terminates his/her services after completion of project but with[in] the period of fifteen (15) months from the starting date of employ[ment], employee shall owe Allied the sum of 10,000 dollars as liquidated damages for time and money spent for recru[i]ting, loss of use and marketing of employee services. Employee agrees to give thirty day [sic] written notice for employment termination. If the employee violates this term, employee shall owe an amount of $5,000.00 (Five thousand dollars) to Allied as liquidated damages . . .[54]

[Court found that damages were not difficult to calculate and the amounts were not reasonable pre-estimates of the probable loss. No evidence showed that sums bear any relation to actual damages that could be incurred from breach.][55]

53 Resource Technology Corp. v. Congress Development Co., 2003 U.S. Dist. LEXIS 15418 at *3–4 (N.D. Ill. Sept. 24, 2003).

54 Allied Informatics, Inc. v. Yeruva, 554 S.E.2d 550 (C.A. of Georgia, August 28, 2001).

55 *Id.* at 552.

Caveat: Please note that some states may require that a liquidated damages provision be separately initialed by the parties for certain types of transactions (i.e. real property transactions).[56]

8.3 Doctrinal concept: equitable remedies

Principle: In lieu of damages (i.e. money), a party may seek equitable relief such as specific performance or an injunction, meaning that it will ask the court to order the breaching party to perform its obligations under the contract or to refrain from some action.

A court may grant specific performance or injunctive relief at its discretion and only where it finds that damages are inadequate.[57] Damages are inadequate if they are difficult to measure with reasonable certainty, substitute performance would be difficult to procure, or a damages award would be difficult to collect.[58] Specific performance is typically granted as a matter of right where the contract is for the sale of real estate.[59]

Example clause

Receiving Party acknowledges and agrees that Disclosing Party has invested considerable resources in obtaining and developing the Confidential Information and that the Confidential Information provides Disclosing Party with a significant competitive advantage. In the event of breach by the terms of this Agreement by Receiving Party, Receiving Party agrees that Disclosing Party will suffer immediate, irreparable harm for which monetary damages will be inadequate. Receiving Party agrees that Disclosing

56 *See*, for example, Cal. Civ. Code §1677: "A provision in a contract to purchase and sell real property liquidating the damages to the seller if the buyer fails to complete the purchase of the property is invalid unless: (a) The provision is separately signed or initialed by each party to the contract; and (b) If the provision is included in a printed contract, it is set out either in at least 10-point bold type or in contrasting red print in at least eight-point bold type."

57 RESTATEMENT (SECOND) CONTRACTS, §359(1); Tower City Grain Co. v. Richman, 232 N.W.2d 61, 66 (N.D. 1975) (Specific performance is an "equitable remedy" and party seeking it "must clearly show that the legal remedy of damages is inadequate"); Chavin v. H.H. Rosin & Co., 246 A.2d 921, 922 (1968) ("The right to compel the specific performance of a contract is a purely equitable remedy, and is given in substitution of the legal remedy of compensation when it is inadequate").

58 RESTATEMENT (SECOND) CONTRACTS, §360.

59 Kohrs v. Barth., 570 N.E.2d 1273, 1275 (1991) ("Where a contract for the sale of real estate has been entered into without misunderstanding on the part of the buyer and without misrepresentation on the part of the seller, specific performance will be granted as a matter of right"); Kalinowski v. Yeh, 847 P.2d 673, 674 (1993) ("Contracts for the sale of land have traditionally been accorded a special place in the law of specific performance . . . Damages have . . . been regarded as inadequate to enforce a duty to transfer an interest in land") (citing RESTATEMENT (SECOND) CONTRACTS, §360, comment 3, at 174 (1981)).

Party will be entitled, in addition to any other remedies available at law or in equity, to injunctive relief to specifically enforce the terms of this Agreement.

Example clause

Each Party agrees that monetary damages may be inadequate to compensate the other Party for any breach of the confidentiality obligations in this Agreement. Accordingly, each Party agrees and acknowledges that any such breach or threatened breach of this Agreement will cause irreparable injury to the other Party and that, in addition to any other remedies that may be available, in law, in equity or otherwise, the other Party shall be entitled to obtain injunctive relief against the breach or threatened breach of this Agreement without the necessity of proving actual damages.

An exclusive remedy provision may preclude the granting of equitable relief provided that the intent of the parties is clearly expressed, as the following case demonstrates:

CASE HIGHLIGHT

REICHERT v. RUBLOFF HAMMOND, L.L.C., 645 N.W.2d 519 (Neb. 2002)

Rubloff Hammond, LLC ("Hammond") entered into a lease agreement with the Reicherts which provided that Hammond would lease space to the Reicherts for their jewelry store. The agreement contained the following clause:

"So long as Tenant is open and operating its business as provided for in the Lease . . . and is not otherwise in default under the Lease . . . then Landlord covenants and agrees that during the period commencing on August 1, 1999 and expiring on July 31, 2004, no space in the Shopping Center will be leased or allowed to be leased, other then [sic] Tenant's operation, for the primary business of the operation of a jewelry store selling fine jewelry. The foregoing restriction shall not apply to (i) "Anchor Tenants" . . . (ii) any tenant, its successor, assign or replacement, open and operating in the Shopping Center as of August 1, 1999 . . .

Landlord and Tenant acknowledge that in the event of a breach of this restriction, Tenant shall give Landlord written notice of such breach and Landlord shall have thirty (30) days from the date of said notice (or such longer period as may be reasonably required if Landlord is diligently attempting to remedy same) to remedy same. If Landlord fails to

CASE HIGHLIGHT *(continued)*

remedy such breach . . . Tenant shall have the rights set forth in the next paragraph as its sole and exclusive remedy because of such breach . . .

Tenant shall have, as its sole and exclusive remedy under the Lease, the right to either (i) decrease annual fixed minimum rent by 50% during the period such store . . . is open and operating . . . or (ii) terminate the Lease . . . If Tenant elects (i) above, then Tenant shall resume paying full fixed minimum rent on the date such Competing Store ceases violating the restriction. If such Competing Store continues to violate the restriction for 270 days after the date said Competing Store opened for business, then Tenant shall have the further right to terminate the Lease . . . no later than 290 days after the date the Competing Store opened for business . . ."

. . .

Hammond entered into an agreement with Ridco, which would allow Ridco to open a competing jewelry store in the same mall. The Reicherts filed a petition for declaratory judgment and a permanent injunction against Hammond. Hammond argued that the Reicherts were limited to the exclusive remedy in the lease agreement. At trial, the Reicherts presented evidence that Ridco had received a more favorable rent arrangement than Reicherts and that the economy in the region was such that Ridco's presence would have significant negative impact on the Reicherts' sales volume. The trial court found that Hammond intended to give the Reicherts an exclusive right to operate fine jewelry stores in the mall through 2004, that it knew this right was important to the Reicherts, that the Ridco store would force the closure of one of the Reicherts' stores before July 2004 and that the Reicherts would pay substantially more than Ridco for approximately the same store space. Thus, the court found, the reduction in rent was an inadequate remedy and that without injunctive relief, the Reicherts would suffer irreparable harm. Accordingly, the trial court issued a permanent injunction against Hammond from leasing the space for the purposes of operating a jewelry business.

The Supreme Court of Nebraska agreed that the parties intended the lease to provide the Reicherts an exclusive right to operate fine jewelry stores in the mall. However, it disagreed that the Reicherts were entitled to injunctive relief. Although a "contract will not be construed to limit the remedial rights of the parties unless that intention is clearly expressed," in this case, the parties expressly stated that the remedy provided in the agreement was the "sole and exclusive remedy under the Lease." Because the remedy provision was unambiguous, the Reicherts were held to the "plain language of the exclusive remedy provision." The Supreme Court of Nebraska reversed the decision of the trial court and found that "the parties clearly intended that the exclusive remedy in the event of a breach would be the termination of the lease agreements or a reduction in rents."

APPLYING WHAT YOU LEARNED

Contract clauses addressing remedies

Buyer, the winning bidder of auctioned property, signed a Purchase Agreement for the property which contained the following provision:

"[Buyer] agrees to pay therefore the sum of Four Million Dollars ($4,000,000) on the following terms: Cash At Closing Plus 5% Buyers Premium[.] One Hundred Thousand Dollars ($100,000) of said purchase price is hereby deposited as earnest money with Kruse Real Estate, same to be refunded if the above offer is not accepted on or before today or if the title to the above property is found defective and said defects cannot be remedied within a reasonable time. However, if the buyer fails to complete the purchase within a reasonable time due to no fault of the seller, then the earnest money deposited is forfeited, and seller may sue for specific performance."[60]

The Buyer terminated the Purchase Agreement after learning of problems with the property's title and condition. Seller ultimately sold the property for $2,350,000 to another purchaser. The Buyer sued the Seller for breach of contract and conversion and the Seller filed a counterclaim for breach of contract. The Seller sought damages in the amount of $2,468,794, which was the difference between the purchase price in the Purchase Agreement ($4,000,000) and the sale of the property to the second buyer ($2,350,000). In addition, Seller sought the buyer's premium* of $200,000 and prejudgment interest in the amount of $718,794. The earnest money amount of $100,000 was credited to this amount.

Could Seller sue for damages or did the Purchase Agreement limit its right to recover to the earnest money and specific performance? (This case is based upon Dean v. Kruse Foundation, Inc. v. Gates, 973 N.E.2d 583, 587 (Ind. App. 2012)).

* The buyer's premium is the price a winning bidder at auction makes to the auction house.

60 Dean v. Kruse Foundation, Inc. v. Gates, 973 N.E.2d 583, 587 (Ind. App. 2012).

Index